THE IRISH AT GETTYSBURG

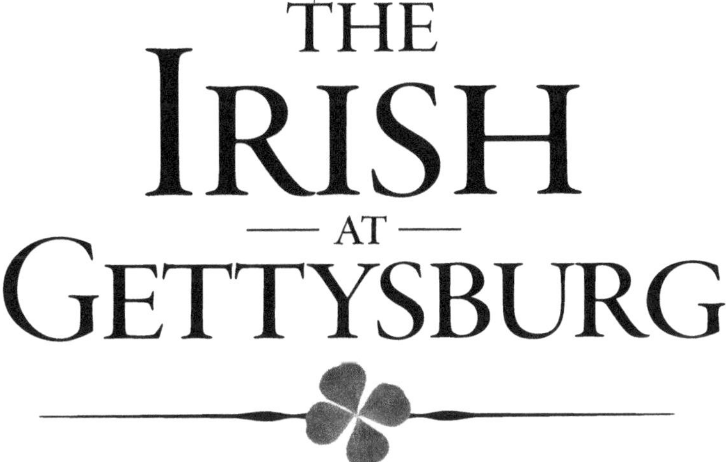

PHILLIP THOMAS TUCKER, PHD

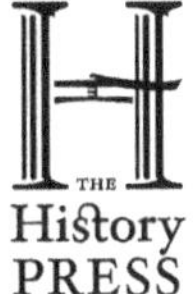

Published by The History Press
Charleston, SC
www.historypress.net

Front cover: *Absolution Under Fire* by Paul Wood. *Author's collection.*
Back cover: *Courtesy of the Library of Congress.*

First published 2018

Manufactured in the United States

ISBN 9781467138529

Library of Congress Control Number: 2017960349

Contents

Introduction

Seemingly everything possible has already been written about the climactic battle of Gettysburg, Pennsylvania—three nightmarish days of intense combat in early July 1863—that determined America's destiny. Because the decisive showdown at Gettysburg was the largest battle ever fought on the North American continent and because of its overall strategic importance, no engagement in the annals of American history has been more deeply investigated from seemingly every possible angle. The longtime publication of a popular glossy journal, *Gettysburg Magazine*, has been exclusively devoted to the epic battle. Clearly, Americans have been fascinated with the dramatic story of Gettysburg far longer than with any other Civil War battle. Quite simply, the history of Gettysburg has become the most thoroughly analyzed and dissected battle in American history; seemingly no stone has been left unturned.

However, the flood of 150th-anniversary books about the great battle that raged from July 1 to July 3, 1863, have basically simply rehashed the same old stories of Gettysburg. Therefore, at this late date, the dramatic story of the Battle of Gettysburg has become very much of a "dead" field of study in Civil War historiography. In 2013, a number of publishers, including from America's leading publishing houses, released anniversary books that were nothing more than the same general histories about the showdown at Gettysburg. Consequently, for people craving something new beyond the standard narrative so often repeated throughout the past, they were sorely disappointed by the new Gettysburg titles released for the 150th anniversary.

In fact, this unfortunate situation that has fully revealed the overall sterility of the Gettysburg field of study has resulted in the writing of this book to fill this significant void in the historical record. Discovering a long-overlooked and -forgotten Gettysburg chapter of importance has been possible because some of the best Civil War history can still be found, even in this crowded field of study, by digging deeper into the historical record. Hidden stories often reveal more fascinating nuggets than can be found in the most popular narratives of traditional Gettysburg history.

Consequently, this groundbreaking study will prove the validity of this reality by focusing on a little-known subject that has been long ignored despite its overall importance: the story of the Irish and their key roles at the battle of Gettysburg. This important chapter about the vital contributions of the most uniquely ethnic and obscure fighting men, especially in the ranks of the Army of Northern Virginia, has not been previously revealed in full, even in books about the most written-about and decisive confrontation in Civil War—and American—history. Therefore, this analysis of the importance of the Irish role at Gettysburg represents one of the final frontiers of Gettysburg historiography.

Clearly, at this late date, a detailed exploration of the contributions of the most forgotten soldiers at Gettysburg has been long overdue. Like no other previous book to date, this specialized study will focus primarily on the long-overlooked roles of the South's most obscure soldiers, who represented the single largest immigrant and ethnic group not only in the South but also in General Robert Edward Lee's Army of Northern Virginia. Because of their longtime absence from the historical record, the contributions of these young Irish men and boys at the decisive Battle of Gettysburg will be explored for the first time in a single volume.

Besides exploring the significant Irish contributions, including the North's famed Irish Brigade, on the first two days of combat (July 1 and July 2), this book will also analyze the unforgettable story of the large number of Irish Confederates who played leading roles in the most climactic moment of the battle, "Pickett's Charge," on the hot afternoon of July 3, 1863. These young men and boys from Ireland, especially the most recent immigrants, were literally caught between two worlds—the ancient homeland and the New World—when they stoically advanced across the open fields in the ranks of Lee's greatest offensive effort. The Irish on both sides included soldiers who still spoke ancient Gaelic of the Emerald Isle.

Other Green Isle soldiers spoke with thick Irish brogues of the Irish peasantry (mostly Irish Catholics) and middle class (mostly Irish Protestants or Scotch Irish, the majority of Celtic soldiers who served in the Army of Northern Virginia). These hopeful and optimistic immigrants from the Emerald Isle had made their dreams come true in the South. Large numbers of Emerald Islanders marched to their deaths during the audacious bid to pierce the right-center of the Army of the Potomac at a weak point of the Cemetery Ridge defensive line.

All in all, to provide a representative example, this book will explore the unforgettable story of great courage and high sacrifice of Irish Confederates during the South's last-ditch effort to win it all. On that fateful July 3, Lee knew that he had to go for broke in a desperate bid to reap a decisive victory before it was too late, because the manpower-short Confederacy was trapped in a brutal war of attrition. This book will reveal some of the best hidden history of the Battle of Gettysburg by focusing on this long-overlooked Irish contribution on both sides in determining the nation's destiny in Adams County, Pennsylvania. Indeed, Yankees from Ireland, especially men serving in Pennsylvania units, played a key role in thwarting the attackers at the crucial moment that became known as the "High Water Mark of the Confederacy."

Before the most famous attack of the Civil War, Irish Confederates played leading roles in equally determined assaults on the second day at both ends of Major General George Gordon Meade's lengthy defensive line centered on the expanse of Cemetery Ridge: East Cemetery Hill on the north, where large numbers of Louisiana Irish Rebels charged the heights with the war cry "We are the Louisiana Tigers!"; and in the all-important showdown for possession of strategic Little Round Top, where Irish soldiers of the Alabama Brigade and the Texas Brigade performed magnificently in determined assaults on the line's southern end.

One forgotten factor that made the showdown at Gettysburg so murderous was the result of a highly respected intellectual who influenced an entire generation of Union and Confederate leaders, Dennis Hart Mahan. What has been most overlooked about Mahan was the fact the he was the son of Irish Catholic immigrants. He was the influential professor who taught at the United States Military Academy at West Point, New York. From 1827 and throughout the antebellum period, he brilliantly articulated his tactical theory that partly shaped the thinking of Civil War leaders, including Irish officers on both sides, at Gettysburg and the kind of aggressive tactics that led to three days of bloody combat.

This most revealing story about the Irish Confederates at the Battle of Gettysburg has been overlooked for more than a century and a half: a remarkable development in an overcrowded field of study. Unfortunately, this negligence was in no small part the result of the dominance of postwar "Lost Cause" mythology that incorrectly portrayed Confederate soldiers as the most racially pure of all Anglo-Saxons (or "true Americans") in an attempt to demonstrate the Southern people's alleged superiority over their Northern rivals. In truth, the South was actually an Anglo-Celtic (not largely Anglo-Saxon, like the North) region. Correspondingly, Lee's troops at Gettysburg consisted of a largely Anglo-Celtic fighting force that included thousands of immigrant Irish and the sons and grandsons of Emerald Isle transplants, who were mostly Scotch-Irish.

Nevertheless, this popular romantic stereotype of a homogenous South and Army of Northern Virginia of noble Anglo-Saxon fighting men (a postwar development) has played a large role in transforming tens of thousands of Irish soldiers into the Civil War's most forgotten soldiers. Indeed, while the Irish in blue who served in Northern armies, especially the famed Irish Brigade, Army of the Potomac, have become well known to Americans, such has not been the case for the Irish Confederates, who still languish in undeserved obscurity.

Even at this late date, the Civil War's historiography has been woefully inadequate and incomplete in regard to the glaring absence of the important roles of the Irish who fought for the South. This omission is especially ironic because the Irish, mostly lower-class products on both sides of the Atlantic, were the least slave-owning and most ethnically distinctive group of the South. Therefore, the Irish experience in the South was an atypical one, and this distinction alone makes them worthy of greater study.

As mentioned, enduring myths and stereotypes, both wartime and postwar, have obscured the historical record to ensure that the largest group of so-called foreign soldiers of Lee's Army of Northern Virginia were the most overlooked fighting men in the annals of Civil War historiography. Ironically, the Irish soldiers were often the butt of jokes and racial stereotypes among the non-Irish, providing a source of soldiery humor across the South. Even the famous diarist Mary Chesnut, who had her own Irish servants, wrote how she saw the Irish nurse of the President Jefferson Davis family "weeping and wailing as only an Irish woman can."

Most important, the significant contributions of these Sons of Erin were far greater than the vast majority of historians, especially non-Irish ones without a serious interest in Irish history, have realized to this day. This unfortunate situation has developed because of a lack of an appreciation for the overall Irish experience, in part due to the lack of documentation about the Irish Confederates, because so many immigrant Irish were illiterate (especially Irish Catholics, due to English anti-literacy laws enacted in Ireland to limit the rise of revolutionary leadership).

Sadly for the historical record, these Emerald Islanders have left us with relatively few letters, diaries or memoirs in private collections and archives around the United States, an unfortunate development that has doomed these Sons of Erin and their notable battlefield achievements to obscurity, especially in relation to the Battle of Gettysburg. In fact, no aspect of Gettysburg historiography has been more overlooked than ethnic studies that have revealed new insights into the overall American experience. This has been an ironic development because of the important roles of Irish Confederates during the three days at Gettysburg, providing additional evidence of an especially rich field of study.

Although a forgotten and untold story to this day, the fascinating odyssey of the Irish Confederates at Gettysburg is an important one that is long overdue. By 1861, the largest immigrant group in the South was the native Irish (Catholics) and Scotch-Irish (Protestants). Contrary to the stereotype that the South consisted of a homogenous Anglo-Saxon society transferred from England, the South was overflowing with hardworking and devout Emerald Isle immigrants. Descended from the Green Isle's inhabitants ("Hibernia," as it was known to the ancient Greeks and Romans), who were the Gaels before they were defeated by invading Celts, the Irish were a distinct Celtic-Gaelic people who possessed their own distinctive and vibrant culture. They possessed a rich heritage and unique value systems, including a warrior ethos, which were transferred to the South as a result of a massive migration that began before the American Revolution.

Most of all, these Sons of Erin revered a distinct warrior ethos from a distant past (generations of ancestors who had bravely defended the Emerald Isle from numerous invaders) and a deep-seated tradition of egalitarianism rooted in ancient common law (Brehon Law) before imperialist England gained its first colony after conquering Ireland by the most ruthless means. Because of the longtime oppression of the native Irish Catholics by the Anglo-Saxon conquerors, America had initially offered the intoxicating idealistic vision of a promised land in the New World for the subjugated Irish people before the American Revolution.

In a striking paradox (because of their general obscurity throughout the course of the Civil War), no contributions of any distinct ethnic people in the South have been more disproportionate and important than those of the Irish Confederates. This is in contrast with the comparable widespread contributions of a disproportionately large number of patriotic Sons of Erin who fought in the American Revolution from beginning to end. The longtime obscurity of Irish Confederate contributions was also partly the result of the thorough Americanization of the Irish people after the war, when they were acclimated into the mainstream of American society. Indeed, in time, Green Islanders lost their distinctive Irishness and unique Celtic-Gaelic cultural qualities in the North and South after merging into the overall flow of American life. After the slowing of postwar Irish immigration to the South (they instead migrated to the West for greater opportunities and to avoid economic competition with the newly freed blacks), the Irish became more thoroughly American, losing their closeness to the Celtic-Gaelic past, ethnic qualities, and distinctive cultural identities.

For such reasons, the presentation of fresh historical views about the Battle of Gettysburg has been nearly impossible in regard to the significant Irish contributions. So much has already been published about Gettysburg for more than a century and a half that it seems that no stone has been left unturned. But fortunately, this is not the case. Therefore, new views are especially much-needed today to provide new insights and fresh perspectives on the traditional story of Gettysburg, America's most overworked field of historical study.

However, as fully demonstrated by this book, even the excessively overcrowded field of Gettysburg historiography can offer rare finds of pure historical gold if a determined historian will spend the extra time to dig deeper into uncharted regions of the historical record. In a striking paradox of Civil War historiography (and unlike the Irish who wore the blue, especially in the ranks of the hard-fighting Irish Brigade), the Irish Confederate contributions have also been lost because the war's winners, as in all wars, wrote the history from a Northern point of view. This time-honored axiom was especially valid in the case of the forgotten Irish Confederates. Equally damaging, the losers across the South wrote an romanticized and embellished Lost Cause history that was overly Anglo-Saxon focused, oriented to bestow perceived racial and cultural virtues of an exaggerated nature. All in all, this was a dual historical development that has obscured the importance of Irish Confederate contributions from 1861 to 1865, including in the most important battle of the war.

As mentioned, the extensive romanticism of the Lost Cause transformed the South's fabricated image into a white Anglo-Saxon Protestant (WASP) bastion of a righteous and racially pure American society, which allegedly made it morally superior to Northern society. This postwar development has led directly to the obscuring of Irish contributions from 1861 to 1865. But thoroughly contradicting this postwar historiography and Lost Cause mythology—long accepted as fact—were the South's demographic and cultural realities at the time of the war's beginning. By 1860, the South was a multicultural and multiethnic nation that mocked the postwar stereotype of the homogeneous Anglo-Saxon (or Aryan) population that allegedly represented Anglo-Saxon purity—one of the greatest and most enduring Lost Cause myths of the Old South. As the largest immigrant group in the South in 1860, the Irish people and their vibrant Celtic-Gaelic culture added the most colorful component of what was a true heterogeneous mix, which mirrored the demographic realities of the South's population and, in turn, Confederate armies, including the Army of Northern Virginia.

Unfortunately, the romance of Lost Cause myths has greatly obscured the South's ethnic realities and complexities, especially the disproportionate Irish wartime contributions in a great silencing of the historical record. Offering a comforting psychological explanation and moral justification in order for the vanquished Southern people to minimize their humiliating defeat and subjugation, these persistent racial myths were developed by an active group of postwar southern writers, ex-Confederate leaders, and historians to explain their disastrous defeat and to regain the moral high ground lost by slavery's defense. Southerners stubbornly clung to the comforting myth that the South's Anglo-Saxon people—actually Anglo-Celtic—were vanquished because of superior numbers of non-Anglo-Saxon mercenary (or "foreign") soldiers and immigrants, especially Irishmen (an estimated 150,000, thanks in part of Ireland's Great Potato Famine that generated an exodus from the Green Isle) and Germans who served in large numbers.

Enduring to this day in the South, the myth was created that native-born Americans had been decisively defeated by hordes of European-born soldiers and not fellow Americans of a shared cultural and national heritage. In much the same way, generations of western European historians, such as the famed British historian Edward Gibbon in his classic work *The History of the Decline and Fall of the Roman Empire* (1776), emphasized how Rome's fall primarily resulted from the invasion of foreign barbarian hordes, including Celts, and the erosion of Roman society from within by the empire's embrace of too many foreign citizens.

CONTRADICTING THE POPULAR IMAGE held by most contemporary Americans that the South was a homogeneous Anglo-Saxon bastion of racial intolerance (certainly for oppressed black people because of the evil of slavery, but not for the Irish), the South possessed a lengthy history not only of greater widespread ethnic diversity, but also a greater overall acceptance of immigrants from distant lands, especially Ireland, than in the North. This intolerance toward the Irish was especially prevalent in the North's major cities, especially New York, Philadelphia, and Boston. The thriving Mississippi River port of New Orleans, Louisiana, was the most multicultural city and the third-largest city in America. For the immigrant Irish of the antebellum period, the South offered far more social and economic opportunities for obtaining true equality and the American dream than did the North, especially in the large northeastern cities.

Consequently, the South, especially the bustling urban centers of New Orleans; Mobile, Alabama; Richmond, Virginia; and Charleston, South Carolina, teemed with thousands of immigrants from Ireland by 1860. Distinctive Celtic-Gaelic communities and enclaves abounded not only in the South's major cities but also across the rural countryside. Here, ancient values, belief systems and ideals of a distinct Celtic-Gaelic society and past were kept alive by the transplanted Sons of Erin so far from their homeland.

Fortunately for the Confederacy in terms of its war-waging capabilities—in a parallel that had been seen in the thirteen colonies just before the American Revolution—the South possessed a vast Irish manpower pool by 1860. Tens of thousands of immigrant Irish had flooded into the South, especially major urban areas (most of all New Orleans) because of the exodus created by the Great Potato Famine of 1845–1849. Known as the An Gorta Mor—ancient Gaelic for "The Great Hunger"—this tragedy resulted in the loss of an estimated one million lives from disease and hunger (the potato crop was the population's main staple), while another one million Irish departed, primarily for America. Ironically, considerable reserves of food stored in warehouses were denied the starving Irish people by the British government, and these products, especially meat, were instead exported to England to reap high profits. This greatest natural and manmade disaster in Irish history not only changed the face of Ireland, it also continued the process of transforming the South into a largely Anglo-Celtic region by 1860 because of the Irish tide of migration.

Unlike in major northeastern cities, the much easier assimilation of Irish immigrants into the overall mainstream of a more open and tolerant Southern society—the unity of whiteness in a slave society enhanced equality—ensured a deep loyalty, including Democratic Party adherence, to their adopted homeland and a widespread wearing of the gray. Most revealing, during the 1850s, ugly anti-Irish riots swept through the ethnic slums and ghettoes of New York City, Philadelphia and Boston and even targeted Catholic churches, while the Irish were accepted as full-fledged citizens in Richmond, Mobile and Charleston. Clearly, this was a significant difference not lost on tens of thousands of Sons of Erin across the South with their adopted homeland's call to arms in April 1861, after the firing on Fort Sumter in the harbor of Charleston, South Carolina.

Therefore, the majority of the Irish people found that the South, not the North, was the true land of liberty, offering greater social and economic opportunities and easier access into the overall mainstream of everyday life. Indeed, since before the nation's founding in the fiery forge of a people's revolution, the South and its people—not only in the cities but also in the rural areas and in the western frontier regions (as far west as the plains of west Texas)—were fully receptive to the Celtic-Gaelic refugees from hard economic times, famines and British oppression.

Fortunately for America, the massive Irish exodus from the horrors of the Great Famine of the 1840s was nothing new. Significantly, the historic diaspora of the Irish people to America began long before the outbreak of the American Revolution, when they began to emerge into the pulse of Southern society. By the time the first shots were fired between the defiant colonists, including men of Irish ancestry, and redcoat regulars on Lexington Green on April 19, 1775, the transplanted Celtic-Gaelic people had already settled the South (like in the middle colonies, especially Pennsylvania along the western frontier) in overwhelming numbers.

Significantly, the Irish had early served as the vanguard of the vigorous push toward the setting sun and in the overall process of the "winning of the West," settling along the western frontier, especially in the South, decades before the American Revolution. The vast majority of these Sons of Erin fought as patriots from 1775 to 1783 to bestow a distinguished martial legacy and solid claim to full American citizenship that was not forgotten by the Irish on both sides during the Civil War. Consequently, the Irish, especially the descendants of earlier immigrants as opposed to the more recent Famine Irish, were aware that they were continuing a noble tradition of resistance to the rule of centralized authority on both sides of the Atlantic, including centuries of Irish uprisings against the British in Ireland.

Often overlooked by historians was that the South only became generally less tolerant of immigrants after the war partly because of economic hard times (migration went elsewhere) and the greater closure of Southern society to outsiders, who were far fewer in number than before the war: an unfortunate development that has also clouded the many distinguished Irish wartime contributions, including at the Battle of Gettysburg. Not only among the Southern population in general, but also throughout the Confederacy's armies, the strong anti-Irish, anti-Catholic and anti-immigrant sentiment—far more prevalent in the North, especially in the northeastern cities—was largely absent.

Mostly members of lower and middle classes of Ireland, these Sons of Erin were the South's most illiterate and uneducated immigrants, which ensured that large numbers were engaged primarily in menial labor, including the building of railroads, during the antebellum period. But middle-class Irish not only retained their social status on American soil, but they also were often able to seamlessly move up in Southern society and in the army's leadership ranks. For a host of reasons, therefore, the Irish-friendly South saw a disproportionate representation in the Confederate army, a situation that paved the way for disproportionate Irish contributions on America's battlefields, especially at Gettysburg.

Revealing how members of this multicultural and ethnic society rose up to lofty levels in the government and military across the South, the Confederacy's brilliant secretary of war and secretary of state was a Hebrew revolutionary, Judah P. Benjamin of Louisiana. The gifted Benjamin, a former lawyer, was only the most visible representative of the widespread support from the South's Jewish community, where worshippers at synagogues prayed for Confederate victory. Ironically, like the Irish communities of the North and South, so the Jewish people in America were equally divided by the war primarily because of where they resided.

Even more revealing, Major General Patrick Ronayne Cleburne became the Confederacy's highest-ranking Ireland-born officer. He commanded a crack division of the Army of Tennessee during some of the hardest-fought battles in the western theater. Like so many Irish immigrants across the South, Cleburne had made his American dream come true in the South. A respected attorney from Helena, Arkansas, the dynamic Irish general fell while courageously leading his veteran division in the Army of Tennessee's desperate assault on the strong defenses of Franklin, Tennessee, on the bloody afternoon of November 30, 1864 (despite knowing that the attack was suicidal). Here, just south of Nashville, more than six thousand Confederates, including a good many Irish soldiers, were cut down in one of the greatest butcheries of the Civil War.

In total, an estimated forty thousand Irishmen fought for the Confederacy. But, in fact, a far greater number of Rebels of Irish descent, especially Protestant Scotch-Irish whose families had been in America for generations, served in the ranks of every Southern army. However, Lee's Army of Northern Virginia contained the most Irish fighting men, including soldiers who served in forty-five distinctly Irish companies. Although the North possessed a larger overall Irish population because of its immense size and larger urban areas, especially New York City, where immigrants had long concentrated in distinctive ethnic communities for safety and mutual support, the South's Irish served in a far higher overall percentage compared to the North's relatively small contribution. Ironically, the Irish were the most underrepresented ethnic group of immigrants in the North's military machine—the antithesis of the far greater Irish contribution in overall percentage terms in the Southern military. This significant discrepancy resulted in part because so many Irish viewed the North's war of conquest as the same as England's conquest of Ireland. However, the excessive focus on the story of the Irish Brigade, Army of the Potomac, to this day has overshadowed the far more important and extensive Irish contributions for the South.

In another one of the war's classic ironies, the soldiers of the famed Irish Brigade hailed mostly from large northeastern cities, where the Irish suffered greater prejudice and discrimination than did the South's Irish immigrants, even in the waterfront communities and slums of New Orleans. Nevertheless, with a remarkable display of valor, around one thousand Irish Brigade soldiers, mostly Irish Catholics, were cut down in attacks on the impregnable defensive positions of the Sunken Road at Antietam on September 17, 1862, and at Marye's Heights in mid-December 1862 at Fredericksburg. Ironically, many defenders, especially among the Georgians at the Sunken Road, were Irish Confederates who were mostly Protestants.

Overshadowing the distinguished roles played by the Irish Confederates during the bloody three days of the war's most important battle, the best-known Irish story at Gettysburg has long centered on the Irish Brigade's role in the struggle for possession of the Wheatfield on July 2, 1863. Colonel Patrick Kelly, who had migrated to America in 1850, led the Irish with distinction during the slugfest at the Wheatfield after Father William Corby, the chaplain of a New York regiment of the Irish Brigade and the son of an Irish immigrant, bestowed his blessings and a solemn general absolution on hundreds of kneeing soldiers of the Irish Brigade. During the anniversaries of the Battle of Gettysburg, talented members of the National Park

Service have continued to conduct popular tours of "The Irish Brigade at Gettysburg" to enlighten visitors about the bravery and sacrifice of the Irish in blue. Consequently, what least of all comes to mind, even among today's historians and visitors to Gettysburg, is the far more significant role of the Irish at Gettysburg, including at the zenith of Pickett's Charge.

DURING THE CLIMAX OF the bloody showdown at Gettysburg, large numbers of Ireland-born Confederates marched forth in lengthy formations that flowed with mechanical-like precision over the open fields during Pickett's Charge following the Irish Brigade's high sacrifice (more than 200 Irishmen of the 530—all that remained of the 3,000 who had originally enlisted—at the day's beginning) in the Wheatfield on the previous day. Thousands of the attackers in Lee's greatest offensive effort of the war were the sons, grandsons or great-grandsons of Irish immigrants who had seen America as the fulfillment of a great dream. Most of all, what the Irishmen of Pickett's Charge represented was not only an ancient Celtic-Gaelic homeland across the sea, but also the largely Celtic, or Anglo-Celtic, South that consisted mostly of Scotch-Irish from Ulster Province, north Ireland.

As mentioned, fighting against centralized authority had become a way of life to generations of Irish, and the Civil War was only the latest chapter of what had become almost a cultural tradition to the Sons of Erin. The ancestors of many Irish Catholics of the Army of Northern Virginia (ironically, like the blue uniformed men of the Irish Brigade) had been liberty-loving rebels who had risen up against English invaders centuries before on the ancient homeland. Consequently, during Lee's assault on the afternoon of July 3, these Sons of Erin were still proud of carrying on the distinguished revolutionary heritage of Irish rebels that extended back far beyond America's own revolutionary heritage.

During what was actually only their most recent revolution against the domination of centralized authority (now located in Washington, D.C., and not London, but still a faraway power that represented arbitrary rule) and a dissimilar opponent, Irish Confederate companies of numerous regiments attacked over the open fields of Gettysburg with colorful battle flags of green emblazoned with ancient patriotic slogans while unleashing Celtic-Gaelic war cries that had been heard on Ireland's most famous battlefields in a storied past.

Irish commands (companies) represented all corners of the South, including as far west as Texas, especially the port of Galveston, where many Irish immigrants had landed to start anew. Irish regiments like the Tenth Tennessee Confederate Infantry Regiment, whose color bearers carried an emerald green banner in the forefront, earned distinction in the western theater. Large numbers of St. Louis and rural Missouri Irish from the Missouri River country and elsewhere across the state served in the First Missouri Confederate Brigade, which evolved into one of the finest combat units of the war. This hard-fighting brigade was decimated (the highest percentage loss suffered by any brigade, North or South, during the war) in the slaughter at Franklin, where Ireland-born General Cleburne was killed on the last day of November 1864.

Symbolically, these cherished flags of hard-fighting Irishmen across the South were emerald green, which had been the national color of revolutionary and nationalistic Irishmen for centuries. These distinctive war banners were also most often distinguished with a gold Irish harp and ancient Gaelic slogans long revered by nationalists in the bloody course of Irish history. More than any other Irish symbol, the harp was the symbol of not only Ireland and the native Irish but also the fiery faith of Irish nationalism. This longtime hatred of the Irish for their Anglo-Saxon conquerors and occupiers had been intensified by England's failure to assist the starving Irish people during the Great Famine, including not distributing readily available relief. (Ireland had been officially part of Great Britain since 1808.)

This distinguished legacy of vibrant Irish revolutionary and martial traditions was carried forward by the attackers in their desperate bid to split the Cemetery Ridge defensive line in two during Pickett's Charge. As in so many battles waged for centuries against invaders, including the Vikings from the north, on Irish soil, the Army of Northern Virginia's Irishmen during the three days at Gettysburg fully realized that everything was at stake, including the life of their infant republic, on the afternoon of July 3. Such often-overlooked factors provided an additional guarantee that the Green Isle soldiers would give their maximum effort during the most iconic charge in American history.

In regard to explaining the common motivations of the Irish soldier that were atypical compared to other Southern soldiers, no Confederates at Gettysburg fought in general less for slavery than the Irish. After all, the vast majority of these Irish immigrants in gray and butternut were relatively poor and primarily menial workers of the lower class—the former peasantry of the so-called old country. These tough men had been mostly common laborers who had worked on the docks, railroads, levees and small farms of the South. Consequently, relatively few Irish (more the case of Catholics than Protestants—the Scotch-Irish—especially the Great Famine Catholics) in the South owned slaves by 1860. In fact, by inclination, the Irish, especially Catholics, in general were the least likely to be slave owners, in part because they had hailed from a long-oppressed minority and were more empathetic than Anglo-Saxons, who possessed a long history as conquerors.

In truth, these Irish also fought from a sense of sincere gratitude to a Southern society that had accepted them and treated them more fairly than Northern society. Consequently, they were infused with a vibrant new nationalism of a kind experienced by their Celtic-Gaelic ancestors in battling the English invaders over the centuries. Because the South had so thoroughly accepted Emerald Islanders (Catholics and Protestants) for generations and given ample economic opportunities for them to advance up the social ladder unlike in northeastern cities, this path of upward mobility helped to open up many leadership positions in Confederate armies.

One of the myths of the Irish experience in America was that immigrant Irishmen were "duped" by unscrupulous northern recruiters to enlist in Union Armies. This pervasive perception has been most recently reinforced and popularized in Martin Scorsese's magnificent 2002 film *Gangs of New York*. In truth, these Irishmen eagerly enlisted to fight for the honor of Ireland and to reap the social and economic benefits of serving the country and becoming a United States citizen in a land of opportunity compared to impoverished Ireland. Quite simply, the Irishmen, especially those of the Irish Brigade, were not ignorant and manipulated pawns as generally believed, because of long-existing anti-Irish stereotypes.

Because of an emphasis on slavery, what has been generally overlooked was the fact that Irish labor, especially skilled, had long served as a pillar of the South's economy. For generations, the Irish workforce had proved vital to the overall economic development of the largely rural regions of the South. Consequently, the majority of the transplanted Sons of Erin possessed a solid stake in the Southern dream, unlike the large number of Irish in major northeastern cities. Emerald Islanders supplied most of the white manual labor in southern cities, in Atlantic and Gulf ports and in small towns in the South's vast interior, while also providing farms and plantations with more highly motivated workers than slaves, who often employed passive resistance to reduce production, for obvious reasons. Irish immigrants in the South tended to gather in large urban areas on both sides of the Mississippi River, especially New Orleans (the first port of entry into the fertile Mississippi Valley), but also upriver in Memphis and St. Louis, after pushing north by steamboat farther up the "Father of Waters."

To defend this adopted Southern homeland, from the east coast to as far west as the Texas prairies, thousands of Irishmen poured forth to do their patriotic duty in the spring of 1861. The adopted homeland below the Mason-Dixon line was seen as comparable to Ireland—a distinct agrarian region of hardworking common people who viewed themselves as under threat from an authoritarian and powerful centralized government located far away. For the average Irishman of the South, by April 1861, the threat that had long emitted from London was seen as little different from the perceived threat posed by Washington, D.C.

Most of all, a vibrant sense of Irish nationalism evolved smoothly into the overall mainstream of Southern nationalism by 1861, because the two revolutionary struggles of the common people were seen as largely one and the same, despite existing on opposite sides of the Atlantic and separated by thousands of miles—a righteous, if holy, struggle for self-determination ("home rule") by the common people. Significantly, the disproportionate Irish role in Confederate armies also mocked the stereotype that the typical Irish soldier, including the men of the Irish Brigade, was nothing more than an opportunistic mercenary only eager for a steady payday. For the most part, this popular view was a product of the enduring legacy of the exiled Irish Catholic Jacobites, the famed "Wild Geese," who had long fought with distinction for Europe's Catholic monarchies (Catholic France and Spain and other nations), serving far from Ireland but mostly on the European mainland. An estimated half-million Irish served in the Irish Brigades of France and Spain from 1585 to 1818. The legendary Irish soldiers fought and died around the world while serving with distinction under the "green flag of St. Patrick"—the patron saint of Ireland.

A host of distinctive Irish cultural ideas, belief systems, and traditions were also carried by the Emerald Islanders north of the Potomac River and during the army's most audacious assault on the ill-fated afternoon of July 3, 1863. And no enduring idea from the pages of history and a misty Celtic-Gaelic past was more foremost in the hearts and minds of hundreds of these brave Sons of Erin than that Ireland's centuries-long struggle against the oppression of Great Britain was the same as the Confederacy's struggle for self-determination: a determined bid of a largely agrarian people to fulfill their long-held dream of winning independence. For the Irish soldiers, dual revolutionary and historical legacies from both sides of the Atlantic—unlike non-Irish Civil War soldiers—inspired them to perform beyond the call of duty during the three days of combat at Gettysburg.

Significantly, the distinguished Irish Confederate role in the Civil War was mirrored in the equally significant Irish contributions in the war for a new nation's independence. During the darkest days of America's revolutionary struggle, a disproportionately large share (generally around 40 percent, but perhaps as high as 50 percent at the lowest ebb of America's fortunes) of General George Washington's Continental Army consisted of Irish soldiers, including Pennsylvania's famed "Line of Ireland" of crack regular regiments: Scotch-Irish Protestants from Ulster Province, north Ireland, and Catholics from the other three-fourths of Ireland. Not unlike Irish Confederates, America's diehard Irish patriots, including more than twenty generals who played a key role in winning a new nation's independence, have been largely forgotten today. Not surprisingly, therefore, the Irish fighters of the losing effort would become far more forgotten in American memory and public consciousness.

Even the most popularized leader of the most famous charge of the Civil War, Major General George Edward Pickett, who led the Virginia Division on the attack's right wing, rode forth with a story about Irish humor in mind: a symbolic example of deep-seated Irish influences in Southern society, especially since he now commanded so many Irish soldiers from across Virginia, including city boys and recent immigrants from Richmond. In the end, no Confederate soldiers in Lee's army had come farther (more than four thousand miles across the Atlantic) to engage in the largest battle ever fought on American soil than did the Irish.

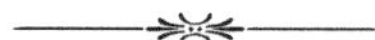

IRONICALLY, WHILE THE TENACIOUS struggle of the Irish Brigade, Major General Winfield Scott Hancock's Second Corps, for possession of the embattled Wheatfield on July 2 before General Dan Sickles' Third Corps had been routed from the Peach Orchard salient, has become celebrated in the annals of Gettysburg historiography, the much more important role played by the Irish on both sides during Pickett's Charge has been long overlooked. A close survey of the military service records at the National Archives of the young soldiers of Pickett's Charge (the "Pettigrew-Pickett-Trimble Charge" is the more proper name) has revealed a disproportionate and high percentage of Irish fighting men among not only the attackers, but also among the casualties.

Of course, this proven demographic reality of Pickett's Charge was perfectly in keeping with the fact that the South was largely a Celtic (or Anglo-Celtic) nation by 1860. The many Irish names of the Confederates at Gettysburg (Kelly, Sullivan, Ryan, Murphy and Fitzgerald) and the even larger number of names with the prefixes "Mc" (such as McMahon) and "O" (such as O'Reilly) have provided additional evidence that the Army of Northern Virginia was most of all an Anglo-Celtic army.

Sadly for the historical record, these hard-fighting Irishmen, except in regard to the Irish Brigade, and their key contributions at Gettysburg have proven almost entirely elusive to even leading Gettysburg historians for more than 150 years. As mentioned, this development can be partly explained by the systematic fading away of Irish identity across the South in the decades after the war and the fact that relatively few immigrant Irish (especially Catholics who had long been denied education by English law) could read or write even as late as the 1860s. Consequently, they left behind relatively few letters, diaries and memoirs, ensuring a forgotten history even in regard to the most important battle of the Civil War.

Therefore, out of necessity because of this overall obscurity about the Irish of the Army of Northern Virginia, this book that has closely analyzed the distinguished role of the Irish Confederates during the three days at Gettysburg has immeasurably benefited from the casual references to Irish soldiers from mostly non-Irish Confederates in their letters, diaries and memoirs. Because of his distinctive and colorful Celtic-Gaelic qualities, the Irish soldier was a source of seemingly endless fascination to many non-Irish Confederates, especially among those men from rural areas. They still embraced the old prewar stereotypes about the Irish in part because more Emerald Islanders lived in the cities than in the countryside. However, in the end, the courage and high sacrifice of the Irish destroyed many lingering anti-Irish stereotypes among the most prejudiced and narrow-minded Southern soldiers, especially those from rural areas but also among officers of the upper class.

This sizeable void in the historical record about the Irish Confederate role during America's true national Iliad is especially ironic today, because the Irish soldier and his wartime capabilities were well known at the time across the Confederacy (and in the North to a lesser degree to mirror the Irish Brigade's widespread recognition for combat prowess) as the hardest-fighting men in the Army of Northern Virginia. In fact, the reputation of the combat prowess of Irish Confederates had spread to the Federal army by the time of the showdown at Gettysburg. Clearly, the average Son of Erin was a unique and distinctive fighting man in Southern armies that served on both sides of the Mississippi.

The well-deserved reputation of the Irish fighting men of the Army of Northern Virginia (a reputation for combat prowess that had been earlier faithfully duplicated by generations of Irish volunteers in Europe's armies, especially those of France and Spain) has made the longtime oversight of their stirring roles at Gettysburg even more incomprehensible. After all, the distinguished role of the Irish on both sides during the climactic moment of Pickett's Charge should have been a focus of historians long ago. (Of special note is the dramatic story of the courageous Irish in blue—Sons of Erin of the Philadelphia Brigade, that was the Second Brigade, Second Division, Second Corps—meeting Irish in gray and butternut at a decisive turning point during the struggle at the clump of trees, which was the "High Water Mark of the Confederacy.") This has not been the case, however.

Instead, these Irish Confederates have become the most forgotten story of not only Gettysburg but also Pickett's Charge, although many Irish attackers were stopped and hurled back by the Irish soldiers in blue in and around the "Angle," just north of the clump of trees. Because of a biased lens focused on a less important showdown, the primary focus of historians has long been the Irish Brigade's story at the Wheatfield on July 2, although far more Irish were participants in Pickett's Charge on the following day. (It is even more of an Irish story when counting Irish defenders on Cemetery Ridge, especially in the ranks of the Philadelphia Brigade.)

The contributions of the mostly Irish Catholics of the Irish Brigade (who hailed mainly from the three quarters of Ireland outside Protestant Ulster Province, north Ireland) have long been memorialized in songs, books, films, paintings and poems. However, the even more crucial story of the Irish, mostly Protestants—primarily Scotch-Irish Presbyterians—from north Ireland, but also immigrant and second-generation Irish, of Pickett's Charge have been overlooked and forgotten.

THE VAST MAJORITY OF Sons of Erin at Pickett's Charge, both recent immigrants and those whose families had been in America for generations, were Scotch-Irish from north Ireland. The term *Scotch-Irish* derives from the fact that their ancestors had been migrants from the lowlands of southern Scotland (an embattled borderland for generations) who later settled in north Ireland (Ulster Province) as part of England's early colonization attempt to transform a hostile land of Irish Catholics into a Protestant bastion and a productive region that could be exploited.

Nevertheless, the Irish Brigade of mostly Catholic warriors has become the most famous ethnic unit of the Civil War, despite representing relatively few Sons of Erin in the overall context of the Civil War. Unlike the achievements of the Irish Confederates, the Irish Brigade's combat record has been romanticized and embellished by historians and writers for generations. Casting a giant shadow over the Irish role in the Civil War, this excessive focus of historians on the heroics of the Irish Brigade has played a role in bringing a dark obscurity to the Irish Confederates—almost as if they were entirely absent from Gettysburg during three bloody days in July—while fostering the still-dominant misconception that the Irish fought almost exclusively for the North.

However, as mentioned, the Irish in blue served in a far smaller overall percentage in regard to the total Northern population than did those in the South, where the Irish were disproportionately represented in the ranks, especially in the Army of Northern Virginia. This wide disparity is best exemplified in regard to the Battle of Gettysburg, because far more Irish served in Lee's ranks than in the Army of the Potomac, contrary to popular perception and conventional wisdom.

Clearly, some fundamental truths about the Irish role have been grossly distorted and obscured, due in part to the excessive recognition of only a relatively small number of Irish Brigade soldiers by discounting a larger number of the South's Irish who fought at Gettysburg. As mentioned, this overemphasis on the much-glorified role of the Irish Brigade—mostly soldiers from northeastern cities—has masked the fact that the Irish were the most underrepresented societal and ethnic group in the Union armies—the exact opposite situation of the Irish Confederates, especially in regard to the Army of Northern Virginia at Gettysburg.

What has been most unrecognized by historians is the fact that, because the South was largely a Celtic or Anglo-Celtic region, the overall Southern and Confederate experiences can often be better understood by looking at key aspects of Civil War history through an intensified Irish lens to guarantee a sharper focus into uncharted territory. In this sense, the American and Southern experiences can be more fully appreciated by taking a closer look at the complexities of the Irish experience on the Green Isle to derive relevant lessons and examples. These Irish fighting men descended from Celtic people (Irish, Scots and Welsh, in regard to those who lived in the South and served in Confederate armies) who were scattered from the western plains of Texas to the Atlantic coast. This rising up of the Irish population in 1861 occurred along a united front that extended across the South for more than fifteen hundred miles.

Symbolically, these Sons of Erin lived in towns across the South with distinctive Irish names, like the tobacco port of Kinsale, Virginia (named after the County Cork port in southern Ireland), and Dublin (in a number of Southern states). Therefore, in a most symbolic representation revealed by demographics and military service records (National Archives, Washington, D.C.) of men who served from the states of Virginia, Tennessee, North Carolina, Alabama, Georgia, Mississippi and Florida, Pickett's Charge was in fact very much a traditional Celtic attack, especially in terms of its overall dominant ethnic composition. Mirroring the Irish demographics of the South and of the Confederate armies in general, this undeniable reality has been one of the most forgotten aspects of the Battle of Gettysburg.

As could be expected in the Confederacy's primary eastern army that protected Richmond and possessed the best chance of winning a decisive victory, some of the best and brightest of the South's Irish (Catholics) and Scotch-Irish (Protestants) served in the Army of Northern Virginia. In this sense, Pickett's Charge was perhaps the most representative and most symbolic example (and certainly the most important) of these disproportionate Irish Confederate contributions on any battlefield during the four years of war.

Additionally, the bloody showdown at Gettysburg revealed the fratricidal nature of the war for the Irish that was an ugly and forgotten reality of the fighting across America. For instance, the brother of Ireland-born Major General Patrick Cleburne wore the blue with pride. The horrors of a conflict that pitted brother against brother were especially the case among the badly divided sons of the Green Isle. Indeed, this was a long-overlooked miniature civil war within the context of the larger Civil War. In this regard, Pickett's Charge has provided the most significant example of the true nightmare of the brothers' war among the Irish people on American soil. (The clash of the Irish in blue and gray at Gettysburg is even more poignant than the Irish Brigade's famous assault directed at overrunning the high ground of Fredericksburg's Marye's Heights, defended by a large number of

Georgia Irish, who slaughtered their fellow Green Isle countrymen without mercy, despite attacking under the waving green battle flags of Ireland that revealed a shared heritage, culture and native homeland.)

FROM THE COBBLESTONE STREETS of Philadelphia (called the "Irish capital" during the American Revolution because of its ethnic demographics and for having been a source of a large number of Green Isle patriots, including the merchant class), the Pennsylvania Irish of the Philadelphia Brigade defended the copse of trees on Meade's right-center when Pickett's attackers pierced the thin defensive line and poured up the slope in a desperate bid to capture the strategic crest of Cemetery Ridge. These determined Philadelphia Irish soldiers, such as Ireland-born Sergeant James Hand of the Sixty-Ninth Pennsylvania Volunteer Infantry, who fell to leave behind a pregnant wife who gave birth to their son shortly after his death, played a leading role in hurling back the onslaught of the large number of Virginia Irish and Scotch-Irish attackers who had broken through the lines at the Angle and farther south at the clump of trees. Here, the Irish engaged in the most savage of little civil wars within a larger Civil War, and this tragic paradox of the Irish experience was most poignantly demonstrated at the "High Water Mark of the Confederacy."

Even this cruel example of Irish killing their fellow countrymen without remorse during one of the most iconic and defining moments of the American experience has long been ignored by historians and relegated to a brief footnote in even the most scholarly works about the Battle of Gettysburg. In one of the Civil War's most classic ironies long overlooked by historians who have failed to fully appreciate the complexities of the Irish experience, the last sight on earth for many attacking Irish Rebels at the very apex of Pickett's Charge was a lengthy battle line of their fellow Sons of Erin (Pennsylvanians mostly from Philadelphia) in blue fighting and dying under the green flag of Ireland—an absolutely shocking sight that reminded surviving Virginia Irish of their distant Celtic-Gaelic homeland while revealing in full the ultimate tragedy and paradox of the Irish experience in America.

Indeed, as a strange fate would have it, the foremost of the counterattacking Union Irish, who hurled the Rebels back across the stone wall that was situated on the slope just below Cemetery Ridge's strategic crest and killed two of Pickett's finest brigade commanders (Brigadier Generals Lewis

Addison Armistead and Richard Brooke Garnett) were Irishmen of the Sixty-Ninth Pennsylvania, Philadelphia Brigade.

As mentioned, the Sixty-Ninth Irish carried a magnificent emerald green battle-flag (the only Pennsylvania regiment to have the permission to do so) that certainly shocked the powder-streaked Confederate Irish at the decisive moment when they believed they had won a decisive victory in splitting the Union army in half. This beautiful silk banner was distinguished by the traditional Irish coat of arms and nationalistic symbols long revered in Irish society, culture and lore. These cherished symbols, well known by Irishmen on both sides, included a round tower, ancient belfries of stone churches seen across Ireland, the swift Irish wolfhound and a yellow sunburst (inspired by the ancient warriors of Irish mythology, the Fianna, who referred to themselves in Gaelic words that meant "sunburst").

This distinctive war banner of emerald green had been donated by the citizens of Philadelphia, which was under threat from General Lee's 1863 northern invasion and would have been doomed without the repulse of Pickett's Charge. After these Irish Catholics had made the sign of the cross to renew their spiritual faith and in the hope of gaining divine protection in the heat of battle, large numbers of Confederate Irish were sacrificed for no gain on the murderous afternoon of July 3, 1863, which played a part in ensuring that their roles in their own words would never be told.

For the first time, therefore, this book will present the story of the Irish at Gettysburg and the Confederacy's most forgotten soldiers, who marched over the green fields of summer during Pickett's Charge in the hope of winning for their adopted homeland the dream that had been denied their ancestors for centuries: the independence of a new nation, a people's republic. Indeed, they were not fighting for the wealthy upper class and slave-owning elite, who were not unlike Ireland's rich English landlords who had long treated the common people with contempt or worse. As generations of their ancestors had fought and died battling against a host of invaders from different lands to the ancient war cry of "Erin go Bragh!" ("Ireland forever"), the Irish Confederates attacked with the same inspiring cry during the height of Pickett's Charge, when it had seemed that the Confederate dream of a Southern nation was about to become a reality.

This book will also tell the story of the little-known Yankee Irishmen who stopped the attackers, especially the troops of Brigadier General James L. Kemper's Virginia Brigade and veteran regiments like the First Virginia Infantry, at the very apex of Pickett's Charge. Despite a shared reverence and love for the green flag of Ireland and the ancient homeland so far away,

Irish fighting men in blue and gray met each other in a nightmarish flurry of vicious hand-to-hand combat with a ferocity seldom seen on that afternoon. Quite simply, Gettysburg served as the highly visible stage of America's own Irish civil war to reveal the complexities of an Irish experience long-ignored.

Supreme sacrifices at Gettysburg were made by a disproportionate number of Celtic-Gaelic men, despite the nagging reality—understood by Irish soldiers on both sides—that this increasingly brutal war for the heart and soul of America was very much a "rich man's war but a poor man's fight." The ancient axiom (more pronounced for them because this was a tragic legacy of Ireland's conquest and subjection by the English) certainly applied to the Army of Northern Virginia's Irish soldiers, who had fought against the same kind of centralized government that had long abused them and their ancestors on the Atlantic's other side.

Clearly, the unparalleled heroics and sacrifices of the Irish (on both sides) at Pickett's Charge is one of the best untold stories not only of the Battle of Gettysburg, but also of the Civil War. The dramatic story of the Irish at Gettysburg has revealed that some of the most neglected and forgotten aspects of even the most famous events in American history can provide some of the greatest revelations about not only the Irish experience, but also the American experience. For more than 150 years, therefore, this remarkable story of the Sons of Erin in gray and butternut at Gettysburg has been lost not only to the general public but also to historians, who have not taken a close microscopic look at this aspect of the famous battle to this day.

In consequence, no monument to the large number of fallen Irish Confederates can be seen today on the most monument-covered battlefield in the world. To be sure, one monument at Gettysburg has proudly displayed the Irish shamrock, but this impressive statue was dedicated to the boys of the famed Irish Brigade. Likewise, an Irish harp is carved into the top of the stone monument dedicated to the heroics of the Sixty-Ninth Pennsylvania, Philadelphia Brigade. Today, the Irish Brigade's role has continued to be told with great enthusiasm to visitors by historians and guides who regularly conduct tours and present programs at the battlefield. But ironically, no such recognition has been bestowed to the Irish Confederates, who have remained the forgotten soldiers of the Battle of Gettysburg to this day.

In the twenty-first century, only the relatively few metal detectors searching Civil War battlefields and Confederate campsites can only occasionally find a physical reminder of Irish Confederate soldiers when discovering an old Irish coin, a clay pipe decorated with an Irish harp, a rusty brass harp insignia worn on hats, a Irish button, or a rare coin (recently found at the site of a Confederate encampment near where the Battle of Shiloh, Tennessee, was fought) that denounced Queen Victoria's June 28, 1838 Coronation in London with the words that accused her of "Trampling on Liberty" (Irish) to gain the English throne.

Indeed, the Irish Confederates have become the most forgotten men of a famed revolutionary Southern army—the most victorious fighting force of its day—that consisted of numerous ethnic groups. When they are mentioned at all, the Irish have long been unfairly stereotyped (as in civilian life, especially in the North and to a lesser degree in the South) in ugly racial terms to obscure the nuances and complexities of the Irish experience on both sides of the Atlantic.

In many ways, the Irish common soldiers of the Army of Northern Virginia who fought at Gettysburg were already outsiders and rebels, long before Southern cannon opened fire on Fort Sumter. In this sense, the Irish of 1861–1865 were actually in the overall mainstream of the American experience by emulating the role of America's revolutionaries—including so many Irish patriots—when another young republic on American soil had struggled for life from 1775 to 1783. Even more, these Irish fighting men were natural rebels by way of heritage, culture, tradition and even religion. As their Holy Bibles had taught them, these men never forgot that Jesus Christ was a defiant rebel against corrupt and abusive Roman authority that had long oppressed the Hebrew people in ancient Judea. Consequently, to the average Irish Confederate, the term *rebel* far exceeded—in its inspirational, spiritual, emotional and psychological meaning—what it meant to the typical non-Irish Rebels of the Army of Northern Virginia at Gettysburg.

Most of all, the Irish had long played a key role in leading the way, especially during the three-day showdown at Gettysburg. The disproportionate Irish performance at Gettysburg, including Pickett's Charge, was in the mainstream of the overall Irish experience from 1861-1865 and most appropriate in terms of continuing a distinguished martial legacy of heroic sacrifice—a continuation of equally impressive martial legacies that had existed for generations on Irish soil. The unforgettable story of the Confederate Irish, the Confederacy's and the army's most invisible ethnic group, reached its zenith at Gettysburg unlike the Irish Brigade, whose members fought under a green flag of a harp and sunburst.

Ironically, when the Irish Confederate survivors of the terrible bloodletting at Gettysburg surrendered at Appomattox Court House on April 9, 1865, few, if any, of these men realized that the nearby Sweeney farm had been settled by an Irish immigrant family from County Mayo, Ireland. They had changed their name by dropping the "Mc" from McSweeney to become more Americanized, and the ambitious immigrants later established the Sweeney Tavern at Appomattox. Joel "Joe" Walker Sweeney (the talented older brother of dark-haired Sam Sweeney of Company H, Second Virginia Cavalry, Army of Northern Virginia, who was fated to die of smallpox on January 13, 1864) had played a key role in fusing slave music (banjo) based on ancient African traditions with the rich musical heritage (fiddle) from Ireland to create the popular tunes that had been sung by confident Confederate troops on the march to a rendezvous with a cruel destiny at a little market and crossroads town in Adams County, Pennsylvania, named Gettysburg.

At long last, it is now time to take a closer and more detailed look at one of the most fascinating chapters of the hidden history of the largest battle ever fought on the North American continent to bring a fresh perspective and new aspect of Gettysburg's history to life while filling a long-existing gap in the historical record. Consequently, this book has explored and emphasized the lives of the individual fighting men in the ranks to provide a better understanding of the overall Irish and Civil War experience. Like no other work to date, this book has restored the forgotten Irish and their significant contributions in the Battle of Gettysburg to their rightful and well-deserved place in the historical record.

1

The Forgotten Irish of the South

No soldiers of the Confederacy were more enthusiastic or highly motivated to fight to win the independence of their adopted homeland than those of the South's largest ethnic group, because the Irish had more to prove to themselves and their non-Irish comrades. The Irish fighting man was a product of dual cultural and historical influences on both sides of the Atlantic. But, perhaps because of the striking paradox of their dual heritage that played a part in their outsized role in the Civil War, the part played by the Irish Confederates has been long ignored or minimized by generations of historians, especially in regard to the Battle of Gettysburg.

The South had early bestowed these Emerald Islanders with greater equality and better opportunities than in the North, especially compared to the major northeastern cities. In addition, breaking away from the grip of the arbitrary power and whims of a faraway centralized government had been the primary Irish dream for centuries, after English armies conquered the Green Isle isolated on Europe's westernmost edge in the late 1600s. By 1861, to the thinking of the vast majority of Irish across the South, the looming threat of an autocratic centralized government was no longer posed by London, but by a newly elected Republican president in Washington, D.C., Abraham Lincoln.

The Confederacy's desperate struggle for independence was so warmly embraced by the transplanted Irish across the South precisely because it was so similar to what generations of Irish—themselves, their fathers, grandfathers, great-grandfathers and great-great-grandfathers—had experienced in attempting to overthrow English domination and to escape autocratic Anglo-Saxon rule.

For the Irish, therefore, the South's struggle for self-determination was not novel or new, because the act of rising up in revolt against the government had become a way of life for generations of Irish. A deep-seated nationalism and a longing for liberty had never died among the common people, especially Catholics, of Ireland. Quite simply, the most ancient of Irish aspirations had been faithfully resurrected on Southern soil in 1861. Here, the South's warrior ethic was largely a Celtic-Gaelic one, because the antebellum South was an Anglo-Celtic region. Ireland's tragic fate as a subjugated land had been determined by its conquest by the crusading Protestants of England in 1690. This brutal conquest of the native Irish people (Catholics) had even resulted in the persecution of priests, who had long served as inspirational revolutionary leaders among the common people. Leading a Puritan army of crusading Protestants who viewed Catholicism as evil, Oliver Cromwell proved to be an absolutely ruthless leader who was determined to rid the Emerald Isle of so-called heretics (or Catholics) by purging the land by committing systematic massacres with his New Model Army in the name of God and England's so-called civilizing mission. The worst slaughter occurred at Drogheda, located just north of Dublin, in 1649, when the city ran with blood when around four thousand Catholics, men, women, and children, were slaughtered by Cromwell's Protestants, after they breached the city's walls.

Despite the heroic efforts of hard-fighting Irish revolutionaries who battled against the odds and a more advanced military armed with superior weaponry, the common people's revolts over the course of hundreds of years were repeatedly crushed by English might. What followed each smashed rebellion were ghastly reprisals fueled by religious hatred. In stubborn defiance, the Irish refused to relinquish their native Catholicism, ancient cultural ways, and Gaelic language to a succession of powerful invaders who lusted for Ireland's fertile lands: the Vikings who founded Dublin, the Normans and the English (the most lethal and determined to achieve a permanent conquest). The Irish people were hardy survivors of a tortured history and tragic past that was foreign to Americans who had emigrated from England. Most of all, the long-suffering Irish had been early preconditioned for rebellion and molded into an ideal soldiery who possessed the unfulfilled dream of an independent nation.

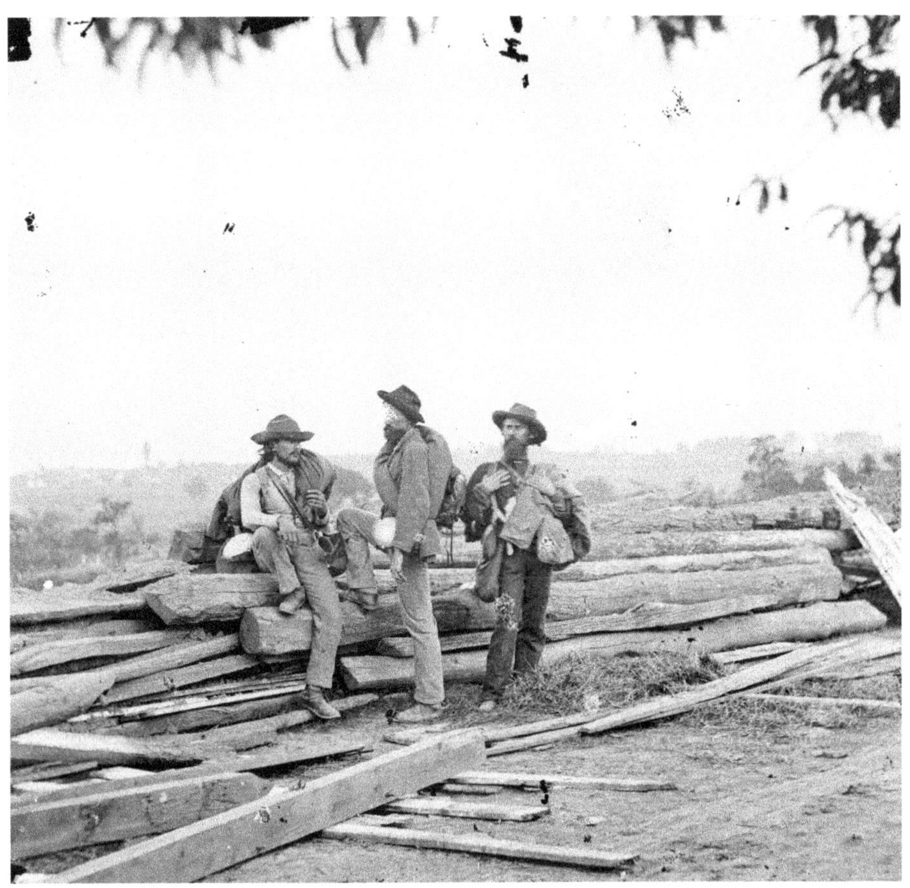

Three veterans of the Army of Northern Virginia captured at Gettysburg. Mathew Brady's photograph of these three defiant-looking Confederates on Seminary Ridge was taken two weeks after the battle. *Courtesy of the Library of Congress.*

The Irish of the South had gained a keen knowledge of historical analogies that still haunted them in 1861, fueling a desire to rush to arms and fight against the newly elected Abraham Lincoln and his Republican Administration. As they had learned from the British, the transplanted Irish in the South feared the evils of a strong centralized government and despotic leaders. After English armies completed the conquest of Ireland, the English and Anglo-Irish elite had established permanent control (the so-called Ascendency) over the impoverished Gaelic-Celtic Catholic masses, whose fertile lands, owned since ancient times by this agrarian people, had been confiscated by the victors. The English imposed harsh restrictions on everyday life, including religion (priests were correctly seen as potential revolutionary and nationalist leaders who held wide influence among the common people) and Gaelic culture in what was an early form of cultural cleansing. In consequence, the Irish became the most oppressed and impoverished people in the western world.

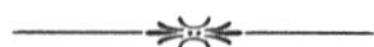

ABUSIVE CONTROL AND HIGH rents (unaffordable by lowly tenant farmers, who were basically peasantry) forced hundreds of thousands of Irish to depart their homeland in two great waves: first, the Ulster Province Irish from north Ireland before the American Revolution; second, Irish Catholics from 1815 to the 1840s. This Irish exodus reached a peak in the 1840s as a result of the Great Potato Famine. Ireland's impoverished people were forced to escape a host of evils, including government abuses, famine, rising rents and economic hard times. Fleeing the ancient homeland to save themselves and their families, the Irish immigrants were, in general, more kindly welcomed in the South than in the North, especially in regard to the major northeastern cities.

Because of the mass exodus of the common people from Ireland for economic, social, and political reasons—mostly Scotch-Irish (Protestant) and then Irish (mostly Catholic) during the Great Potato Famine in the 1840s—the South evolved into primarily a Celtic (or Anglo-Celtic) land, even by the time of the American Revolution. Indeed, by 1861, the South consisted primarily of Celtic settlers (lower and middle class) from Ireland and Scotland, as well as people from other Celtic lands like Wales. From before the outbreak of the American Revolution, the generations-long westward expansion across America had been led by poor settlers, mostly Irish and Scotch-Irish, who had to push toward the setting sun to reach the fringes of settlement and secure land as squatters. Lasting for generations, this was one of the great migrations in human history, with mostly Celtic settlers pushing the limits of the western frontier and their own physical endurance.

Contrary to pervasive stereotypes that still exist today, the South was not (and never had been) a homogenous white, Anglo-Saxon Protestant (WASP) land, according to the romantic legend. This popular myth, born largely from postwar Lost Cause romance, was created in the organized effort to bestow a sense of righteousness and nobility upon a vanquished people who had lost a nation and a way of life. However, this enduring stereotype has played a role in guaranteeing that the Irish Confederates were the most forgotten soldiers not only of the Civil War but also of the Army of Northern Virginia.

Indeed, the creation of die-hard revolutionaries by 1861 was a searing evolutionary process that had begun long before Southern guns opened fire on Fort Sumter. From before the American Revolution, the tide of Celtic settlers who pushed west carried with them their ancestors' traditional anti-English and anti–central government values based on hard-earned experience. Time-honored Celtic-Gaelic qualities, values and legacies, including the celebration of St. Patrick's Day in honor of the Apostle of Ireland, early took firm root in the South's backcountry (including west of the Appalachians in today's east Tennessee even before the American Revolution). What has been most forgotten about the saga of America's relentless expansion west is the fact that Celtic settlers thrived in this new and demanding land in part because of their harsh experiences on the Atlantic's other side, to the point that the Southern people were largely a Celtic people by 1860.[1] Quite simply, the Irish (mostly Scotch-Irish Protestants, as opposed to Irish Catholics) and other Celtic people, especially the Scots, became the very "defining fabric of the South" from the beginning, up to the Civil War.[2]

Therefore, the disproportionate Irish Confederate war effort reflected their predominance in the general population of the South before the fratricidal conflict. Irish contributions from 1861 to 1865 were so widespread that, in the accurate and insightful words of one Confederate soldier, many "gentlemen from the Emerald Isle [were well represented in Confederate Armies], not a few of whom were in every regiment in the service."[3] In fact, the core concepts of the South's militia tradition traced its roots in part to the traditional gatherings of the ancient Celtic-Gaelic clans, especially in Scotland and Ireland, because the Celts had so often gathered to defend homes and families from invaders bent on pillage and conquest.[4] In general, aspiring Irishmen of the middle class across the South most often organized militia companies that had been named after Irish nationalist leaders and heroes like Robert Emmet and Patrick Sarsfield, who both died for the dream of Irish independence, while lower-class men from the Emerald Isle usually served in the enlisted ranks.[5]

Without exaggeration, a journalist with the *Memphis Daily Appeal* told the truth of the Southern war effort that has so often escaped the history books and popular memory: "when the banner of resistance to despotism was raised in the South, the generous, chivalrous Irishmen flocked to its fold, offering their lives in its defense. None are truer patriots—none are more willing to suffer martyrdom in freedom's cause than the oppressed sons of Erin's Isle [who have been] exiled from the land of his nativity by oppression."[6]

Consequently, the disproportionate Celtic-Gaelic demographic of the South—the Irish, especially the Scotch-Irish who outnumbered Irish Catholics unlike in Ireland—fought in the struggle of "the Confederacy, whose culture [and traditions] had been shaped by the clannish, leader-worshiping, militaristic [Sons of Erin and their descendants, who had then actually and in essence] fought a Celtic war" against the United States from 1861 to 1865.[7]

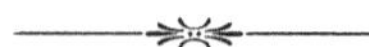

THE CENTRAL MOTIVATION OF this large percentage of Sons of Erin who wore the gray (an estimated forty thousand men who represented the South's largest immigrant group) was perhaps best explained by fiery Irish nationalist and die-hard Southerner and Irish nationalist John Mitchel. Expounding upon the common viewpoint of so many Irish across the South, he emphasized the distinct "parallel [that existed] between the condition of the Southern states and that of Ireland"; therefore, there was only one solution, "as in Ireland...*Repeal of the Union*."[8] As the radical editor of the newspaper *Nation*, he had urged Protestants and Catholics to unite again the English and openly preached the gospel of revolution across the Green Isle before his exile by the alarmed British Government: "The people's sovereignty—the land and sea and air of Ireland for the people of Ireland—this is the gospel that the heavens and earth are preaching, and all hearts are secretly burning to embrace....It is the mighty, passionate struggle of a nation hastening to be born into new national life."[9]

Clearly, Mitchel's great dream of liberation and redemption (the oldest of Irish nationalist aspirations) was rekindled—in an entirely new form—in the South's life-or-death struggle of self-determination. Mitchel's militant nationalism and pro-revolutionary stance had led to his imprisonment in 1848 by British authorities, who feared the force of his powerful words. But the resourceful Mitchel escaped his exile far from Ireland and relocated to the American South after five years of captivity.[10]

Most of all, the Irish saw the South's struggle as the same as that of Ireland's centuries-long fight against another strong centralized government of an imperialistic Anglo-Saxon people who believed that God had bestowed on them the moral right to rule other people and possess their lands.[11] For political exiles from Ireland like the diehard Mitchel, who hated England with an unbridled passion, the transition from Irish revolutionary to fiery patriot on American soil was a seamless one, thanks largely to the searing Irish experience and the lessons derived from it. After all, in many fundamental ways because of the central tragedies of the Irish experience and with roots in the Irish peasantry or farmers, the average Irish rebel of George Washington's Continental army was not altogether different from the typical Irish rebel of General Robert Edward Lee's Army of Northern Virginia in ideological, psychological and motivational terms. After all, both of these wars were people's struggles for self-determination, and the American Revolution was actually similar to the Irish liberation efforts on the Atlantic's other side for generations of lowly Irish.

In both 1775 and 1861, the Irish fought to preserve the life of an infant people's republic against the might of a centralized, distant government (London and Washington, D.C.). Even as they fought for self-determination and the independence of the world's newest republic, Irish soldiers brought their cultural ways and value systems to their military experience, especially a warrior ethos. From the American Revolution to the Civil War, Irish fighting men also maintained their religious faith and celebrated St. Patrick's Day in honor of Ireland's patron saint with the same zeal that they displayed in opposing the soldiers of a centralized government. All the while, they retained elements of ancient Irish aspirations and a sense of Green Isle nationalism, rooted in the Celtic past, which never faded away on American soil, battling in the hope of defeating their enemies that would guarantee a long life for a new independent nation to bring a brighter future.

IRISH ANTECEDENTS IN THE AMERICAN REVOLUTION

The exodus of tens of thousands of Scotch-Irish to America's shores from north Ireland that peaked between 1770 and 1775 ensured that General George Washington's ranks were overflowing with Irish Protestants and Catholic patriots. These soldiers represented a large share (at least 40 percent, very likely even higher at times) of the Continental army, including during the Revolution's darkest days. Since the early eighteenth century, when it was first celebrated in Boston by Ulster Province immigrants (not

Irish Catholics) in Boston in 1737, St. Patrick's Day became a time-honored tradition that was revered by the Irish across the South.

St. Patrick's Day, therefore, was enthusiastically celebrated during the war years by thousands of Washington's Irish soldiers, both Catholics and Protestants (mostly Presbyterians), who were united as one against their longtime oppressor, England. Ironically, the sacred Irish holiday was likewise celebrated by many Sons of Erin in the British army (as in the Union army), which contained a high percentage of Irish soldiers who had enlisted primarily for economic reasons. Military parades in honor of St. Patrick were seen on March 17 in major cities like New York; Charleston, South Carolina; and Baltimore, Maryland, during the American Revolution. Most important, the republican influences and egalitarian legacies of the American Revolution inspired future generations of Irish on both sides of the Atlantic, fueling nationalist aspirations to lofty levels across the South by the time of the Civil War.[12]

Even in the darkest days, Ireland's revolutionary past and St. Patrick were never forgotten by the Emerald Islanders of Washington's Continental army or Lee's Army of Northern Virginia. The hard-fighting son of Scotch-Irish immigrants from north Ireland, Colonel Francis Johnston—who led so many Emerald Islanders of the crack Pennsylvania Continental Line (crack regular regiments) that it was known as "the Line of Ireland"—issued the most culturally appropriate order to his largely Celtic-Gaelic fighting men: "The commanding officer desires that the celebration of the Day [St. Patrick's Day] should not pass by without having some rum issued to the troops [and] While the troops are celebrating the bravery of Saint Patrick in innocent mirth and pastime, he hopes they will not forget their worthy friends in the Kingdom of Ireland [because] like us [they] are determined to die or be free."[13] In revealing the link between two revolutionary struggles on opposite sides of the Atlantic, the Pennsylvania regiments of the Line of Ireland were invaluable to Washington in battling experienced European professionals during a lengthy war of attrition because the Irish "provided the backbone of the American army."[14]

From the American Revolution to the Civil War and in keeping a distinguished martial tradition alive, the Irish perpetuated the revered values of an ancient warrior ethos that had been part of their distinctive Celtic-Gaelic society since ancient times, and this unique cultural legacy led to the well-deserved sobriquet of the "Fighting Irish." This popular name for the hard-fighting Irish soldier was symbolized by one of Ireland's national symbols, the Irish wolfhound, known for its tenacity and combativeness in the pages of Irish lore and legend so revered by the Irish people. The bloody course of Irish history has provided seemingly endless chapters of the combativeness and feisty spirit of the Irish fighting man in the most adverse and no-win situations, but far more from necessity, crisis and emergency requirements than from an alleged genetic disposition of an irrational aggressiveness that had become a negative Irish stereotype (like an alleged excessive drunkenness and laziness).[15]

During key turning point moments of the American Revolution, Washington's Irish soldiers not only dominated the enlisted ranks but also the officer corps of the patriotic men who wore the Continental blue with pride. In total, twenty-two generals of the Continental army were either born in Ireland or were the sons or grandsons of Irish immigrants.[16] Ironically, in an unfortunate historical continuum in regard to two revolutions, the disproportionate roles and numbers of the Irish who fought in the ranks of General Washington's army have been as forgotten as the disproportionate numbers of Irish Confederates.

This distinguished legacy of Irish contributions to the winning of liberty was not lost to the Civil War generation. Irish leaders and communities across the antebellum South kept the truth alive about the significant Irish contributions in winning America's independence. In the words of one of the transplanted Irishmen in Alabama, the "country of Washington owes a large debt of gratitude to Ireland."[17] Therefore, for ample good reason, in regard to the invaluable contributions of the Irish throughout the struggle, especially the low points of America's fortunes, General Washington (like General Robert E. Lee in regard to the Irish of his Army of Northern Virginia) "loved them, for they were companions of his toils, his glories, in the deliverance of his country."[18]

THE RISING OF THE CELTIC-GAELIC CLANS

Thousands of Irish across the South viewed the defense of their adopted homeland against Northern invaders in the same way (a sacred duty) that generations of Irish had viewed nationalistic struggles in defense of their beloved Emerald Isle against invading Norsemen and then Anglo-Saxon invaders from England.[19]

The seamless merger of dual revolutionary influences from opposite sides of the Atlantic was early displayed by the Irish soldiers of the Emerald

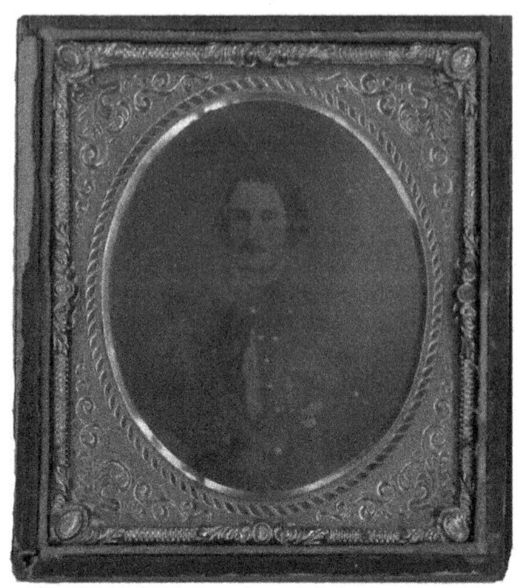

Tintype of a dashing Confederate officer, who is holding the brass handle of his sword. *Author's collection.*

Guards (Company I), Eighth Alabama Infantry, Army of Northern Virginia. The Irish marched off to war with typical Celtic-Gaelic enthusiasm to meet the blue-uniformed enemy, viewing them as little different from Englishmen, especially the New Englanders who had long boasted about their Anglo-Saxon purity. The nucleus of this disciplined Irish company had been the men of the Mechanics Fire Company of Mobile, Alabama. A total of five companies of the Eighth Alabama consisted of men from Mobile. Consisting of both city boys and soldiers from rural areas, the regiment joined General Cadmus Wilcox's Brigade, Army of Northern Virginia just before the 1862 Peninsula Campaign. The Eighth Alabama proved to be a crack fighting command. Along with Wilcox's other Alabama regiments, the Eighth Alabama, including the Irish of the Emerald Guards, played a key role in the dramatic showdown at the Battle of Salem Church, a brick structure on a commanding hilltop. Here, about four miles west of Fredericksburg, Virginia, and performing splendidly under the skilled leadership and tactical brilliance of General Wilcox, the Alabama troops were instrumental in buying precious time by slowing the advance of General John Sedgwick's powerful Sixth Corps from marching west to Chancellorsville to strike the rear of Lee's Army that now faced the forces of "Fighting Joe" Hooker.

At the head of more than one hundred Ireland-born soldiers who wore uniforms of "dark green," representing the blending of Irish and Southern nationalism into one, flew a colorful silk banner of emerald green. This battle flag was decorated with the Irish war cries of "Erin go Bragh!" and "Faugh a ballagh!" and ancient Irish symbols long revered by the people of Ireland. Such long-existing nationalistic symbols inspired these Irish fighting men with memories of old Ireland, fueling their combativeness to high levels against what they viewed as only the latest threat to the Irish people.

Born in Cloyne, Ireland, John Quinlan, Roman Catholic bishop of Mobile, blessed this distinctive Irish battle flag of the Eighth Alabama in a solemn ceremony that fused Irish and Southern nationalism while reinforcing the prevalent view that this was a sacred emblem of a righteous struggle against oppressors. Quinlan migrated to America in 1844 and fulfilled his religious ambitions. The Eighth Alabama, including a good many Sons of Erin, such as the capable Captain William Fagan, age twenty-two and the great-grandson of an Irish immigrant, was part of Brigadier General Cadmus Wilcox's Alabama Brigade, Lieutenant General Ambrose Powell Hill's Third Corps, during the ill-fated offensive effort on the climatic final day at Gettysburg, Pickett's Charge. Other Emerald Islanders served in Wilcox's brigade. A fine regiment of determined fighting men that made Wilcox's Brigade so effective on the battlefield, the Ninth Alabama consisted of nearly one hundred former laborers of the Tennessee & Coosa Railroad from Guntersville, Alabama, especially Company B, which was appropriately known as the "Railroad Guards." Large numbers of Irish laborers had laid iron track and built railroads across the South. Other Alabama regiments, including the First Alabama, were also distinguished by an emerald green hue in terms of their demographics.

These highly motivated Irish of the Eighth Alabama, especially the Irish company known as the Emerald Guards, hailed from the port of Mobile, which was the oldest "Latin town" east of Mexico on the American mainland after the Spanish town of St. Augustine in northeast Florida. Revealing European-influenced qualities and characteristics like those of New Orleans, and also founded by the French, Mobile was distinguished by colonial architecture, elegant brick townhouses shaded by giant live oaks and festive Mardi Gras celebrations in the cobblestone streets. Mobile had long been a cosmopolitan town where Spanish, French and Italian were spoken more than English in the streets. Eager to meet the Yankees, Irishmen of Mobile formed a volunteer unit named in honor of the revered Irish revolutionary martyr Robert Emmet. A victim of the English, who were masters at early crushing Irish revolts, young Emmet had been hanged before a large crowd in Dublin, becoming one of the most revered heroes and revolutionaries of Irish history. The so-called "foreign" population of Mobile consisted of nearly one-quarter of the total populace of one of the South's largest cities. Mobile was one of the largest immigrant-filled cities in the Confederacy, after New Orleans, which was distinguished by its vibrant French Quarter and large Irish community in distinctive ethnic neighborhoods like the Irish Channel.

Symbolically, on one side of the Eighth Alabamians' banner was a hand-painted portrait of George Washington, who had long represented

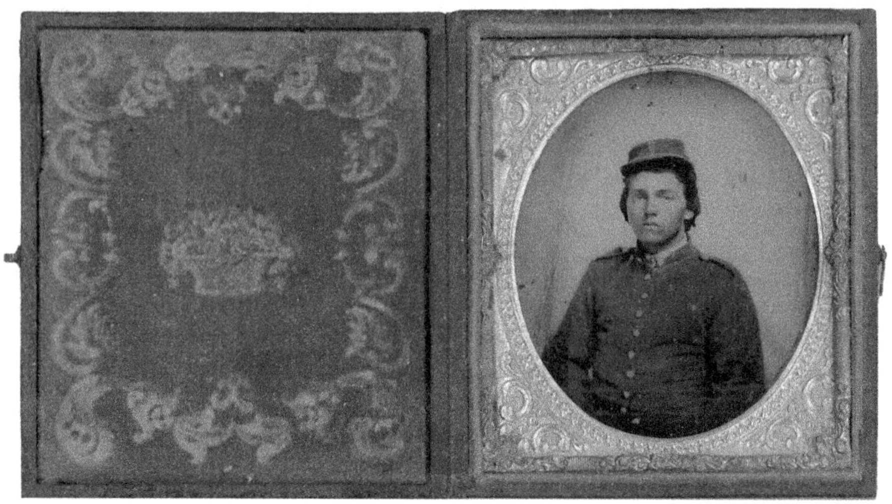

Tintype of a young Confederate private wearing piped kepi. *Author's collection.*

a new birth of freedom to people around the world. On the flag's other side were colorful images that reminded the Mobile Irish of a much older and lengthier struggle against the same opponent, the English who had surrendered to Washington and America's French Allies at Yorktown, Virginia. The most cherished Irish symbols—a wreath of shamrocks, an Irish harp of gold and the Gaelic battle cry "Erin go Bragh!"—decorated this beautiful battle flag of green. Ironically, this same war cry and Gaelic nationalist slogan were distinctive features of the flags of Union Irish regiments, especially the mostly Catholic fighting men of the Irish Brigade, Army of the Potomac. Like the Irish Confederates, the Irish Brigade soldiers were also profoundly influenced by the memory of Ireland. Color Sergeant Peter Welsh, Irish Brigade, penned in a letter how: "When we are fighting for America we are fighting in the interest of Irland (sic)" in this war.[20] Across the South, the emerald flag possessed a magical "control over the brawny sons of the Emerald Isle," fueling their determination to fight to the bitter end.[21]

In every battle, the inspirational influence of Irish flags was powerful, reinforcing a deep emotional, historical and symbolic appeal to the average Irish soldier of both the North and South. Indeed, "the green flag seemed to exert a magnetic control [and] their fondness for their own companies is explicable: the Irishman fights better shoulder to shoulder with Irishmen as comrades, and always yearns to reflect honor on 'Ould Ireland.'"[22]

The combat prowess of the Sons of Erin ensured that Irish companies were often designated regimental color companies, which led the way in attacks, including during all three days at Gettysburg. This development can be seen in the Irish color companies of the following combat commands: the Virginia Hibernians of Company B and from Alleghany County, Twenty-Seventh Virginia Infantry; the Irish Volunteers of Company K and from Charleston, First South Carolina; and Jackson Guards from Atlanta, Company B, Nineteenth Georgia.[23]

A CRACK SOLDIERY

Ironically, as demonstrated during the slugfest at Gettysburg and on other battlefields across America, the long-established reputation of the Irish soldier as a superior fighting man, especially in key combat and crisis situations, revealed a central paradox of the overall Irish experience. Indeed, in the words of one historian who revealed one of the great contradictions in Irish history, "History gives evidence of the combat characteristics of the Irish; yet it might equally well be argued that, left to themselves, the Irish were never given to militarism."[24] Nevertheless and most significantly, "the bulk of the Confederate Army, including most of its leaders" was in fact fighting men of Scotch-Irish descent, including in Lee's Army of Northern Virginia at Gettysburg.[25]

To the average Irishman of the South, this was a sacred struggle for liberty, but this was one that bitterly divided the Irish across America. One North Carolina Irishman hoped and prayed with a righteous sincerity that "an over-ruling Providence [would kindly] save" his fellow Irishmen of the North "from the guilt of raising their hands against the Southern people" who fought for the establishment of a new people's republic.[26] But most Irish Confederates believed that killing their fellow countrymen was far more of a necessary requirement for the winning of the Confederacy's independence than attempting to convert them by reminding the Irish Yankees of their shared revolutionary and cultural roots. On some of the bloodiest battlefields of the war, meeting in bloody reunions that revealed no hint of a mutual heritage and ties of brotherhood, Emerald Islanders shot down their fellow Irishmen in blue with a grim intensity that caused one astounded Southern officer to ask an Irish common soldier why he killed so many fellow Sons of Erin with impunity. In reply, the seasoned fighting man simply answered with homespun fatalism that "they must all take it as it comes."[27]

Such a wide variety of complex emotional, psychological and moral factors not found among the non-Irish, especially when combined with the desire to demonstrate loyalty to the Confederacy and prove worthiness as equal citizens, made the Irish Confederates the best fighting men of Lee's army by the time of the showdown at Gettysburg. Known for their determination to reap victory at any cost despite the odds or disadvantageous combat situations, the Emerald Islanders established legendary reputations for heroics not only in the army but also on the home front.

However, the widespread recognition of the combat prowess of the Irish came at a frightfully high price from 1861 to 1865, resulting in disproportionately high casualty rates among the Sons of Erin: the identical tragic fate that befell the Irish Brigade that became legendary across the North. While noted for a feisty defiance toward autocratic authority (including occasionally toward the officer corps of the Confederate army, including generals) and a sometimes belligerent, quarrelsome nature that was the flip side of their well-known merriness and well-honed sense of humor demonstrated both on and off the battlefield, the Irish soldier in gray and butternut transformed liabilities into assets that placed in the shadows the lack of discipline—far more off than on the battlefield—and defiance toward authority.

Most of all, the Irish fighting man was known for rising to the fore during the most severe challenges and crisis situations on the battlefield, such as during the three days at Gettysburg. Consequently, these Sons of Erin (still very much Old World men fighting in the New World so that their new country would not become like their subjugated homeland) earned a lofty reputation for superior combat performances in the most severe contest, becoming the talk not only of the army but also across the South. Rising splendidly to the challenge in one key battlefield situation after another on both sides of the Mississippi, the Irish Rebels fought their hardest and performed their best beyond the call of duty most often when the situation was the most critical, such as during Pickett's Charge.

Years of invaluable prewar militia experience gained by middle-class Irish (who mostly served as officers, like lower-upper-class members in general) and lower-class Irish—primarily serving in the enlisted ranks—in major Southern cities from Richmond to New Orleans prepared them for the stern challenges of war. The importance of this often overlooked militia experience that instilled invaluable training also fueled pride in the men's distinctive

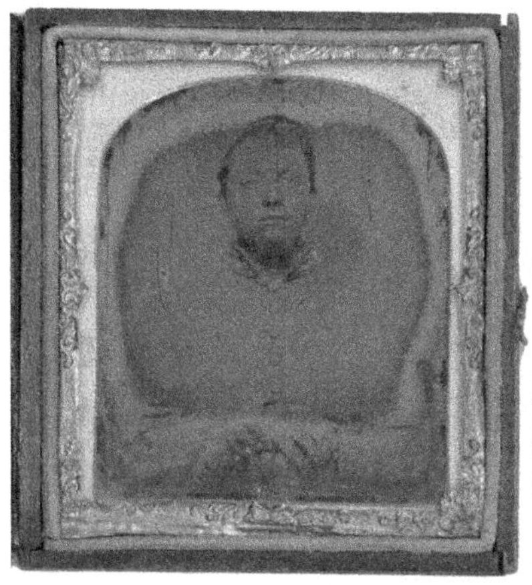

Pious North Carolina soldier holding the Holy Bible in his hands. Wartime tintype. *Author's collection.*

Irishness, ancient martial traditions, and the distant Celtic-Gaelic homeland that was always in their hearts and minds.

For such reasons, the Irish fighting men—officers of mostly middle-class status (primarily artisans and merchants in civilian life) and enlisted soldiers of the laboring class—made for ideal Southern soldiers committed to fighting to the bitter end so that the South would never suffer Ireland's dismal fate. The Irish soldier was distinguished by superior combat capabilities, resiliency, and flexibility on the field of strife while garnering a well-deserved reputation for physical and mental toughness and, especially, resourcefulness on the battlefield. The lofty reputations of the Irish for bravery and high sacrifice were repeatedly verified in highly visible roles in key combat situations, as when Sons of Erin led the charge as color guard members or banded together in protecting regimental colors from capture during close-quarter combat—especially if that battle flag was a cherished green one.

Whenever the battlefield situation was darkest and the odds against them were the longest, Irish soldiers were widely known for standing fast and firm amid the fiercest combat, continuing a legacy of fighting to the bitter end for God and country. The Irish fighting man especially excelled in the tactical offensive, when he charged a foe with a well-known abandon while unleashing ancient Gaelic war cries of "Faugh a ballagh!" ("Clear the way"). The penchant for unleashing tactical offensive in a manner that bordered on recklessness was the best-known quality of the Irish soldier, extending back centuries and becoming legendary on both sides of the Atlantic. The Irish Brigade, Army of the Potomac, became famous for its costly assaults at Antietam and Fredericksburg.

But the Irishmen in gray and butternut possessed another quality that helped to make them the most unique and distinctive ethnic soldiers of the Army of Northern Virginia and the South. The high spirits and lively humor of the Irish fighting man was the common coping mechanism of an oppressed and longtime underdog people who had long suffered on the Green Isle. Such a distinctive and keen humor, marked by a distinctive cutting-edge wit, satire, ribaldry, and cynicism born of lives dominated by hardship and adversity, was evident among Irish soldiers even in the most daunting battlefield situations. The Irish also possessed a sharp sense of fatalism that often merged with humor. Not long before the attack on Marye's Heights at Fredericksburg, where the Irish Brigade was cut to pieces, one member of the Irish Brigade promised in a letter how he expected "the ball will [shortly] open [and] we will make them dance" to their Irish tune. Other than black slaves, no people in America had faced greater hardships and difficulties than the mostly lower-class immigrants from Ireland, more so in the North than in the South. The extremely challenging and overall toughening process of the Irishman helped to create a highly durable and excellent fighting man without peer in the armies of North and South.[28]

THE ARMY OF NORTHERN Virginia was filled with thousands of Irish soldiers, from immigrants to the sons, grandsons and great-grandsons of Celtic-Gaelic immigrants who had fought in America's previous wars. As a result, General Lee's Army, from lowly privates to the highest-ranking leaders, was primarily a Scotch-Irish fighting force that especially excelled in the tactical offensive. Under Lee's aggressive leadership since the Seven Days' Battles, the Virginian's distinct penchant for achieving excellence in the art of the tactical offensive was especially evident during the victorious Confederate assaults at Second Manassas and Chancellorsville.[29] Perhaps historian James Webb, in his book *Born Fighting*, said it best in regard to truly understanding what made Lee's Army of Northern Virginia the successful fighting machine that repeatedly defeated the Army of the Potomac: "the bulk of the Confederate Army, including most of its leaders, was Scots-Irish."[30]

However, since so much focus of generations of historians, North and South, has been placed on the dramatic story of the three brigades of the Virginia Division of Pickett's Charge at the expense of the heroics and sacrifices of thousands of North Carolinians, Alabamians, Tennesseans, Floridians and Mississippians, the Irish Confederates who served in these other fine combat units that advanced to the Virginians' left during Pickett's Charge were even more forgotten. Indeed, Pickett's Division cast a giant shadow to obscure significant contributions of Irish attackers to the north.

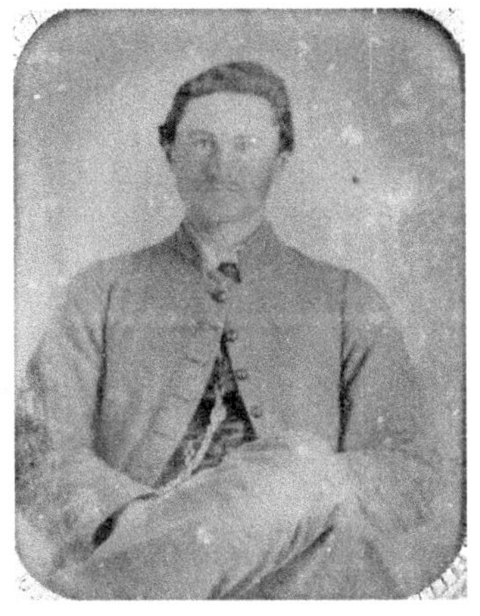

Tintype of young private wearing standard uniform coat with Confederate "I" infantry buttons. *Author's collection.*

But despite the importance of the distinguished roles played by the Irish Rebels and their disproportionate battlefield achievements on both sides of the Mississippi, the contributions of these Irish fighting men have become lost in the mainstream portrayal of America's national *Iliad*, even though they were among the South's most enthusiastic defenders who fought and died in disproportionate numbers. This widespread enthusiasm for the South's struggle for independence was forthcoming despite the fact that the vast majority of the Sons of Erin, especially those of the lower class, had no direct connections to slavery or the planter class elite before Confederate guns opened on Fort Sumter.

Quite simply, what has been most forgotten about the Confederate experience was that these mostly lower-class Irishmen were not primarily motivated by or interested in defending either slavery or the wealthy upper-class elite (like the English and Anglo-Irish elite who ruled Ireland), because they were part of neither. In truth, the deep bond of the Irish to their adopted homeland of the Confederacy was largely an ideological, psychological, emotional and political one that had little if anything to do with the institution of slavery. In this sense, therefore, the Irish in gray and butternut were perhaps the most atypical and unorthodox soldiers of the Confederacy—a key distinction long overlooked and ignored by historians.

OLD PREJUDICES AND STEREOTYPES

Ironically, then and even today, a certain degree of prejudice against the Irish has continued to exist from non-Irish historians and writers, further obscuring their key contributions from the American Revolution to the Civil War, almost as if the large number of immigrant volunteers who hailed from a small Green Isle on Europe's western edge was an absolute impossibility. In this regard, the strength of the powerful Anglo-Saxon myth—or America's traditional history—has continued to dominate the general thinking and common assumptions about the South and the Confederate soldier who fought to defend the land he loved.

Therefore, generations of Southern and Civil War historians have continued to routinely dismiss this vital contribution of Emerald Islanders on all levels during the struggle for the independence of an infant nation conceived in violent revolution. But most of all, generations of mainstream and traditional historians have routinely ignored the fact that the Confederacy was very much a Celtic (or Anglo-Celtic) region and nation due to the heavy volume of immigration that had poured in from Ireland since before the American Revolution.

This unfortunate development in the field of history is much like the common portrayal of longstanding Anglo-Saxon-dominated myths that guaranteed the persistent lack of recognition for Irish contributions in not only the American Revolution but also America's saga of westward expansion. To address this glaring negligence in American history that has continued unabated to this day, a revealing book by Myles Dungan, *How the Irish Won the West*, has recently helped to bring a new awareness and proper recognition to the importance of Irish contributions in America's story. He correctly emphasized how Irish contributions to the West's settlement have been overlooked because of the enduring myth that the western experience was entirely a white Anglo-Saxon Protestant (WASP) one. Only recently, historian Phillip Thomas Tucker, Ph.D., has likewise bestowed long-overdue recognition upon the forgotten Irish and their vital roles during the struggle for independence in his *How the Irish Won the American Revolution* (Skyhorse Publishing, 2015).

As mentioned, a comparable general assumption and stereotypical view from a distorted lens has resulted in the lack of focus on the Irish Confederate contributions at all levels, especially in regard to the climactic showdown at Gettysburg. After all, Pickett's Charge was largely a Celtic attack (like the largely Southern Celtic or Anglo-Celtic Confederacy itself) in terms of its overall dominant composition and cultural characteristics and even in regard to providing a partial explanation of the heavy reliance on offensive tactics. If hundreds of Irish attackers had broken through the weak Union right-center on the crucial afternoon of July 3, 1863, perhaps a future book could then have been written under the appropriate title of *How the Irish Won the Battle of Gettysburg*.[31]

2

Virginia's Hard-Fighting Irish

As the contours of history and as the gods of war would have it, an ill fate seemed to dog the long-suffering Irish people for generations on the much fought-over Emerald Isle—the "old sod"—because of the tragic legacies that stemmed from England's subjugation and abuse of the population. Perhaps no famous slogan has been more misplaced for the Irish than "the luck of the Irish" unless it was meant to be sarcastic. The unpredictable patterns of history had not been kind to the Irish people on both sides of the Atlantic. In truth—and because it seemed as if there was a dark "curse on ould green Ireland," in one immigrant's insightful words—migration to America had long offered the only solution for escape and salvation not only for impoverished Irish but also for Emerald Islanders of middle-class status.[32]

The Great Famine of the late 1840s and early 1850s flooded the American South with immigrants, who rejoiced upon successfully leaving the Green Isle. For good reason, the Irish had been embittered at the lack of humanitarian assistance and effective food distribution from the apathetic centralized government in London, which ruled Ireland with an iron hand and a righteous arrogance. Without a government of their own, the Irish were completely at the mercy of the aristocratic whims of England. Even Americans, Quakers, Jews and even the Choctaw Nation sent food to Ireland, but this was not enough to stem the crisis. Almost in a token display, London established food distribution centers in major cities that proved inadequate and ineffective. Many English believed that an angry God had decided to smite the Irish for their alleged character sins and that the famine was a righteous retribution to punish the Irish people. An estimated one million Irish died of starvation and disease. Catholics, the native Irish, were more impoverished than Irish Protestants and suffered the most during the famine.

John Mitchel said it best in regard to this simmering hatred toward abusive big government, which still viewed the Irish as savages of a different race and placed them last in terms of priorities and interests. Increasing numbers of outraged people on both sides of the Atlantic claimed a deliberate policy of genocide had been orchestrated by England to rid the island of tenant farmers to transform agricultural regions into far more profitable stock-raising areas. "The Almighty sent the potato blight, but the English created the famine" by withholding timely assistance, especially food (stored in warehouses or exported to England to reap hefty profits) that could have saved thousands of men, women and children.[33] The mass exodus flowing from Ireland made America, especially the already largely Celtic South, even more Celtic-Gaelic in terms of overall demographics.[34]

But, as mentioned, large numbers of immigrants had migrated to the South long before the Great Famine, even before the American Revolution. In 1832—nearly a decade and a half before the potato famine—among the tens of thousands of Irish immigrants without prospects or high expectations, John Dooley immigrated to the South. He boarded a sailing ship bound for America at one of Ireland's principal ports, probably Limerick on the Shannon River but perhaps Galway on the west coast, when he was nothing more than "a poor immigrant" along with a group of other hopeful Irish that included his future wife, Sarah Jane.

The two were cousins, and a close bond existed between them. As in this case, the long trip across the Atlantic was often an extended family undertaking for the lowly Irish, who pooled their meager resources for the difficult crossing that took weeks. John and Sarah hailed from the same bustling market town of Limerick, located in the green countryside of southwest Ireland. Limerick possessed its own connection to the Atlantic with its strategic location at the head of the wide estuary of the Shannon River (Ireland's longest watercourse). The town had been founded by Vikings, who became the masters of Ireland's waterways. Contrary to popular stereotypes, the Vikings were far more settlement- and commercial-minded than the popular image of plunderers bent on mindless destruction of villages and churches. They established trading and farming communities across the Emerald Isle that eventually evolved into Ireland's leading cities, including Dublin.[35]

Along with other Dooley family members, the two cousins departed picturesque Limerick (known as "Luimneach" in Gaelic), drawn by the irresistible pull of the golden dream of a better life in America. It carried them on a watery journey of more than four thousand miles and lasting more than a month. For almost all of these hopeful immigrants, the perilous journey across the Atlantic was a one-way trip, because they were leaving Ireland forever. Like their fellow emigrants, Dooley family members knew that there was no turning back or returning to Ireland. They left behind everything that they had ever known in pursuit of making the great dream of America a reality.

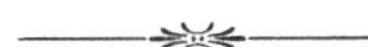

JOHN DOOLEY AND HIS group of immigrants were part of the centuries-long diaspora of the Irish people escaping religious and political persecution, English abuses, famine and hard economic times. Large numbers of the best and brightest Irish moved far away from the Green Isle, and America benefited more than any other nation. Symbolically, the Shannon River town of Limerick had been the scene of an earlier struggle for liberty when the besieged town became the last center of Catholic Jacobite resistance against an invading English army in 1691.

At this memorable turning point in Irish history, the town's citizens, including defiant Irish women who loved Ireland as much as the men, had hurled rocks and bottles at attackers in the fight to save their beloved city. But spirited resistance and valor had not been enough to save the ancient town along the clear waters of the Shannon. Limerick's surrender and the vanquishing of lofty nationalistic aspirations of the Jacobites in early October 1691 ended the bloody religious conflicts known as the Jacobite Wars. This decisive defeat of the Catholics guaranteed England's complete subjugation of the bountiful and beautiful lands of Ireland. This turning point in Irish history had made America the destination of choice for generations of Irish to escape the ugly realities of a dismal life as a conquered people under foreign rule.[36]

During this period, a flood of hopeful Irish immigrants entered the major ports along the Eastern Seaboard, including Baltimore, Maryland, and cities situated along the Gulf of Mexico, like Mobile but especially New Orleans, Louisiana (the "Crescent City"), on the Mississippi River. The Seventeenth Virginia Infantry, Major General George Edward Pickett's division, was distinguished by Irish soldiers of the Emmet Guards and the

O'Connell Guards. These men from the "old sod" hailed from the busy port of Alexandria, Virginia, on the Potomac River, across from Washington, D.C., and just north of George Washington's Mount Vernon.

In September 1836, John and Sarah Jane Dooley were married—it was common for cousins to wed in this day—in a solemn ceremony at a Catholic church (almost certainly St. Joseph Church) located in the heart of Alexandria. Living at this longtime tobacco port—from where Virginia's earliest primary cash crop had been sent down the Chesapeake to lucrative markets around the world—was one of General George Washington's most faithful staff members during the American Revolution, Ireland-born Lieutenant Colonel John Fitzgerald. Known for his merry personality and love of good jokes, he had emigrated from County Wicklow, Ireland, in 1759 and settled in Alexandria.

Later in 1836, to take advantage of greater economic opportunities, John and Sarah Jane Dooley settled permanently in Virginia's busy capital, Richmond, which was situated on the muddy James River in the Tidewater and not far from the Atlantic: the heart of the Old Dominion's tobacco country. As expected by the new transplants because the Irish were clannish, the Dooley family found a thriving Irish community in Richmond. Irish immigrants had first settled along low-lying Shockoe Creek section of town (the Shockoe Valley on Richmond's west side, before the creek flowed into the James River).

The bustling state capital offered plenty of jobs in the tobacco warehouses along the river and in the flour mills. Here, the immigrant Irish labored long hours and then went home to the bleak and rough-and-tumble working-class community known as Butchertown, which consisted of rows of tanneries and slaughterhouses in the unhealthy part of Richmond. Meanwhile, middle- and upper-class Richmonders lived on the healthier higher ground, including Shockoe Hill, which was swept by fresh river breezes and overlooked the majestic James River. These older residents had moved higher up in the social order, unlike the most recent immigrant Irish. Virginia, known as the Old Dominion, contained a "foreign" population of more than 35,000, including more than 16,500 Irish citizens, out of a population of just over 38,000 people in 1860.[37]

Embarking on a fresh start in a new land of a promise on a scale unknown in Ireland, John and Sarah were part of the dominant trend of Irish immigrants who settled primarily in Southern cities, which offered greater economic opportunities than could be found in large Northeast urban areas at this time and encouraged the growth of vibrant Irish communities.

A highly social people who closely embraced family, the Irish tended to congregate in Irish communities and enclaves in the larger Southern cities. Indeed, because the Irish in general were "a gregarious people [they were naturally] drawn to city neighborhoods where there was a sense of community reminiscent of the rural villages where they grew up" in the picturesque countryside of the Green Isle.[38]

With hard work and determination, John Dooley achieved success as a hatter and furrier, benefiting from the general prosperity of Virginia's capital and its thirty-eight thousand residents in 1860. Just as important, the Dooley family was early embraced in full by the people of Richmond. They encountered little, if any, of the anti-Irish or anti-immigrant animosity that was so prevalent in large northeastern cities, especially New York City and Boston. In time, Dooley's popularity and business success elevated the family to upper-class status, guaranteeing entry into the city's social elite and a world of prosperity.

Accomplishing in Richmond what would have been virtually impossible for an Irish immigrant family to duplicate in a major northeastern city, Dooley was part of a true success story seen by other Sons of Erin across the South. In a relatively short time, he had moved up from impoverished immigrant status to a highly respected member of Richmond's upper class. This kind of smooth evolution and social mobility engendered a deep love for the South in successive generations of Irish immigrants. The success story of the Dooley family has provided a very good representative example of the more abundant opportunities and easier assimilation that existed for immigrant Irish, both Protestant and Catholics, in a more tolerant South than in the North.

A healthy brood of fun-loving children (five daughters and two sons) grew to maturity in the Irish-friendly environment of Richmond. Born on July 12, 1842, John Edward Dooley Jr. was the most promising child of the extended Dooley family. Dooley's large home became not only a popular center of social activities for Irish and Irish Americans in Richmond but also a special place that bestowed a host of Irish historical and cultural legacies upon the children. Here, along the sluggish James River, the memories of the history of Ireland were kept alive, including a distinct sense of Irish nationalism and cultural pride in the ancient homeland so far away.

Clearly, despite success in the mainstream of Irish social life in Richmond, the Dooley family never turned their backs on any aspect of their Celtic-Gaelic heritage or their Emerald Isle past. They cherished the richness of their family's Irish legacies so that they continued to exist as faithfully as the rising sun glimmered over the James River on a hot summer morning. As with so many Irish who had found a fresh start and a new home in the South, the Irish past was something that was revered by these opportunistic new Americans who had taken full advantage of the ample economic and social opportunities that were presented to them. Here, the Dooley family celebrated time-honored Celtic-Gaelic military traditions, cultural values and folkways (like St. Patrick's Day, which promoted a distinctive Irishness and helped to fuel the spirit and faith of Southern nationalism by 1861 among the Irish across the South). Most important, an ancient warrior ethos from the Green Isle was likewise transferred across the Atlantic, taking root among the Irish across the South and playing a role in preparing them for the nightmare of the Civil War.

The Making of Irish Rebels on American Soil

The Dooley home and family were always open to lower-class Irish immigrants whom the family often assisted with the process of acclimating to a new life. More important, John Dooley early on struck up a lasting friendship with the leading Irish nationalist, advocate of Ireland's independence in America and foremost Irish political exile of the day, John Mitchel. He was a frequent visitor to the Dooley home, where the memories of old Ireland came alive and never died. Here, the fires of Irish nationalist and revolutionary zeal were stoked by the outspoken Mitchel, whose rants against England, which he described as "the most base and hostile tyranny that has ever scandalized the face of the earth," had made him famous. He influenced the Dooley family and the Irish community of Richmond in general with his fiery radical rhetoric denouncing the abuses of centralized authority and England as "a ferocious monster."[39]

Like Dooley's father (of the same name) who served as the volunteer company commander, John Mitchel was not only a close friend of the Dooley family but also an inspirational revolutionary example who deeply influenced young John Edward Dooley Jr. to wear the gray with the call to arms. As a young lieutenant of the Emerald Islanders of Company C (Montgomery Guard from Richmond), First Virginia Confederate Infantry Regiment, Dooley proudly marched off to war with his mostly Irish comrades in green uniforms, which represented the old country and cherished Celtic-Gaelic cultural values and revered martial legacies that refused to die on American soil. He was one of the lucky ones, surviving service in the hard-fighting First Virginia, including the Army of Northern Virginia's greatest offensive effort (Pickett's Charge).

Dooley and other Irishmen across the South were inspired by Mitchel and his revolutionary activities against British rule in Ireland that were well known on both sides of the Atlantic. Born in 1815 near Dungiven, County Derry, located in the middle of the top of north Ireland, Mitchel was the cynical son of a Unitarian minister. He viewed England much like his father viewed evil in causing trouble in the world. Mitchel later became the leader of the nationalistic "Young Ireland" movement. This radical movement had been the day's most revolutionary and militant organization, actively promoting the liberation of Ireland from British rule by the most violent means.

Representing a new generation of revolutionaries, the "Young Irelanders" of 1848 espoused the vibrant dream of a free Ireland and the growing nationalistic sentiment on both sides of the Atlantic, including in Richmond, during the antebellum period. Mitchel had been exiled in 1848 for his incendiary words, which were rightly deemed treasonous by alarmed British authorities who feared still another people's revolt on the Emerald Isle. They knew that Mitchel's revolutionary influence—a leading voice of the "Young Ireland Movement"—should be removed from the long-suffering Irish people, who only needed such a catalyst to light a spark. As the editor of Ireland's most radical newspaper, *United Irishman*, Mitchel had called for a great social upheaval to remove an aristocratic and oppressive order of the English and Anglo-Irish ruling class. Clearly, Mitchel needed to be eliminated without transforming him into a new martyr. Arrest and exile provided the answer.

After escaping imprisonment and exile on the island of Tasmania, located just off the coast of Australia, Mitchel had then founded the newspaper known as the *Citizen* in New York City ("the Dublin of America"), which contained America's largest Irish population. Because he was so vehemently against the British government, which had a long reach, in his writings and speeches, the backlash for his radical outspokenness eventually forced Mitchel to flee New York City. Exiled not only from Ireland but also from the North, Mitchel eventually settled in the more Irish-friendly environment of Richmond without the hostile followers of the anti-Irish and anti-immigrant Know-Nothing Party that existed in major northern cities. Here, like the Dooley family and so many other Irish who had migrated to the South, the wandering Irish exile found greater tolerance and acceptance than in any other place in America.

In Richmond, Mitchel openly operated not only a Southern nationalist newspaper but also a leading "Irish American newspaper." Representing the popular views of Irish Catholics and Protestants across the breadth of the South, he became the revered leader of Richmond's vibrant Irish community. In this sense, the spirit of revolution was already in the air in the South, especially Richmond, long before the creation of the Confederacy. The Dooley family played a leading role in a host of community activities in the state capital, including those at which Mitchel either presided or was present to extend his radical influence.[40]

Mirroring the transformation of so many lower- and middle-class Irish immigrants into full-fledged American citizens across the South, the Dooley family's success in the overall process of integrating fully into the upper levels of Richmond society benefited the children of this dynamic Irish immigrant family in America. And few sons of Ireland benefited more from Richmond's ample opportunities—eagerly embraced by these Old World transplants—than John E. Dooley Jr., who had been named after his father.

The Irish family excelled both socially and financially in Richmond, but the most tangible expression of the successful transition from Irish immigrants to American citizens was young John's entry into a prestigious American college. Demonstrating that Irish Catholics of recently immigrant and lowly status could rise up in Southern society (more friendly at multiple levels in general than northern society, especially in the major northeastern cities) by receiving the best education in the land, John E. Dooley Jr. made this first step forward in gaining higher education, bringing great pride to his family.

John achieved this first-time lofty status for the Dooley family when he proudly entered Catholic Georgetown College (today's Georgetown University, situated just outside Washington, D.C.) in the fall of 1856 at age fourteen. Symbolically, this highly respected Jesuit school of higher learning was located on property that had been settled by a banished Scottish Jacobite rebel and immigrant named Ninian Beall. Like so many other Celtic revolutionaries who had been forced into exile for fighting against an abusive centralized power, he had paid a high price for attempting to keep Scotland free of English rule. Georgetown was one of the best academic schools in the East, and young John Dooley Jr. benefited immensely from the overall experience.[41]

BUT IT WAS NOT the heady environment of Georgetown College that most influenced the future course of young Dooley's life, fundamental faith and core beliefs. Instead, it was the passionate and spiritual-like Irish revolutionary influences, as personified by the family's revolutionary friend, John Mitchel, which had the most profound influence on young Dooley and on a new generation of the sons of Irish immigrants across the South.

Symbolically, after the Southern states split from the Union during the secession winter of 1860–61, the Irish of Savannah, Georgia, continued to keep sacred a host of cultural traditions and values by celebrating St. Patrick's Day in 1861 with the popular John Mitchel. This development has provided additional evidence of the fusing of a vibrant revolutionary heritage of Ireland with the radical values of the new Southern republic conceived in revolution, because these dual struggles had a great deal in common.[42]

This recognition of Ireland's foremost revolutionary agitator and radical—who continued to voice his strong opinions about freeing Ireland by force on American soil—revealed how completely the respective causes of Ireland and the South (a distinct people's self-determination and the yearning for independence in both cases) had essentially become one and the same by the start of the Civil War. Indeed, Mitchel had long emphasized how there existed a distinct "parallel…between the condition of the Southern states and that of Ireland."[43] Most important, in emphasizing dual revolutionary and home-rule struggles for the self-determination of a culturally distinct people, he had implored in no uncertain terms that the only solution for the South "as in Ireland is *Repeal of the Union*."[44]

Because of this fusion of Irish and Southern nationalism (a symbiotic relationship) that embraced the same lofty republican goals based on self-determination and liberation in the Age of Enlightenment spirit of 1776, young Dooley was thoroughly radicalized and militarized (thanks in part to Mitchel's revolutionary influence and that of his father, a nationalist and a highly respected Richmond militia officer) as early as 1858. At that time, the young man had joined a volunteer company of pro-Southern cadets from Georgetown College, the premier Jesuit institution of higher learning in the East. After demonstrating solid judgment and leadership abilities that had impressed his peers, Dooley was elected to a lieutenant's rank. His paramilitary experience prepared him well for serving as a lieutenant of the Celtic-Gaelic soldiers of the Irish Company C (Montgomery Guard), First Virginia Confederate Infantry, Army of Northern Virginia.

Symbolically, the First Virginia Regiment, consisting of many soldiers from Richmond, Henrico County, had been organized by Colonel Patrick Theodore Moore. He had migrated from the port of Galway on Ireland's west coast in 1821. A prominent Richmond merchant, Moore had then led the young militiamen of Richmond's Irish company, which became the pride of the Irish community, during the antebellum period. At the Battle of Blackburn's Ford on Bull Run Creek on July 18, 1861, when the advancing Army of Northeastern Virginia, which had departed the defenses of Washington, D.C., and attempted to cross Bull Run Creek, the First Virginia Irishmen responded with a typical Irish fighting spirit. A father of nine and forty-nine years old, Captain John Dooley Sr. played a key role in the hot fight at Blackburn's Ford, risking his life for his adopted country and inspiring his men in the vortex of battle. His gallantry made his son, company and regiment proud, while becoming the talk of Richmond.

During the attack that smashed into the Yankees, the ancient Celtic-Gaelic war cry of "Faugh a ballagh!" of the First Virginia Irish soldiers echoed through the dark woodlands along Bull Run Creek and the humid July air. Before falling wounded on the sacred soil of the Old Dominion with a nasty head injury, Colonel Moore led the charge that resulted in a successful defense of the ford. During the attack, which demonstrated that the best defense was an aggressive tactical offensive, he had been the first soldier to raise the ancient Irish war cry, which symbolically united the destinies of two peoples in dual separate struggles for self-determination on opposite sides of the Atlantic.

Most important, the sparkling success of the Virginia Irish at Blackburn's Ford then set the stage for the July 21 Southern victory at First Manassas, because the Federal army had been forced by the sharp setback to move farther west in attempting to cross Bull Run Creek. By the time of the showdown at Gettysburg two years later, this seasoned Confederate regiment from the Old Dominion had earned widespread renown in the Army of Northern Virginia as "the *bloody First.*"[45]

Most significant, the Dooley family of Richmond offers one of the most representative examples not only of the key link between Irish nationalism and Southern nationalism and two people's struggles for self-determination on opposite sides of the Atlantic but also the disproportionate Irish contribution in the Confederacy's service. Therefore, the Dooley family has provided a fascinating microcosm of the overall Irish Confederate experience in the South and the merger of two revolutionary movements that motivated Irishmen to fight from 1861 to 1865.

Besides the vibrancy of Irish revolutionary influences, still another legacy (the most obscure and forgotten one) also played a role in galvanizing resistance among the Sons of Erin in 1861. With the first call to arms, the popular French revolutionary anthem that had been long sung by revolutionaries, the "Marseillaise resounded through the streets" of Richmond.

At that time, John Dooley Sr. commanded Company C (Montgomery Guards), First Virginia Confederate Infantry, and his two sons, John and James, served under his command that proudly represented not only Richmond but also Ireland. Indeed, almost as if they were going to war on Irish soil, these Irish of the Old Dominion donned the green to also fight for Irish liberty and ancient Irish legacies like their rebel descendants before them. James Dooley fought beside Richmond's Irish until he fell wounded at the battle of Williamsburg (May 5, 1862) on the Virginia peninsula, when the Army of the Potomac pushed aside the town's defenders and then marched north toward Richmond during the 1862 Peninsula Campaign.

Only his young age and studies at college had kept John Dooley Jr., who was as enthusiastic about fighting for the South as his father was, from having earlier departed Georgetown to go to war. He was only a freshman at Georgetown College when the war erupted to forever change his world as he knew it. The likeable and personable Dooley, a member of Richmond's elite, was known affectionately by the boys in the ranks as "Gentleman Jack" after he became a Confederate soldier of the First Virginia. Of course, the young man's education at a prestigious college had something to do with this lofty sobriquet. John Dooley Jr. was a sensitive and introspective young man despite his belligerent views when it came to Yankees. He possessed an especially strong anti-British attitude, like other family members, thanks to Ireland's enduring legacies and partly to Mitchel's revolutionary influence. After he decided to play his part in fighting for God and country on the front lines, Gentleman Jack left behind the world of books and scholarship, walking away from Georgetown College's popular Cricket Club in August 1862 before completing his studies.

Beyond the usual motivational forces that influenced the non-Irish to fight for the Confederacy, the key factors that drove young Dooley into service of the Confederacy and to join his father and brother of the Montgomery Guard (Company C, First Virginia) were the omnipresent historical lessons and legacies from the Atlantic's other side that were not lost to the Irish across America: "They had seen their old lives destroyed by a 'foreign' government and were not going to let that happen again. They now had parallel struggles, one to be fulfilled at some stage in Ireland and one much more pressing because it was closer to home."[46]

Consequently, an estimated forty thousand Irish from across the South—from Richmond on the East Coast to the western frontier more than one thousand miles away—served in Confederate armies on both sides of the Mississippi. The Irish fought faithfully year after year beside their non-Irish comrades in the gray and butternut ranks of virtually every regiment of the South. However, nearly fifty distinctive Irish companies of regiments from numerous states were counted in Lee's Army of Northern Virginia alone, which was a significant representation of a distinct Irish identity. These men of the South's primary eastern army identified with their distinctive Irish culture and the lengthy history of an ancient Celtic-Gaelic people's many rebellions to free themselves from British rule. In much the same way, and as mentioned, Irish across the South perceived a most serious threat in what they considered to be a despotic central government located in Washington, D.C., which was seen as a most ominous threat that had to be met with armed might.[47]

Symbolically, to set the stage for the forgotten war—a fratricidal conflict within the context of a larger Civil War—among the Irish people of America, the Irish played a leading role in the Southern war effort from the beginning. On April 12, 1861, Irish gunners were among the first Southern artillerymen who pulled lanyards to open fire on Fort Sumter. The fort's garrison that manned an island in Charleston Harbor contained a large share of Irishmen (63 percent). As fate would have it, and most symbolic in regard to the overall Irish experience, the Civil War's opening guns resulted in the war's first fatality: a Son of Erin in blue.[48]

AS MENTIONED, THE DOOLEY family provides a classic example of the wholehearted Irish commitment to the Confederacy and the extent of the motivational sources from both sides of the Atlantic: father, John Sr., and his two sons, John and James, served together in the heavily Irish First Virginia Confederate Infantry, General James Lawton Kemper's Brigade, General George Edward Pickett's Division, Army of Northern Virginia.[49]

The Dooley family of Richmond represented an undeniable situation noted with some dismay by Englishman Colonel Arthur Fremantle, His Majesty's observer of America's fratricidal war, who had been assigned to report on the performances of Lee's army. After viewing large numbers of Irish in the ranks of the Army of Northern Virginia, the aristocratic Briton, who had long worn a scarlet uniform of the British Army, specifically emphasized the bitterest of ironies and tragedies for the Irish people in America from 1861 to 1865: "Southern Irishmen make excellent 'Rebs,' and have no sort of scruple in killing as many of their northern brethren as they possibly can."[50] And, most symbolically, this punishment (the cruelest of all Irish tragedies on American soil during the four years of war) was delivered with unbridled enthusiasm on the war's major battlefields by large numbers of Irish Rebels attacking Union Irish soldiers of combat units that carried not only the U.S. flag but also regimental flags of green in a proud display of ethnic and cultural heritage.[51]

When Captain John Dooley Sr. led his volunteer company, First Virginia, from Richmond to the seat of war, Company C was the regiment's most heavily Irish company (the Montgomery Guard). This well-trained command of Richmond soldiers overflowed with zealous Sons of Erin who hailed from the upper class to the lower class, representing a wide variety of occupations. Like so many other Celtic-Gaelic commands that earned distinction on both sides of the fratricidal struggle, including the Irish Brigade, Army of the Potomac, this fine company had been named in honor of an Irish hero, specifically, America's first Irish fighter for liberty, Ireland-born General Richard Montgomery.

Despite prophetic warnings about his impending death, and knowing that he possessed little chance for success in overwhelming one of the most formidable defensive positions on the North American continent with so few attackers, this highly respected Irishman fell while courageously leading the desperate attack of his ragtag forces on Quebec during a driving snowstorm in late December 1775. But before he was fatally cut down on a snowy street by the blast of a British cannon at close range, Montgomery nearly won Canada (the possible fourteenth colony if captured by the determined attackers) for the infant American republic in one of the most audacious offensive efforts of the American Revolution. Montgomery became America's first martyr and first Continental general to die on the battlefield. Like so many Irish soldiers in the American Revolution and the Civil War, including those at Pickett's Charge, General Montgomery was killed in a bold tactical offensive effort when he was going for broke.

As mentioned, Captain Dooley's Irish company had been organized by Richmond's Irish citizens on April 21, 1861, with the first calls to arms. When the Irish of Company C, First Virginia, marched through Richmond's streets on the way to the front, they wore fancy uniforms of emerald green in the martial tradition of generations of revolutionaries of old Ireland. These Irish Confederates of Richmond fulfilled the Irish patriot's longtime ambition of wearing of the green to represent the ancestral homeland while battling in what they believed was a just and righteous cause comparable to that of Ireland's longtime struggle for liberty.[52]

Of course, the relatively few Unionists of Richmond, such as the ever-defiant Elizabeth Louisa Van Lew—later a clever Union spy who assisted in the intelligence war and seemingly always kept her head—saw the rallying of the Richmond Irish without the pervasive Southern nationalistic hue or any links to the Irish past: "Think of a community rushing gladly, unrestrainedly, eagerly, into a bloody civil war!...Surely what madness was upon the people!"[53]

Of Dutch (as her last name indicated), French and German heritage, Elizabeth was not aware, despite her keen intelligence and fine education (gained in Philadelphia with other members of the upper-class elite), of the in-depth meaning and overall importance of the Irish experience to the average Irishman who had enthusiastically rallied to go to war.[54] While most of Richmond's Celtic-Gaelic fighting men marched away from the James River country to fight for God and country, other Irish soldiers of Company C, Nineteenth Battalion Virginia Heavy Artillery guarded the array of earthen defenses that protected the Confederacy's capital.[55]

Harsh realities and tragic fates awaited a large percentage of Irish soldiers on battlefields across the South. As a cruel fate would have it, Company C, First Virginia was thoroughly decimated during Lee's last-ditch bid to win it all on the final day (July 3, 1863) at the bloody showdown at Gettysburg. Among the experienced and highly capable Irish officer corps, Captain James Hallinan, a young, lowly laborer who eventually commanded the Irish company because of outstanding leadership abilities, was killed during the assault, while Lieutenant John E. Dooley Jr. was cut down while leading the way for the charging Irish soldiers at the company's head. Among a dedicated group of noncommissioned officers, three Irish sergeants of Company C fell in Lee's greatest attack of the war, when everything was at stake: Edward Byrnes, a thirty-eight-year-old mechanic, was killed; Charles Kean, thirty-four, a Richmond saddler, also fell to rise no more; and John Moriarty, a twenty-eight-year old laborer, was wounded and captured. Likewise, the enlisted ranks of this hard-fighting Irish company were decimated during Lee's desperate bid to reverse the war's course before a brutal war of attrition waged by a vastly more powerful opponent consumed and destroyed his army and nation.[56]

With skill and ability, the Irish immigrant family patriarch, John Dooley Sr., the commander of Company C (Montgomery Guard), had briefly led the First Virginia in late 1862 as acting commander. The regiment that the senior Dooley, the Irish immigrant who had helped to mold the Irish soldiers for such a supreme challenge as they faced at Gettysburg, advanced at the forefront of Pickett's Charge, represented a defining and iconic turning point in American history.[57]

REMARKABLE, BOLD REBEL IRISH WOMEN

Significant in also playing a role in inspiring Lieutenant John Dooley Jr. and his brothers and father to fight for the Confederacy were a good many patriotic Irish women. Ample documentation has revealed that these feisty Irish Confederate women were as, if not more, militant and diehard as the males of their families. Indeed, the most fanatical of Rebels, these women of all classes were the wives, sisters, and mothers of men fighting at the front. They played key roles in fueling the fighting spirit of these young men and boys who were told to go forth and defend their country. Across the South, Irish Confederate ladies instilled in their sons the urge to do what was right and to do their duty in serving their country on distant battlefields against the invaders of their new republic. Some fire-eating women of Richmond, perhaps from the Green Isle across the sea, implored Confederate soldiers to "kill as many Yankees as you can for me" and to bring back Abe Lincoln's severed head as a trophy, or at least an ear from "Old Abe."

Quite a remarkable woman in her own right and by any measure, Sarah Jane Dooley, the Irish immigrant who journeyed with high hopes to America in 1836, at the time of the Texas Revolution, and later married John Dooley Sr., was a fiery nationalist, both Irish and Southern. Self-sacrificing and stoic, Sarah was, in her son's words, "a great sufferer" who willingly made personal sacrifices like so many other Irish women across America. She proudly sent her husband and sons off to war in newly tailored uniforms because this conflict was considered a holy war. Sarah "was the typical valiant Irish mother, glorying in those jewels, her children [and graced with all] those lovely adornments of the women of Ireland—sweetness, gaiety, and personal charm."[58]

In many ways, when it came to embracing the stern challenges of war, Sarah Jane Dooley and other courageous Irish women were much like the remarkable Ireland-born mother of Andrew Jackson, Elizabeth Jackson. From Castlereagh on the east coast of north Ireland in Ulster Province, the Scotch-Irish Jackson family, headed by hardworking Andrew Jackson Sr., had established deep roots on Southern soil in the largely Scotch-Irish settlement of the Waxhaws in the fertile Piedmont of South Carolina.

As fate would have it, the Jackson family had moved to this wilderness region just in time to find themselves caught up in the swirling vortex of the American Revolution. This conflict—actually a civil war, especially in the South—was particularly savage in South Carolina, where more skirmishes and battles were fought than in any other state. The British and Loyalists (actually more ruthless than English soldiers) attempted to crush the rebellion in the most ruthless manner, including burning down the Presbyterian churches of the fiercely patriotic Scotch-Irish and by no-quarter warfare. It was England's same brutal formula that had smashed so many Irish revolts for hundreds of years.

Her husband died not long before Andrew's birth into a harsh world for Irish immigrants. The senior Jackson had attempted with all his efforts to make the Piedmont's land of the Waxhaws more productive, a task that required endless work (the lowly Irish immigrants were too poor to purchase and own slaves to assist in taming the land like the non-Irish). Elizabeth then became the family's head and the primary provider. She had an unconquerable will (inherited by Andrew Jackson), and her "harrowing" experiences as a free-spirited woman living in north Ireland ensured that Elizabeth's hatred of the British knew few bounds. Therefore, Elizabeth early on steered her boys, including the lanky teenager with sharp facial features and typical Scotch-Irish looks named Andy, toward the patriot cause, which she warmly embraced like a holy shroud thanks in no small part to the enduring legacies of generations of Ireland's revolutionaries that remained alive and well on American soil.

Most important, this "fresh-looking, fair-haired, very conservative… Irish lady" was the fieriest revolutionary of the Jackson family and a guiding light to her boys, including young Andrew, who idolized his mother. Especially after her husband died from too much hard work and exhaustion in attempting to tame the land, she thoroughly molded the character of her sons. Like their mother, who still spoke with an Irish brogue, the Jackson boys became die-hard patriots of South Carolina. Thanks in part to how thoroughly she had shaped him, one of Elizabeth's sons became a respected general by the time of the War of 1812 and, eventually, the seventh president of the United States, "Irish Andy" Jackson.

Like her patriotic sons, Elizabeth Jackson displayed uncommon heroics during a crucial period of America's struggle for liberty in war-torn South Carolina. After journeying to Camden, South Carolina, in the rolling hills of the Piedmont, she convinced the aristocratic British commander to exchange her captive sons, Andrew and Robert. At this time, they were in extremely bad shape and needed immediate medical care. After the common Ireland-born pioneer woman gained their release from the Redcoats' clutches, which was no small accomplishment, Elizabeth then brought her two sick sons back home after a perilous trek through a region ravaged by war. However, Robert Jackson died of disease shortly after his return home. Andy was much more fortunate than his brother. He miraculously survived the most harrowing of ordeals by the narrowest of margins. Then, after her ill-advised trip to Charleston on still another errand of mercy to assist badly neglected American prisoners, Elizabeth fell victim to disease. She died of cholera far from home. A true American heroine and Angel of Mercy who gave her life for her sons and the Patriot cause, this remarkable Irish woman had been fatally stricken while selflessly attending to the multitude of helpless and sick captives, including two sick nephews, who suffered severely from multiple aliments in the oven-like hulls of hellish prison ships anchored in Charleston Harbor.[59]

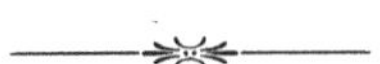

GENERAL ANDREW JACKSON SUCCESSFULLY met the greatest challenge of his military career in defeating thousands of attacking British regulars at the Battle of New Orleans on January 8, 1815, during America's most one-sided victory of the War of 1812. Thereafter, Jackson had only a single regret in his distinguished life of repeatedly overcoming insurmountable odds and seemingly impossible situations. This is testament to his Scotch-Irish toughness, willpower and resourcefulness that were the most common characteristics of the Irish fighting man from the American Revolution to the Civil War.

General Jackson's farmers, hunters and regulars decimated the neat formations of the hated English regulars and Scots on the plain of Chalmette, located just south of the Crescent City and part of the Mississippi River floodplain, and this was also a stirring tribute to his courageous Irish mother. After all, Elizabeth had long detested the sight of British soldiers, who had brought so much misery to her family on both Ireland's and America's soil. In regard to his remarkable victory at New Orleans, "Irish Andy" Jackson said without exaggeration and with sincere regret that never left him: "I wish she could have lived to see this day. There never was a woman like her. She was gentle as a dove and as brave as a lioness."[60]

The feisty spirit of this amazing Scotch-Irish woman, born among the green, rolling hills of north Ireland and buried in the lowlands around Charleston at a location unknown to this day, was mirrored in the Irish Rebels who volunteered to fight for the Confederacy, including volunteers from the bustling port of Charleston. The New Irish Volunteers of the port city consisted of Irish companies like the Jasper Greens, Meagher Guards, Sarsfield Light Infantry and Montgomery Guards. The unit later became the First South Carolina Volunteers under General Maxcy Gregg. The hard-fighting Gregg was destined to be killed at the Battle of Fredericksburg, Virginia, in December 1862. To the beating of drums and the playing of fifes, these Irish soldiers had marched off to war from South Carolina with expectations for easy victory under a green-and-white banner decorated with an Irish harp and a shamrock.[61]

Like the Irish revolutionary and cultural legacies that were alive and well across the South, large numbers of equally remarkable Irish women like Elizabeth Jackson were found in Irish communities throughout the Confederacy. In Winchester, Virginia, a starved Army of Northern Virginia veteran, John W. Stevens (who had been recently wounded at Antietam), and an equally seasoned comrade departed a Confederate hospital without authority. They were eager to rejoin General John Bell Hood's Texas Brigade, which was destined to play a key offensive role at the southern end of the battle line at Gettysburg on the afternoon of July 2. Stevens wrote how he and his comrade fared very well, when "we met an Irish woman…and we laid our case before her in true hungry soldier style. Her warm Irish heart responded to the tune of six big fat biscuits" that were eagerly devoured.[62]

Symbolically, on the journey to rejoin his command—one of General Robert E. Lee's elite brigades and the army's only combat brigade from west of the Mississippi—Stevens feasted on what he had gathered from "a fine Irish potato patch" before rejoining his Fifth Texas Irish comrades in time for the next round of bitter fighting.[63] Another Texas Brigade soldier of Hood's crack command, Joseph "Joe" Benjamin Polley, never forgot the noble efforts of the "Irish ladies of [New Orleans, who] could not do too much for us."[64] Like countless other Irish women across the South, another aged Irish mother sent her son, Patrick, to the front with pride mixed with tears despite the fact that she feared "I'll niver see my boy again."[65] The largest number of Irish Confederates from Texas hailed from Galveston, which was the state's largest city and busiest port in 1861.[66]

FORGOTTEN IRISH REVOLUTIONARY LEGACIES CREATED DIE-HARD CONFEDERATES

But even more than the John Dooley family of Richmond, the best example of the strong connection between Irish and Confederate nationalism was evident in the John Mitchel family. As mentioned, John Mitchel was not only a leading Irishman of Richmond, he was also the leading advocate for violent revolution in Ireland to overthrow British rule. A distinctive people's self-determination that had fueled the motivations of thousands of Irish across the South was also a product of the most recent revolution that shook Ireland to the core. Like many Irish of the Civil War generation, Mitchel's uncompromising radicalism was born of the greatest revolution in Irish history. This was the massive people's revolt of Irish Catholics and Protestants that erupted during the summer of 1798.

This nationalist uprising was led by the guiding hand of the revolutionary organization known as the Society of United Irishmen, founded in Belfast, north Ireland, in October 1791. These die-hard Irish nationalists of the late eighteenth century echoed the words of Thomas Paine, the Age of Enlightenment political philosopher who had inspired American Patriots, including many Irish immigrants, during the American Revolution.

To the thinking of Irish Confederates across the South, the great Irish revolt of 1798 had been resurrected in 1861 in a region that was largely Celtic. Erupting in late May 1798 in County Wexford in southeast Ireland and led by inspirational religious leaders like Fathers Michael Murphy and John Murphy, who encouraged their parishioners to rise up in a holy war, this was a lower-class uprising of the common people, mostly oppressed Catholics who were Ireland's second-class citizens. Without artillery or muskets in a tightly controlled land that had been transformed into England's first colony, these Irish rebels were armed mostly with pikes, pitchforks and scythes against a well-equipped opponent.

Besides the longtime abuses of wealthy landlords whose lands were farmed by lowly tenant farmers, a new generation of Irish revolutionaries were inspired by American and French revolutionary and egalitarian traditions. (America was the foremost inspirational influence partly because so many Irish on both sides of the Atlantic supported America's rebellion against the ancient enemy, England.) Born in 1815 (the same year that "Irish Andy" Jackson won his remarkable victory at New Orleans) near the small market town of Dungiven, County Derry, Mitchel had been inspired by the words of his patriotic father, a fiery Unitarian minister who served as a holy warrior in the revolution of 1798.[67]

The role of Mitchel's father as a "Young Ireland" revolutionary leader and United Irishman in 1798 revealed how closely religion was connected to revolution in Ireland—essentially one and the same to the long-suffering Irish people, evolving into something close to a cultural tradition. Besides the revolutionary actions of Mitchel's minister-father, egalitarian-minded Catholic priests emboldened their parishioners from the pulpit, where they preached revolution, and then occasionally into the fire of battle. Father Michael Murphy was killed by a blast of British cannon fire while leading his County Wexford revolutionaries, including former parishioners, in a headlong charge under the flowing folds of an emerald-green battle flag decorated with revolutionary sentiments of "Liberty or Death!" during the Battle of Arklow, Ireland.[68] On the bloody battlefields of the Green Isle for generations, the Irish Rebels were inspired onward by "the national flag of the future, the green flag showing the harp" of ancient Ireland.[69]

Because of such revered revolutionary legacies, soldiers of four Irish companies (the Jasper Greens, Montgomery Guards, Sarsfield Light Infantry and Meagher Guards) united to create the Irish Volunteers of the First South Carolina Volunteers. The colorful battle flag of the Irish

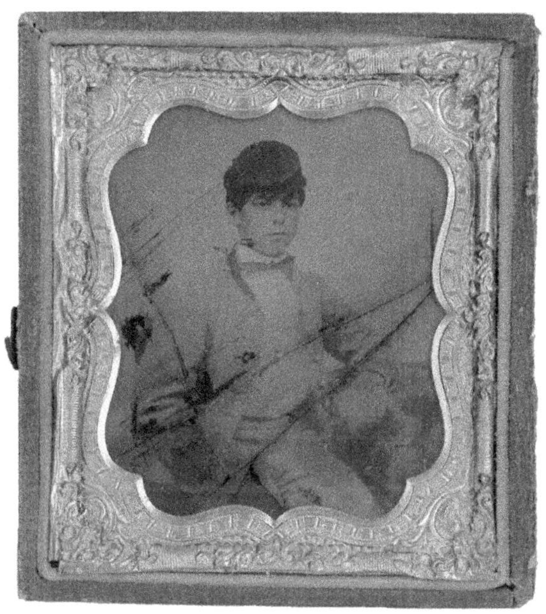

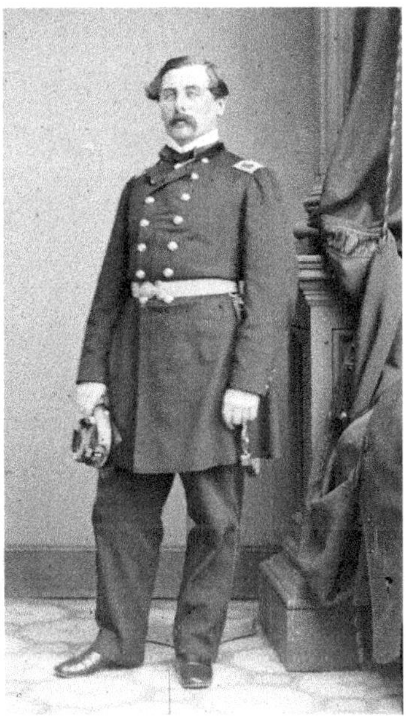

Left: Tintype of Confederate soldier in gray coat and dark kepi. *Author's collection.*

Right: Born in Waterford, Ireland, Brigadier General Thomas Francis Meagher, nationalist leader of the Young Irelander Movement of 1848 and the inspirational commander of the Irish Brigade, Army of the Potomac, in 1862. *Courtesy of the Library of Congress.*

Volunteers, the senior Irish company of Charleston, was blessed by Ireland-born Bishop Patrick Lynch of Charleston. Decorated with a harp, wreath, and shamrock, this silken flag had been sewn by the Sisters of Our Lady of Mercy at Charleston.

The Sarsfield Light Infantry was named in honor of the young Irish patriot Patrick Sarsfield. Holding the title of the first Earl of Lucan, he fought with distinction as a hard-hitting cavalry commander of Irish troopers on behalf of Catholic James II. The dashing Sarsfield died of wounds in 1693 at the Battle of Landen, Ireland, becoming still another Irish martyr on a list that seemed endless. Meanwhile, the First South Carolina company, known as the Meagher Guards, was named after "Young Irelander" and Irish nationalist Thomas Francis Meagher from Waterford, Ireland.

In one of the great ironies of the Irish experience in America, Brigadier General Meagher led the Irish Brigade against Irish Confederates on some of the bloodiest battlefields of the war. After distinguished service as the commander of the Irish Brigade and surviving Antietam and Fredericksburg, Meagher died mysteriously by falling off of a steamboat into the Missouri River on July 1, 1867, while serving as the acting governor of Montana Territory. The exact details of Meagher's tragic end are unknown to this day, remaining one of the greatest mysteries in the history of the American West. But what was known was that Meagher had legions of enemies, especially among the English who had old scores to settle.

REVOLUTIONARY BROTHERS FROM THE EMERALD ISLE

Before Meagher's tragic demise in the swirling, dark currents of the Missouri, he had a charmed existence, having lived a dozen lives and repeatedly dodging death. Well-educated and hailing from a wealthy family, he was one of Ireland's most distinguished revolutionary leaders who rivaled Mitchel in fame and reputation. Meagher and Mitchel, revolutionary comrades—"Young Irelanders" of 1848—became mortal enemies in the bitter struggle that raged from 1861 to 1865 on American soil. Mitchel had abandoned his legal career to join Meagher, a native of Waterford, Ireland, in their holy war against England. As fate would have it, Meagher was only a reluctant leader of the famed Irish Brigade, having a good many Irish friends in the South. Having grown up along the Liffey River, he was a romantic and an idealist. As a true Irish Catholic nationalist and longtime Democrat, Meagher closely identified with the Southern people's longing for independence because of the analogies to Ireland's historical plight.

In fact, Meagher supported the South all the way up until the firing of Confederate guns on Fort Sumter. Mitchel's revolutionary legacy inspired large numbers of Irish to rally across the South, including in South Carolina, which had been the most militant state since the early 1830s. As usual, the green flags especially drew enthusiastic Irishmen to the ranks in large numbers from across the South.

From the picturesque city of Charleston, the Palmetto State Irish of the First South Carolina Volunteers served under an Irish battle flag distinguished by a "Cross [and] an Irish harp encircled by a wreath of oak leaves, palmetto and shamrock combined," while underneath was painted the words of the battle cry "Liberty or Death."[70] One of the greatest tragedies and ironies of Irish history, mirroring America's own deep divisions in this fratricidal

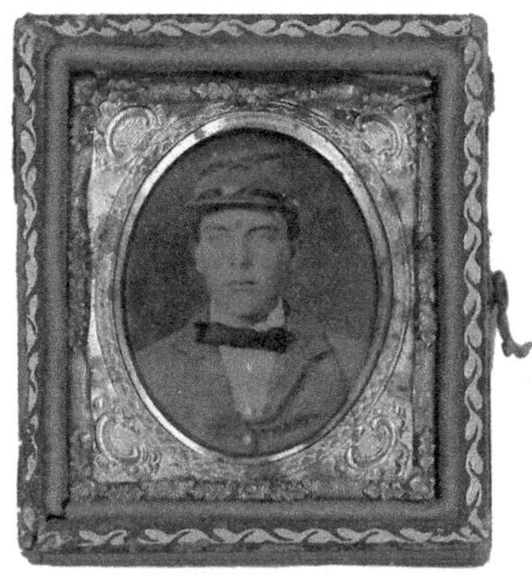

Small tintype of young North Carolina private early in the war. *Author's collection.*

war, these two nationalists of Ireland, Mitchel and Meagher, became enemies on American soil in fighting for what they believed was right.[71]

But desperate bids to gain nationhood came at a frightfully high price for rebels in Ireland. Like so many other Irish revolts over the centuries and the Confederacy's own struggle for existence, the great Irish Rebellion of 1798 had been doomed to bloody failure from the beginning. The Irish people's arising during the month of "liberty was a futile tragedy." As in most revolutions, regardless of time or place, it was the common people, especially innocent and helpless women and children, who paid the highest price for rising up—especially after it failed. Indeed, the Irish people, including innocent ones, suffered brutal reprisals, including mass hangings (England's traditional means of stamping out rebellion) conducted with typical ruthless efficiency by experts in crushing rebellions. It had become a well-honed skill of England's professional soldiers by this time, and the poorly armed Irish peasants never had a chance of succeeding.[72]

As mentioned, Mitchel evolved into the inspirational voice and leading spirit of the "Young Ireland Movement" of 1848 while promoting the most radical and dangerous solution for the long-oppressed Irish people: open rebellion against the most powerful nation in the world. Among the Young Irelanders were the most radical revolutionaries destined to play inspirational roles in fighting on opposite sides during the Civil War: Thomas Francis Meagher and John Mitchel, who were among Ireland's best and brightest. These two dynamic Irishmen evolved into symbolic leaders of the Irish people in the North and South by 1861, when they had become enemies.

As mentioned, the ancient Irish harp was a much-revered nationalist Irish symbol representing an independent national identity and a cherished cultural legacy of "a once-great Gaelic civilization" before the curse of the English conquest. In this sense, the Young Ireland Movement had sought to resurrect the ancient glories of the Irish past and restore the beloved traditions of an independent Celtic-Gaelic culture and civilization so that Ireland could become "A Nation once again."[73]

As the first leader of this new generation of Irish rebels, who continued a tradition of resistance to autocratic authority of a so-called "foreign" power, Mitchel had rejoiced in the creation of the green, white and orange flag of Irish nationalism in 1848. Educated at the premier educational institution in Ireland, Trinity College, Dublin, he emphasized his burning desire "to see the flag one day waving, as our national banner, over a forest of Irish pikes" to be directed at Ireland's British rulers, as during the high-risk Rebellion of 1798.[74]

Articulating the common views of so many Irish, Mitchel's hatred of England was without limit. He reasoned that the English government had deliberately allowed the Great Famine to spread like a wildfire and without sufficient relief in order to depopulate the land of Irish tenant farmers (basically, a case of ethnic cleansing without requiring soldiers to do the dirty work or risking the destruction of property and resources). In this way, the wealthy English and Anglo-Irish landlords converted their fertile lands to the raising of stock for the exporting of meat to England, reaping greater profits to become richer.[75]

Therefore, the rage of the Irish people knew few bounds, including in regard to Meagher and Mitchel. Irish misery on a massive scale was transformed into a positive good to the reasoning of the ruling elite. Many Englishmen, including high-ranking government officials, delighted in what they saw as God's divine hand in ridding the Green Isle of so many troublesome Irish of the lower classes by death and exodus. The surreal horror of more than one million Irish men, women and children dying of starvation and disease was viewed in perverse fashion by many English leaders and aristocrats as "God's punishment of the Irish" for their alleged inferiority and immorality—a Darwinian extermination that was a righteous culling in their minds dominated by racial factors, including notions of Anglo-Saxon superiority. Ironically, fighting for the Confederacy was less dangerous than living in Ireland for many Emerald Islanders.[76]

Therefore, the transplanted political exiles of the failed revolt and of the devastating famine never forgave the English for their sins, finding ample fertile ground to nourish their deep-seated hatreds in America. In the South, the great revolutionary dream of Ireland's eventual liberation was a memory that not only never died but was also resurrected with a passion. Indeed, combining dual revolutionary influences to create a potential Southern nationalism, the Irish in the South became the faithful keepers of the "Spirit of '98," which, in turn, had been inspired by the egalitarian visions stemming from America's own "Spirit of '76."[77] For instance, history-minded Lieutenant John Edward Dooley, First Virginia, Major General George E. Pickett's Division, was still angered over "the fearful cruelties perpetrated by the English soldiery in '98 upon the Irish. Their fiendish acts upon defenceless people will find sometimes to be paralleled by the infamous brutalities of the Yankee mercenaries" of Union armies.[78]

Likewise, John Mitchel's eldest son of much promise, Captain John C. Mitchel Jr., demonstrated the depths of his commitment to the South by emphasizing the analogy between the two revolutionary struggles for self-determination on opposite sides of the Atlantic. After having been hit by Union shellfire from either land batteries and warships during Fort Sumter's defense on July 20, 1864, the Ireland-born captain's dying words, deliberately meant to inspire his fast-working gunners of the First South Carolina Artillery, were eloquent. He emphasized the significance of Ireland in serving as a primary motivator for Irish across the South: "I die willingly for South Carolina, but oh! That it had been for Ireland!"[79]

What has been most forgotten is the fact that Captain Mitchel had been in the forefront of the resistance effort since the first booming of Southern guns at Fort Sumter on April 12, 1861. Indeed, at that time when America's most nightmarish war was sparked, "Lieut. John Mitchell [sic], the worthy son of that patriot sire, who has so nobly vindicated the cause of the South, has the honor of dismounting two of [Fort Sumter's] parapet guns by a single shot from one of the Columbiads, which at the time he had the office of directing."[80]

But perhaps the captain's father, John Mitchel Sr., who had been born near the town of Dungiven, County Derry, in Ulster Province, said it best by making the appropriate analogy. He had made sure that his marble tombstone in Charleston's best cemetery was inscribed with his most heartfelt conviction and deepest regret, which was felt by so many Sons of Erin across the South: "I could not fight for Ireland, so I chose to fight for the South."[81]

Symbolically, by 1861, "the Emerald Isle had contributed largely to the population of Charleston," and these Irish were well represented in South Carolina units (infantry, cavalry and artillery), especially in the Army of Northern Virginia.[82] Therefore, such Irish commands as the "Old Irish Volunteers" organized to fight not only for the Confederacy, but also in the name of old Ireland, which was never far from the hearts and minds of the young men and boys from the Green Isle.[83]

SHOWDOWN IN THE EASTERN THEATER

As with the previous year, 1862 brought no decisive victory for either side, despite the determined attempt of the massive Army of the Potomac, under General George Brinton McClellan, to capture Richmond in the spring and summer. In the end, McClellan was repulsed before the gates of Richmond after having suffered heavy losses from repeated Confederate offensive strikes that had sent the Union army reeling.

In her diary, Mary Chesnut, a South Carolina aristocrat with intelligent insights about Southern life and the upper echelons of the Confederate government in Richmond, lamented the missed opportunity of the Southern army having failed to destroy the Union army during the Peninsula Campaign, when McClellan's forces were hammered by General Lee's repeated blows: "Miriam says she feels like sitting down, as an Irish woman does at a wake, and howling night and day—'Why did [General Benjamin] Huger let McClellan slip through his fingers?'"[84] What Mary Chesnut did not know was that the true Irish wake was given to generations of Green Isle migrants before they had departed Ireland for America, never to return. Friends and family had long gathered to say their final farewells to thousands of Irish immigrants about to depart for America's shores, where St. Patrick's Day was faithfully celebrated with a mixture of reverence and joy in the close-knit Irish communities in the North and South.[85]

Equally of concern to Mary Chesnut, who lived in Richmond with her South Carolina senator-husband and saw the inherent flaws of the Confederate experiment in nationhood during the 1862 campaign on the Virginia Peninsula, was how "we see so many foreign regiments among our prisoners. Germans–Irish–Scotch."[86] Irishman Thomas Conolly was especially shocked by how savagely this civil war among the Irish was waged on American soil. As he penned in his diary while touring the South and learning about the struggle's dynamics, Conolly understood some of the horrors of America's fratricidal conflict for the Irish people: "a number of Yankee prisoners 150 come up under guard & getting into conversation with them I find one half of them [were] Irish" soldiers.[87]

Chesnut made her own appropriate analogy to the Irish if the South was vanquished: "We will be like Irish emigrants, but we can't write poetic laments."[88] She also mocked the behavior of lower-class Irish, who were a common amusement to Americans, especially those of the upper-class elite in both North and South. In fact, white Southerners seemed more prone to mock and make ethnic jokes about lower-class Irish than even their own slaves, whom they often considered part of the family in the typical paternalistic thinking of the day. An amused Chesnut penned how the Irish nurse of President Jefferson Davis's son, "Poor little Joe," five, who was killed in a tragic 1864 fall from the upper floor of the White House of the Confederacy to send a gloom over Richmond, was "weeping and wailing as only an Irish woman can."[89]

Ireland-born Thomas Conolly, the scion of one of Ireland's leading Anglo-Irish families from County Kildare, located just west of Dublin, was impressed by the sight of the Mississippi-born president and Mexican-American War hero who had become a source of criticism for Confederate defeats, especially in the West: "marked head & clearly chisled features of Jeff Davis his hair quite grey & his lantern jaws more thin & sallow than of old but his grey eyes bright & clear."[90]

Like Mary Chesnut, non-Irish soldiers of the Army of Northern Virginia employed a host of analogies to the Irish that were part of the popular lexicon, an enduring testament to the pervasive influence of Irishness and the large Irish presence in Southern society. Upper-class Southerners were amused by the seemingly peculiar characteristics of the lower-class Irish, viewing them with a sense of wonder. Handsome Richard Wright "Dick" Tally, the son of a South Carolina congressman and a member of Company A, Third South Carolina Infantry, wrote his sister upon encountering a fun-loving Irish family after having become briefly lost in the rural countryside while foraging far and wide in search of provisions. He asked the Emerald Islanders for directions: "Washington Albert 'Puts' [Williams] and myself went to ask the way, and I liked to have killed myself talking Irish to them. It was the merriest crowd I ever was in."[91]

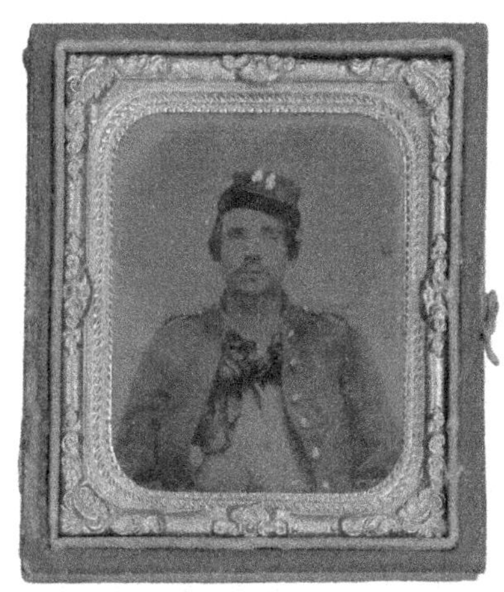

Confederate soldier with open coat, homespun shirt and brass insignia on kepi. *Author's collection.*

Clearly, a good many popular stereotypes—positive as well as negative—about the Irish people, especially recent immigrants who often still spoke Gaelic and possessed all the characteristics of the peasantry, existed among the Southern people. Some of the ugliest of these racial and cultural stereotypes were directed

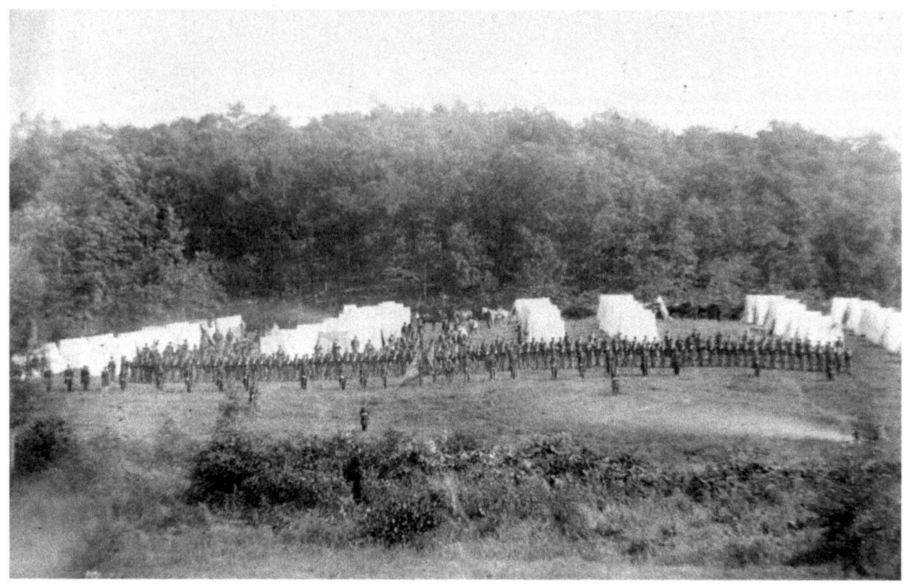

Photograph of Union troops aligned before their tented encampment. *Courtesy of the Library of Congress.*

toward lowly Irish immigrants, who were often unfairly accused and charged with crimes by non-Irish, who embraced British-inspired views of the Irish as born criminals who could not be trusted. As late as 1860, in the backwater of Virginia (today's West Virginia), consequently, the mountain people of this rugged land retained "a great prejudice against the entire Irish population" of immigrants.[92] Among the common people, including many Scotch-Irish whose ancestors had come to America long ago, of this region far from Richmond and the more genteel people of the Tidewater, "the dred [sic] of the Wild Irish" was rampant.[93]

Ironically, the Irish soldiers of the 155th New York Volunteer Infantry embraced some aspects of the same stereotypes about immigrants from the Emerald Isle, turning negatives into positives by nicknaming their command the "Wild Irish Regiment."[94] But more significant, and as the example in western Virginia reveals in regard to the much-feared "Wild Irish" immigrants who seemed beyond control, these Irish of the lower class, especially Catholics and Gaelic speakers of the old language, were often victims of racial stereotyping, becoming a convenient scapegoat for a host of the societal ills. However, this development was far more common in the North, especially in the large northeastern cities, than in the South, which was more welcoming of the Irish.[95]

ANCIENT IRISH LEGACIES AND FORGOTTEN RACIAL WAR FOR THE IRISH

Revealing the complexities of America's forgotten fratricidal conflict—Irish in blue versus Irish in gray and even deep divisions between former Irish leaders (Mitchel and Meagher)—the Civil War was also very much a racial conflict. And, significantly, this racial war had far less to do with black and white in the minds of the average Irish Confederate. A North Carolina Rebel saw this conflict in purely racial terms, viewing it like past rebellions in Ireland, when Puritan armies, especially under the ruthless Oliver Cromwell, marched across Ireland, slaughtering Irish Catholics, especially at the town of Drogheda in 1649, in a bloody holy war. Making the appropriate historical analogy, he wondered with dismay how and why members of the Irish Brigade and other "Irish Catholics of the North [would fight] side by side with the black-hearted Puritan, the enemy of their race and creed."[96]

Extremely "proud [that] I belong to the 1st Va. Regiment," Lieutenant John Edward Dooley Jr. still felt bitterness toward "the *puritan* [the English, who was able to] rob us of our property, devastate our lands, starve the pleading orphan and the broken hearted widow, trample in the dust every principle of right, and crush out completely our identity as a free people."[97]

Such an enduring historical legacy was part of the very being of Irish Confederates, especially recent immigrants. Leaving a permanent imprint on the Irish consciousness and psyche, the Celtic-Gaelic culture and ancient homeland had to be defended against successive foreign invaders in a seemingly never-ending historical process. As a consequence, one of the most distinctive features of the Celts was their well-known combat prowess, born of severe adversity and do-or-die conflicts, which had become legendary. Even the ancient Greeks, who called Ireland *Insula sacra*, or "holy island," and the Romans, who never conquered Hibernia (Ireland), possessed a high "degree of respect for Celtic prowess in battle" from their bitter warfare on the European mainland.[98]

Ancient Greek and Roman writers repeatedly emphasized the ferocity of the Celtic warriors, whose courage and skill in battle were legendary. Displaying excessive martial qualities and aggressiveness on the battlefield, they had long proved "fearless to the point of irrationality." Most of all, these Celts were known for a distinct fondness for launching the headlong charge with a relentless intensity and audacity regardless of the situation or the odds.[99]

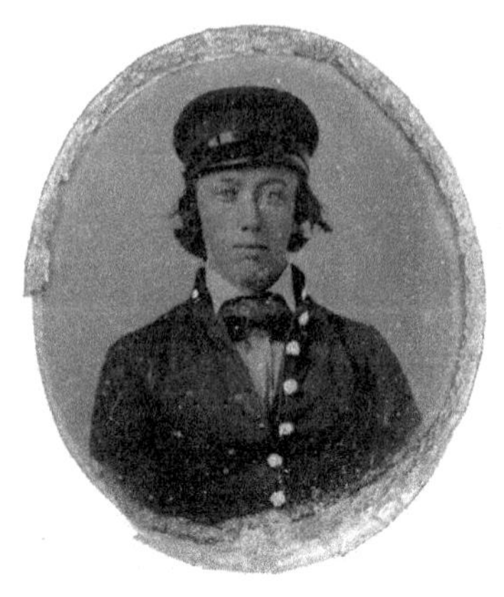

Early tintype of a long-haired zealous Confederate volunteer from the Trans-Mississippi Theater. *Author's collection.*

Therefore, it was no coincidence that this legendary tenacity and never-say-die attitude had been inherited by the largely Celtic-Gaelic (Irish) and Celtic (Scottish and Welsh) descendants serving in large numbers in the Army of Northern Virginia. Quite simply, these were longtime martial traditions passed on to the Atlantic's west side by the tides of migration over centuries as part of a cultural and martial inheritance. In this sense, cultural and historical traditions were key factors that determined behaviors and fueled a highly motivated Irish soldiery. Like their ancient ancestors, these hardy Celtic-Gaelic fighting men in gray and butternut had long won victories across Virginia by relying on the hard-hitting power of the tactical offensive, except during the bloody repulse at Malvern Hill. Here, knowing that this was his last chance to destroy the Army of the Potomac that had advanced too close to Richmond, Lee had attempted to deliver a knockout blow to McClellan's army on July 1, 1862, during the last bloody confrontation of the Peninsula Campaign.

Destined to be shot down and captured during Pickett's Charge, Lieutenant John Edward Dooley Jr. described the historical analogies between Ireland and the South and the ancient foe—the English—who had been now replaced by the hated Yankees (those of English heritage, especially New Englanders). Revealing how Irish legacies were still alive and well during the war years, Dooley was disgusted and angered by the tragic course of Irish history, especially "the fearful cruelties perpetrated by the English soldiery in '98 [the Irish revolution of 1798] upon the Irish. Their fiendish acts upon defenceless [*sic*] people we find sometimes paralleled by the infamous brutalities of the Yankee mercenaries of the present day."[100]

Again, these were not the prejudiced and isolated views of an Irishman embittered about England's bloody subjugation of the Green Isle and driven by a narrow view of history. A distinguished Mexican-American War veteran who had risen to the fore while leading his Mississippi regiment with skill during a turning-point moment of the Battle of Buena Vista, President Jefferson Davis perhaps said it best in revealing the common sentiments of the Southern people, especially those citizens of Irish descent: "England

[as] the robber nation of the earth, whose history is a long succession of wrong and oppressions [especially in crushing the national aspirations of the Scottish and Irish people for centuries], whose tracks are marked by the crushed rights of individuals."[101]

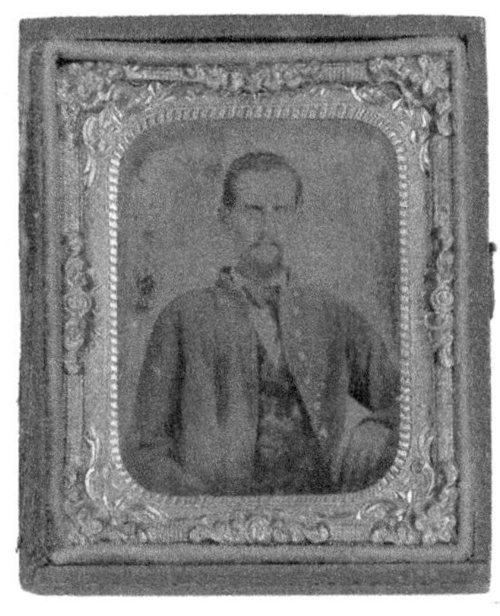

Confederate private in uniform coat and stylish vest underneath. *Author's collection.*

Fueling his motivations, a member of Hood's Texas Brigade (containing a large percentage of men of Scotch-Irish descent), Private John Camden West, Company E (Lone Star Guards), Fourth Texas, coveted "the satisfaction of striking a blow in the holiest cause that ever fired the breast of man, and illustrating by action the feelings which glowed and burned in my little heart, on reading the stories of [Scottish freedom fighter and nationalist William] Wallace." William Wallace was another revered Celtic revolutionary who gave his life in a desperate attempt to free his people from English domination.[102]

To the average Southerner of their largely Celtic nation that was now the Confederacy, the boys in blue were viewed as Yankees (as they were called by the Irish with a race-based contempt deeply rooted in the past), or descendants of England. They had gained the name *Yankees* (or, more properly, *Yankee Doodles*) from their mocking English allies before the American Revolution. A race-minded Louisiana Rebel of French Creole ("Cajun" or Acadian) descent described the view of the typical Confederate soldier (Irish and non-Irish) in regard to their opponent: "the cold-hearted Yankees, fit descendants of the intolerant and murderous race who first landed at Plymouth rock."[103]

Significantly, this deep-seated hatred of the Yankee was not that of the backward "cracker" or hillbilly from the isolated regions of the Blue Ridge Mountains of Virginia but actually a widespread view of people across the South, including in major cities, in 1861. In this sense, for many Southerners, including the Irish, fighting the Yankees was part of a long-existing racial war that had relatively little to do with blacks or slavery, as so commonly assumed by many modern Americans—a generally forgotten historical reality and perspective that has revealed the complexities and nuances of the Irish experience.

In the summer of 1775, in a letter to his brother, an aristocratic Virginia planter, large slave-owner, and former militia commander, on taking command of the nascent Continental army at Cambridge, Massachusetts, felt a deep-seated and traditional Southern disgust toward the New England soldiers, whom he now commanded with some uneasiness. Without considering the wide cultural differences (the antithesis of Virginia Tidewater values and behavior that were in general more Celtic than English, especially when compared to New England) and revealing what was essentially a cultural clash that became part of the Civil War's dynamics, General George Washington denounced the New Englanders (a typical Southern view of Yankees) in no uncertain terms. In a letter that focused on differences of fellow Americans who were the first to fight for liberty, he complained of how the undisciplined New Englanders, who wore civilian clothes rather than uniforms, were "the most indifferent kind of people I ever saw [and] they are exceedingly dirty and nasty people."[104]

Nearly a century after Washington wrote these revealing words in regard to deeply entrenched sectional views and prejudices held by Southerners, Major William Thomas Poague made an important distinction among members of his Virginia battery, reflecting the presence of men of two distinct races that were almost as much pitted against each other in his own command as against the enemy on the battlefield: "If I were asked to select representatives of the two types of men composing our battery [Rockbridge Artillery] I would name Fairfax and McCorkle—the former the [English] Cavalier element, the latter the Scotch-Irish—each the perfect flower of his type."[105]

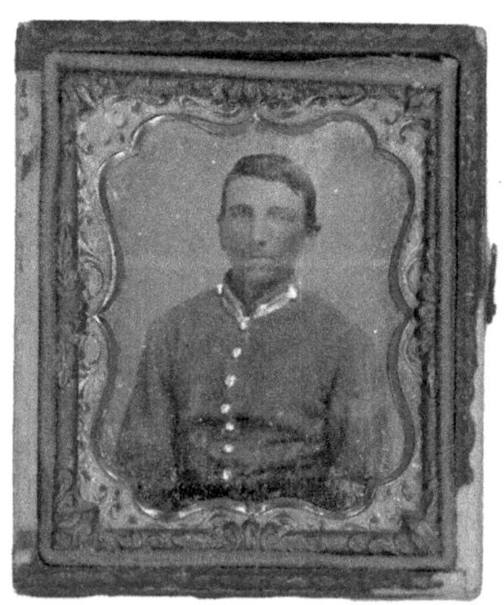

North Carolina soldier in standard uniform coat. *Author's collection.*

Indeed, the bitter conflict of 1861–65 was actually a racial war between English brothers and Celtic brothers in a long-existing historical confrontation that had been transferred to the Atlantic's west side: a cultural clash that significantly shaped the American experience to a degree not generally recognized or appreciated by historians. Because the Englishman (the Yankee of British descent) had long attempted to erode the core foundations of the ancient Celtic culture of Ireland and Scotland, the people of Celtic descent (especially the Irish) had long viewed the English and their descendants (the Yankees, especially New Englanders) as the enemies of their race.[106]

As mentioned, the Civil War was also literally a war between Irish brothers, as proven by a good many notable examples, including at high levels of military leadership. Major General Patrick Ronayne Cleburne, born on St. Patrick's Day 1828 in the port town of Cork in County Cork, south Ireland, and the Confederacy's highest-ranking Irish officer, lamented the fact that his own brother wore the blue.

Nevertheless, Pat Cleburne, who spoke with an Irish brogue and never relinquished his Irish ways, loved his brother until his dying day. This dynamic general was killed on the bloody afternoon on November 30, 1864, when Lieutenant General John Bell Hood's Army of Tennessee was unleashed on the powerful defenses of Franklin, Tennessee. Determined to stand beside his new Southern republic in "weal or woe," this promising former lawyer from Helena, Arkansas, fell to rise no more while courageously leading the suicidal assault of his crack division on a beautiful Indian summer afternoon. This was the Confederacy's most nightmarish offensive effort, resulting in a slaughter. Knowing that the assault was doomed from the beginning because of the defensive strength of the Union position nestled in the Harpeth River Valley and lying before the small agricultural community, a stoic Cleburne led the way in the attack, encouraging his troops onward and into hell itself. (As fate would have it, Cleburne's half brother Christopher, who was also born in County Cork and a promising Trinity College student in Dublin, was also killed during the war.)

General Cleburne embarked on a doomed assault upon Franklin's powerful defenses situated just south of Nashville, Tennessee, in Hood's desperate bid to destroy defending Union forces before they slipped away to the safety of Tennessee's capital. With no illusions remaining, Cleburne's last words to a fellow general, who commanded one of his brigades, emphasized how few of his veterans would ever see their homes again after attacking such powerful fortifications: "if we are to die, let us die like men."[107] With a distinct race of fierce fighters in mind, General Lee paid a tribute to this courageous Irishman, an aspiring son from County Cork whose American dream had been transformed into a nightmare by politics, sectionalism, and fate, emphasizing how the incomparable General Cleburne "inherited the trepidity of his [Irish] race [and] on a field of battle he shone like a meteor in a clouded sky."[108]

But the surreal horror of large numbers of Irishmen killing fellow Irishmen at places like Franklin was nothing new on American soil. Conflict between Irish brothers had been a little-known feature of America's struggle for liberty from 1775 to 1781. The British relied heavily on Irish recruits to fill the ranks of their regiments dispatched to America. Consequently, these Irish soldiers of the British Empire in scarlet uniforms occasionally met their brothers and other relatives who were serving under Washington and his top lieutenants.

This was the tragic case of the Ireland-born Maguire brothers, who faced off at the battle of Saratoga, New York. The two brothers met during the surrender of General "Gentleman Johnny" Burgoyne's Army of British and Hessians at Saratoga on October 17, 1777. Won by the northern army under General Horatio Gates, this decisive success secured the all-important

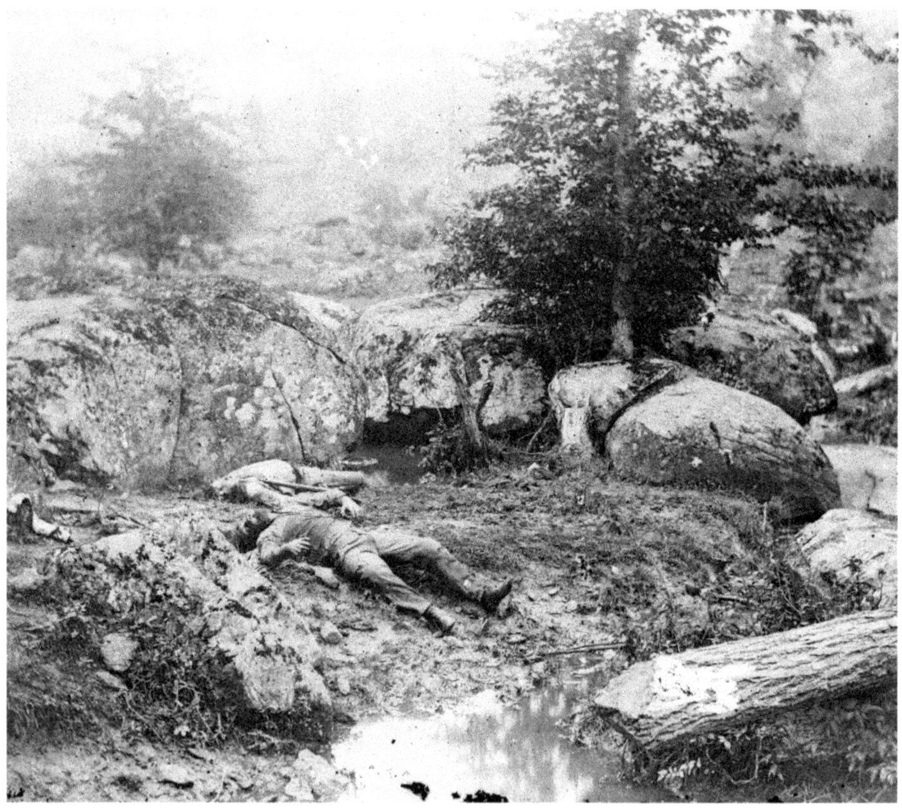

Dead Confederates who had fallen along the clear waters of Plum Run at a location between Big Round Top and the Devil's Den—the appropriately named "Slaughter Pen." Photo taken on July 6, 1863. *Courtesy of the Library of Congress.*

1778 French Alliance. America gained an invaluable ally. The French made the decisive victory at Yorktown, Virginia, in October 1781 possible, thanks to their naval superiority and land army, which united with Washington's Continental army.[109]

In addition, the defiant son of one of the highest-ranking British officials in America, John Johnson, Ireland-born William Johnson led a patriot command that was appropriately named "Johnson's Greens," in honor of the native homeland.[110]

However, this appropriately named brothers' war of 1861–65 more often pitted brothers against brothers among the Irish than during the long struggle of the American Revolution. Major Hugh Garvin Gwyn led the Twenty-Third Tennessee Regiment with a typical Irish offensive-mindedness. He later served as the adjutant for General John Hunt Morgan, who emerged as one of the Confederacy's famed cavalry leaders in the western theater. The son of Catherine Garvin and Alexander Gwyn, Hugh Garvin Gwyn was born in Londonderry, north Ireland, in 1839. He married Mary Valentine in 1864 before returning to the battlefield to fight for his adopted country.[111]

Meanwhile, Hugh's older brother, James Gwynn, served as a major general in the Union army. He was born on November 24, 1828, in the Scotch-Irish city of Londonderry, north Ireland, like his brother. James Gwynn first served as a captain of the 23rd Pennsylvania Volunteer Infantry (ironically, his brother served in an excellent regiment with the same numerical designation, the 23rd Tennessee). James then became the colonel of the 118th Pennsylvania. He was promoted for gallantry in the fighting around Petersburg, including in the Confederate disaster at Five Forks, Virginia, which paved the way for the surrender of Lee's army at Appomattox Court House. James achieved the rank of major general, becoming just another Irishman who won distinction in this war.[112]

PENNSYLVANIA BECKONS IN 1863

In early July 1863, a clash between historic enemies (men of mostly English descent versus men of mostly Celtic, or Irish, decent) was about to rage for three days during the battle—the bloodiest of the war—that determined America's destiny at a small town in southeastern Pennsylvania. Here, the battle-hardened Irish of Lee's Army of Northern Virginia, a largely Celtic fighting force in overall composition, demonstrated a grim resolve to win a decisive victory north of the Potomac at any cost, because time was running out for the Confederacy.

This hard-fighting army had won a series of victories since General Robert Edward Lee had taken command on the Virginia peninsula on June 1, 1862. The showdown at Chancellorsville, Virginia, in early May 1863 had been the most recent success, representing the zenith of Lee's success. The dramatic victory at Chancellorsville provided Lee with the long-awaited opportunity to push north of the Potomac River and win a decisive victory. Consequently, confidence was high among the army's rank and file for achieving a decisive success on Northern soil in the summer of 1863. And for the Irish in gray and butternut, because they knew that everything was at stake, the most pressing requirement for reaping a decisive success in Pennsylvania and breaking the frustrating stalemate that was dooming the Confederacy now required having absolutely "no scruples of any kind in killing as many of their northern breathren [from Ireland] as they possibly could."[113]

The fact that the Irish fought with distinction beside non-Irish in the ranks of the Army of Northern Virginia was not always sufficient to diminish popular stereotypes about the Irish character. When one Texas Brigade soldier wrote a letter home, he expressed worry that the carefully written missive would never reach his wife in the distant trans-Mississippi homeland, because the mail carrier was a recently discharged Irish soldier. In his own words that revealed one of the day's most popular anti-Irish stereotypes (and one that has doggedly persisted for generations among many non-Irish and well into the twentieth century): "I am afraid that the Irishman will get drunk and lose this [letter]."[114]

But the faithfulness and commitment of the Irish on both sides to fight to the bitter end for what they believed was right was no longer questioned by skeptical non-Irish by the spring of 1863, when Lee pushed north toward Pennsylvania with visions of perhaps capturing Philadelphia, if all went well. One Irish Yankee, Thomas Jones, born in 1839 in County Down, Ireland, and a member of the Forty-Eighth New York Infantry, wrote in a letter to his sister: "One fine fellow [perhaps a New York Irishman] hailed up his rifle and said, 'Here is the death of Jefferson Davis' boys,'" including Irishmen in gray and butternut uniforms.[115]

His Ireland-born brother, William Jones, who also hailed from County Down, likewise learned of the brutal side of war when so many Irish killed each other with a ferocity seldom seen on battlefields across America. He wrote back home about how incensed Georgia Rebels, including men from

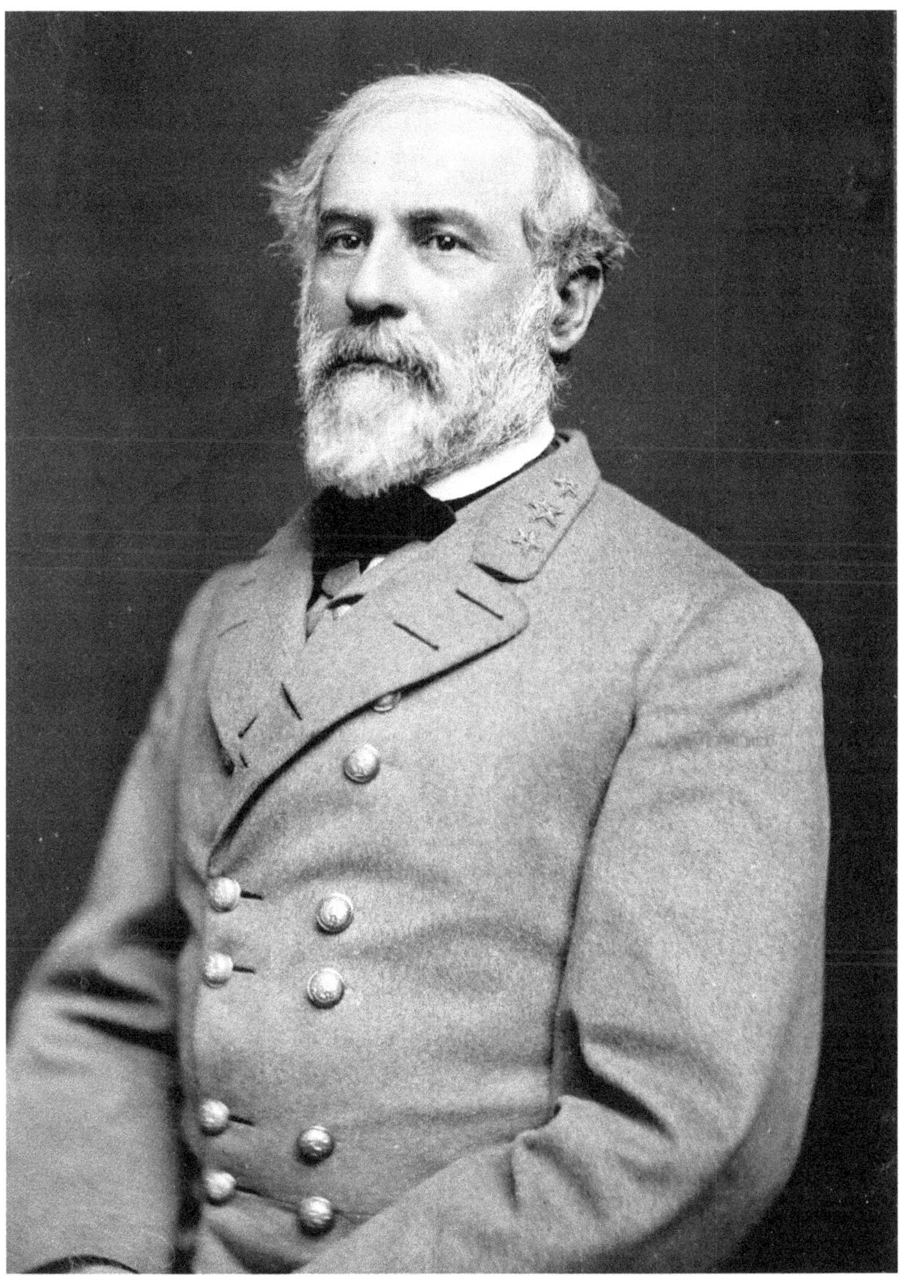

General Robert E. Lee gambled everything in his desperate attempts to destroy the Army of the Potomac at Gettysburg. *Courtesy of the Library of Congress.*

Ireland, "want vengeance on the 48th [New York] and they say they will not leave a man of us alive."[116]

As penned in a September 1863 letter, one Irish soldier in a New York regiment was especially eager to set the sights of his musket on "the arch-traitor General Lee," who was mostly of English descent in the Virginia cavalier tradition. Ireland-born Thomas Conolly revealed the extent of the civil war among the Irish when he wrote in his diary about how Rebels of Irish descent (Scotch-Irish) had captured or escorted Irish prisoners in blue in an unorthodox gathering of the clans.[117] What has been most forgotten about this conflict was the fact that the Civil War was also the bitterest of wars among Irish brothers from the same communities and homes on the distant Green Isle: a bitter irony that has revealed the complexities of the Irish experience seldom explored by either Irish or American historians.

Like the famed "Wild Geese" of Irish exiles who served with distinction in the Catholic armies of Spain and France in major battles on European soil, the Irish in Lee's predominantly Celtic army were also exiles who fought and died far from their native homeland. Symbolically, Lee's Irish were the sons, grandsons and great-grandsons of exiles, rebels and revolutionaries extending back centuries: historical legacies and memories that were sources of pride. Even some of the best Irish poetry and literature was dominated by the themes (sorrow and anguish) of Irish exiles far from their homeland and heroic Irish warriors who died in battle against invaders of the Green Isle.

Perhaps some Irish Rebels, especially educated officers who had gained knowledge at Trinity College, were reminded of the inspirational words from the popular Irish poem "Fair Hills of Eire" by Donnchadh Rua. On the eve of the greatest battle on the North American continent beginning quite by accident on the morning of July 1, 1863, in Adams County, Pennsylvania, they might have reflected on the words that they had heard spoken to them since childhood in the Irish tradition of rich oral history: "Take my heart's blessing over to dear Eire's strand—Fair Hills of Eire O! To the Remnant that love her—Our Forefathers' Land! Fair Hills of Eire O!"[118]

Other cultural influences from ancient Celtic lands across the sea also motivated General Lee's soldiers to perform at their highest level at Gettysburg, where everything was at stake. The historical romance of the popular Scotland-born writer Walter Scott significantly influenced an entire generation of Southern soldiers, including the Irish fighting men, in regard to the importance of traditional Celtic concepts of valor, gentlemanly conduct, and noble sacrifice for God and country. Fated to die during the fierce fighting at Chickamauga, Georgia, in September 1863, Taliaferro "Tally" Calhoun Simpson, a respected Third South Carolina officer of Lee's army, described his enchantment "in reading some of Walter Scott's beautiful stories."[119] In still another letter, this ill-fated son of South Carolina, Congressman Richard F. Simpson, continued to expound upon his admiration for "Walter Scott's fine tales" about "old Scotch characters" of Scottish history, including struggles against the hated English invaders of an ancient homeland.[120]

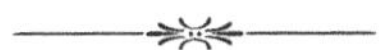

SOME OF THIS APPEAL about the more romantic sides of war played a role in influencing a generation of young Confederates, including a young Scotch-Irish soldier from South Carolina named Richard Rowland Kirkland at Fredericksburg in December 1862. The young man of strong religious faith hailed from a middle-class farming family of Kershaw County, South Carolina. He joined a company known as the Camden Volunteers under Scotch-Irish commander John D. Kennedy of the Second South Carolina Regiment, which was known as the Palmetto Regiment. An excellent commander who had just recovered from a nasty Antietam wound from September 17, 1862, Kennedy commanded the Second South Carolina, Brigadier General Joseph B. Kershaw's South Carolina Brigade, when the Army of the Potomac launched repeated suicidal assaults on the high ground lined with rows of artillery and infantrymen at Fredericksburg during one of the greatest slaughters of the Civil War.

Sergeant Kirkland, age twenty, risked his life in bringing full canteens of precious water to the large number of Federal wounded who lay before the stone wall at the foot of Marye's Heights on the cold morning of December 14. The horrors of America's most murderous war had not hardened the kind Irish heart of Sergeant Kirkland. His heroics and compassion toward the enemy, including fallen Irish Brigade soldiers who had been cut down by the musketry of Irish Confederates, were witnessed by the men of both armies. He jumped over the stone wall and brought relief to fallen Federals amid the open fields of slaughter.

When the veteran soldiers of both sides saw that the brave Kirkland, loaded with comrades' canteens and perhaps recalling the notable examples of ancient gallantry from a time in the misty past that was no more, was assisting the Yankee wounded, a chorus of wild cheers erupted from the admiring soldiers of both sides. He became known as the "Angel of Marye's Heights" for bringing relief to so many enemy soldiers in a highly visible errand of mercy that restored a rare degree of sanity to the insanity of war. As cruel fate would have it, Sergeant Kirkland was killed at the Battle of Chickamauga in September 1863, when no one could help the young South Carolina man of such commendable compassion and faith.[121]

3

CLIMACTIC SHOWDOWN AT GETTYSBURG

As the most successful military commander of his day, General Lee was at his peak by the time of his second invasion of the North during the 1863 summer campaign. Knowing that he had to win a decisive success to break a stalemate and with Southern fortunes sagging in the western theater, Lee was going for broke; the Confederacy was dying a slow death in a war of attrition. For such reasons, Lee's men were highly motivated, believing that their leader would bring them to a sparkling victory north of the Potomac, as seen so often on Virginia soil. In his diary, Irish aristocrat Thomas Conolly described Lee as "the idol of his soldiers & the Hope of His Country."[122]

Ever the opportunist after reaping victory at Chancellorsville that bestowed flexibility and freedom to maneuver, Lee was correctly convinced that the Confederacy's only hope was to secure victory north of the Potomac. If Philadelphia could be captured to reap a significant strategic gain and empower the Peace Democrats, then perhaps the beleaguered Confederacy could negotiate a peace to ensure a new republic's independence. Most of all, Lee realized that the manpower-short South was trapped in a brutal war of attrition that it could not win in the long run. Neither Lee nor his Irish soldiers had any idea that a cruel destiny was about to lead them far north to the town of Gettysburg, which had its own ethnically distinct "Irishtown."[123]

During the army's second campaign north of the Potomac after the disastrous 1862 Maryland Campaign, Lee was destined to rely heavily on his top lieutenant, Lieutenant General James "Old Pete" Longstreet,

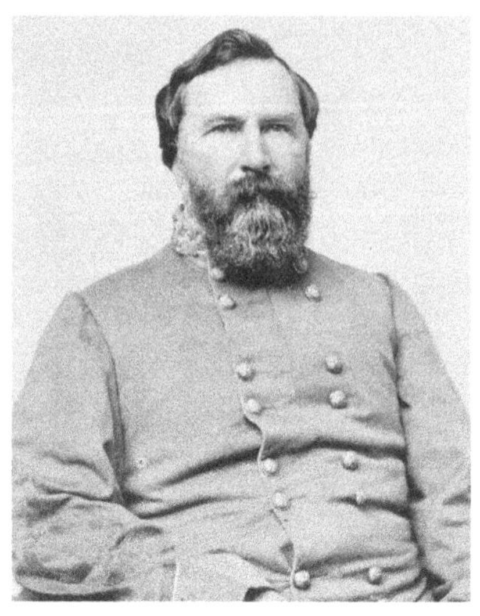

Defensive-minded Lieutenant General James Longstreet, Lee's top lieutenant, strongly disagreed with Lee's offensive plans at Gettysburg. *Courtesy of the Library of Congress.*

who commanded the hard-hitting First Corps, Army of Northern Virginia. Longstreet had risen to the fore after the mortal wounding of "Stonewall" Jackson, whose masterful tactics had been the key to victory, at Chancellorsville in early May 1863, replacing the dour Mexican-American War veteran and holy warrior who seemingly had emerged from the pages of the Old Testament. Irishman Conolly was thoroughly impressed by Longstreet's "honest bluff countenance & thorough soldier-like appearance. His stories of Buffalo hunting &c. [Longstreet] is called the Bull Dog of the army" of Northern Virginia.[124]

With an eye for his fellow countrymen who were now battling on American soil, Conolly also noted a colleague who hailed from the port of Wexford in southeast Ireland, Maurice Kavanah, who served as General Longstreet's body servant and "stud groom."[125] Significantly, Conolly, a privileged member of the upper class unlike the many lower-class Irish in Lee's ranks, was impressed—if not confounded to a degree—by the fact that the lowly "Maurice Kavanah is high in the confidence" of General Longstreet, who displayed no anti-Irish prejudice, to his credit.[126]

After reaping so many victories in Virginia, Lee and his battle-hardened veterans were never more confident for success on Northern soil than with the launching of the summer campaign of 1863. After all, the ever-aggressive Virginian had met with nothing but success in the past, including most recently in the showdown at Chancellorsville. Lee was especially confident in his own abilities and the combat prowess of his men, because the less-than-capable "Fighting Joe" Hooker, whom he had recently defeated at Chancellorsville, still commanded the Army of the Potomac.[127]

With the winning of a dramatic victory north of the Potomac River in the summer of 1863, Lee envisioned the tantalizing possibility of the delivering of a strategic blow, strengthening the Northern peace party, the so-called Copperheads, and deflating the Northern people's will (Lee's psychological target) to prosecute the war to the bitter end. They would then vote Abraham Lincoln, who had failed to crush the rebellion, out of office in November 1864 to lay a foundation for a negotiated peace.[128]

However, Lee should have been less confident of an anticipated easy success north of the Potomac, which many soldiers in his army believed was now inevitable, because of a host of hidden realities. After all, Lee's first invasion of the North nearly resulted in disaster for his badly depleted Army of Northern Virginia (its ranks severely thinned by desertion and disease to a lesser extent) and saw the war's bloodiest day after some of the war's most nightmarish combat, at a small market town nestled amid the rich farmlands of western Maryland, Sharpsburg, on September 17, 1862. Here, amid the pristine countryside drained by Antietam Creek's clear waters located just north of the Potomac, Lee's veterans fought the more powerful Army of the Potomac to a bloody standstill on a battlefield dominated by open fields. But even the Battle of Antietam had been a very close call (nearly fatal) for the South's primary eastern army, which was fortunate in having been able to survive and then limp back across the Potomac to Virginia without being destroyed by superior might.

Nevertheless, when ambitious plans were first formulated at Richmond for a second northern invasion, the abundant ugly realities of the Maryland Campaign of less than a year before were conveniently forgotten and ignored by the new nation's top military and political leaders, in part because of the urgent need to win a decisive victory. As Lee had repeatedly emphasized to President Jefferson Davis, now was the time to gamble because the South was on the losing end of a lengthy war of attrition, and time was of the essence. However, after the terrific bloodletting at Antietam, which paved the way for and guaranteed a three-day slugfest at Gettysburg, one Rebel soldier waxed prophetically about a grim new reality for the Army of Northern Virginia that could no longer be ignored: "the Yankey army is now as good as ours."[129]

An opportunity to fulfill the greatest Confederate ambitions fueled the motivations of thousands of veterans, including soldiers from the faraway land of the shamrock and St. Patrick. They dreamt of once again pushing into the promised land north of the Potomac, of winning the most decisive battle of the war and then capturing major northeastern cities like Philadelphia and Baltimore and, eventually, Washington, D.C. (the greatest prize), guaranteeing a long life for the new republic. A confident General William Dorsey Pender, who led a hard-hitting division of Lieutenant General Ambrose Powell Hill's Third Corps, Army of Northern Virginia, before suffering a mortal wound during the fighting at Gettysburg on July 2, penned with confidence in a letter to his wife, "We might get to Phila. without a fight."[130]

Ironically—if not ominously for future developments north of the Potomac—this had been the identical overly optimistic belief in the march north during the ill-fated Maryland Campaign, when it had been widely believed that "Lee would dictate terms of peace in Independence Square, Philadelphia."[131] But now Lee and his men believed that the Maryland Campaign had only been a trial run for the final fulfillment of Confederate aspirations, especially for achieving a permanent peace, in the decisive summer of 1863. Therefore, an "overweening confidence," in the words of Lee's gifted assistant adjutant general Walter Herron Taylor, who served as Lee's invaluable chief of staff, in the army's ranks had never been higher.[132]

As early as the 1862 Peninsula Campaign, General John B. Magruder had made bold promises to his troops at Yorktown, where Washington and his French allies had won the Revolutionary War's most important victory in October 1781, laying siege to the old tobacco port to force the surrender of Lord Charles Cornwallis's army of British, Hessians and Loyalists. At the time of England's greatest military humiliation in America during its determined bid to retain its thirteen colonies, Ireland-born General Charles O'Hara had handed over his sword in a formal surrender ceremony (Cornwallis had feigned illness), in part because so many Irish soldiers had long served and fought in disproportionate numbers in Washington's ranks, especially during the struggle's darkest days, when many non-Irish had deserted because prospects were so grim. It was the ultimate horror for an arrogant English aristocrat like Cornwallis, who had close connections to King George III and the upper-class elite. In command of the Yorktown defensive line before the Army of the Potomac's advance on Richmond at the Peninsula Campaign's beginning, General Magruder had promised that they would eventually push into the North and "burn its cities" in order to "dictate terms of peace on their own soil."[133]

The chances of Lee's army achieving a decisive success in Pennsylvania were actually quite good in the summer of 1863, representing the best final opportunity to win it all. Especially compared to the disastrous 1862 Maryland Campaign, never before was the Army of Northern Virginia in better overall shape for offensive operations than when its soldiers prepared to push north toward the Potomac River. In the words of Lieutenant John

Edward Dooley Jr., as penned in his journal: "Never before has the army been in such fine condition, so well disciplined and under such complete control. Perhaps never before have we had a larger effective force, sixty thousand infantry with some two hundred pieces of cannon."[134]

Just before the unleashing of Lee's ambitious second invasion of the North, this young lieutenant, a proud son of Richmond and member of Pickett's Division, revealed the depth of his Irish roots when the Army of Northern Virginia displayed its discipline and martial prowess during a grand review: "We begin our march, determined to look as well as possible before our leaders and the *foreigners*. Our Brigade [under Brigadier General James Lawton Kemper] occupies a center position in column, and as we pass these noble reviews I am sure all of us looked our best, bore our arms with all the precision of which we knew, and wondered if the English Lords didn't admire us. In returning to Camp someone suggested that it would be mortifying and a sad joke if the Englishmen whom we had been trying to please so much were only Yankee spies; and I must confess I had myself some doubts about their genuine nobility."[135]

Of course, Dooley's reference to the English as "foreigners" was in keeping with the longtime view about this historic enemy of the Irish people, especially dispossessed Irish Catholics and sons of St. Patrick, who hated the abusive interlopers as detested "Saxon curs" and "Luther's followers" of the Protestant faith.[136]

The Confederate Irish, especially the most recent immigrants of the dispossessed lower class, knew only too well about the abuses of the English and Anglo-Irish ruling class, who had risen during the Ascendancy and ruled Ireland with an iron fist after the last Jacobite (Irish Catholic) rebellion was crushed at the Battle of the Boyne in 1690. After the English conquest, the common people (Catholics) of Ireland were without land (now possessed by the victors as spoils of war) and lived a meager existence as tenant farmers of the great estates of the English and Anglo-Irish ruling class. The haughty conquerors had bestowed almost all of Ireland's fertile lands on relatively few landowners, who were basically feudal lords ruling over serfs.

While marching north toward the Potomac River with high hopes for winning it all, Lee's Irish still recalled the sight of the Georgian mansions of exquisite beauty and in the Palladian style, as well as the great country houses on the sprawling estates of the Anglo-Irish aristocracy. These stately mansion houses usually stood atop hills that offered panoramic views of the fertile countryside. Of course, this wealthy ruling class had the might of the British army and the empire to back their abusive authority over the lowly and landless masses (modern-day peasants). The common Irish had long lived a lowly existence in small, one-room cottages with thatched roofs and survived mostly on potatoes, which was Ireland's one-crop staple for the common people.[137]

A FRESH HISTORICAL PERSPECTIVE

In the most written-about battle in the annals of American history, no previous study has been devoted to the important contributions of the Irish and their vital roles. Like no other fighting men in the largest battle fought on the North American continent, the story of these forgotten soldiers has been absent from the historical record for more than 150 years in a significant omission.

In the revealing words of one Confederate veteran from west of the Mississippi River who knew of the importance of the Irish contributions to the struggle for Southern independence that have been obscured and overlooked for so long, "Whoever tells the truth as to our war will [look to] Ireland in her struggle for self-government for Irish blood asserted itself in our war."[138] Likewise and most significant, neither the Battle of Gettysburg nor Pickett's Charge can be fully appreciated without first understanding the significant impact of the Irish experience and the key role of Irish soldiers on both sides.

Likewise, a South Carolina Rebel from east of the Mississippi emphasized, correctly, that "the land of the Shamrock, as on other fields, contributed its quota on the strongly contested ground" of Gettysburg on July 1–3, 1863.[139] Nevertheless, the extensive contributions of the Irish have been not only minimized but also ignored by generations of writers and historians, despite their significant achievements in America's most popular and important battle of the Civil War.

Ironically, therefore, one of the best stories of the Battle of Gettysburg has been long overlooked in the most popular books: the fratricidal conflict between Irishmen in blue and in gray in the decisive showdown at Gettysburg, including during the height of Pickett's Charge at the embattled Angle and at the copse of trees on the Army of the Potomac's weak right-center.

Lee and his Army of Northern Virginia, consisting of around eighty thousand troops who were veterans who knew how to vanquish Yankees, were going for broke in once again taking the war to Northern territory. With the strategic Confederate bastion of Vicksburg, Mississippi, under threat from General Ulysses S. Grant and his seasoned troops of a seemingly invincible western army, Lee hoped to negate the dire consequences if the Mississippi River was lost of the Confederacy by securing victory on Northern soil: an almost impossible task because of poor Confederate leadership in the West and the lack of Army of Northern Virginia reinforcements having been sent west, thanks largely to Lee's pro–Virginia theater bias, if not obsession. Perhaps guilty more of wishful thinking than of realistic contemplation that weighed the hard facts and harsh realities, Lee was optimistic about the chances for success north of the Potomac, knowing that it was literally a case of now or never for his ever-weakening nation. However, beating "Fighting Joe" Hooker had proved costly, and Lee's officer corps had been decimated. Even worse, the Army of the Potomac was more resilient and tougher than Hooker. In this sense, Lee had more vanquished Hooker at Chancellorsville rather than the Federal Army, which continued to mature and improve more than the Army of Northern Virginia.[140]

Lamenting the past losses of so many comrades of the largely Irish Montgomery Guard, First Virginia, such as Lieutenant John H. Donahue, a hopeful Lieutenant John Edward Dooley Jr. penned in his journal on June 24: "We are moving in the direction of Martinsburg [in today's West Virginia] and learn for the first time that Pennsylvania is our objective point."[141]

In this Northern campaign, the young men and boys of the Army of Northern Virginia had complete faith in their commander and their own proven abilities, because he had beaten one Army of the Potomac commander after another. As mentioned, "Fighting Joe" Hooker was only the most recent victim. Taking the conflict far away from war-ravaged Virginia was a godsend to the beleaguered nation and Southern people, who had already suffered severely from the invasion of their homeland since 1861. Therefore, the spirit of vengeance also accompanied Lee's troops during the push north. In the words of one soldier: "I have got a gruge [*sic*] against [the Yankees and] it is my Honest wish that my Rifle may Draw tears from many a Northern Mother and Sighs from Many a Father before this thing is over."[142]

Clearly, both the nature of this conflict and the men who fought on both sides had been significantly changed since the war's beginning, because the conflict's brutality was on the rise. Early idealism and notions of the romance of war for soldiers had proven fleeting and illusionary, having been long since crushed by the summer of 1863. No longer was this conflict for the average fighting man about martial music, cheers, and kisses from pretty girls or romantic concepts about reaping glory. Instead, this conflict had become about only one thing, and it was an ugly and nightmarish reality: killing and wiping out as many opponents as possible in order to secure a decisive victory.[143]

His faithful followers who marched north toward the Potomac River fully expected Lee to lead them to the war's most decisive victory, which would save the life of the infant Confederacy. This merciless war of attrition was now a race against time for the Rebels. Irishman Thomas Conolly, who hailed from one of Ireland's leading families and lorded as the head of vast estate, Castletown House, in County Kildare, described Lee and his supreme importance to the Confederacy: "the idol of his soldiers & the Hope of His Country...one of the most prepossessing figures that ever bore the weight of command or led the fortunes of a Nation, add to this the prestige which surround his person & the almost fanatical belief in his judgement & capacity wh[ich] is the one idea of an entire people & there stands before you the beau ideal of an accomplished & self reliant chief directing with a firm hand & sagacious head the mighty machine of war."[144]

As could be expected of a provincial-thinking, but brilliant, military man who had decided to fight for the Confederacy only in the hope of protecting the people of Virginia, including his own family, Lee especially revered his Virginia troops, including the Old Dominion veterans of Pickett's Division. The words of Lieutenant John Williamson Finley, an experienced officer of Irish descent, captured the overall mood of the common Rebel soldiers at Gettysburg, especially in regard to Pickett's Charge on the final bloody day: "to every man in our army [Lee] was simply 'Marse Robert.' We would have followed him anywhere—even into the jaws of hell itself...and on the third day at Gettysburg...that is exactly what we did."[145]

Now commanded by Brigadier General James A. Walker, the Stonewall Brigade of Virginians was the pride and joy of General Lee. The brigade included the Irish soldiers of the Emerald Guards, Company E, Thirty-Third Virginia. These veteran soldiers hailed from the Shenandoah County town of New Market (site of the May 15, 1864 battle in which the Virginia

Military Institute cadets won fame in a spirited attack). They also hailed from small middle-class farms across the Shenandoah Valley.

As the revered Virginian, the former commandant at West Point (like Lee before the war) wrote about the Stonewall Brigade: "From its conduct and association this brigade has acquired the affection of the whole Country, & stands high in the esteem of the army."[146] While the Stonewall Brigade has become famous in the annals of Civil War historiography, what has been overlooked is the fact that this veteran Old Dominion command consisted mostly of Scotch-Irish and others of Irish descent. Significantly, this demographic of the brigade was consistent with the overall Celtic demographics of not only the South, but also the Army of Northern Virginia.[147]

Irish Humor

Along with superior fighting qualities, the Irish Confederate soldiers were distinguished by a distinctive brand of Celtic-Gaelic humor that was generally sharper and keener than that of Lee's Rebels of British (Anglo-Saxon) descent because of different cultural realities and historical experiences. Long utilized as a natural coping and survival mechanism to deal with personal setbacks and severe adversity, especially foreign conquest and occupation of their homeland, a well-honed Irish humor was distinguished by its parody, satire, ribaldry and biting wit.

In order to bring a little joy to difficult lives, especially the oppressed landless peasantry, who had been the underdog for centuries, Emerald Islanders even made fun of themselves and mocked life itself. This highly developed Irish, or Celtic, sense of humor was also evident in soldiers of Celtic heritage from other lands, especially Scotland, where nationalism and determined bids for independence, including by William Wallace, had been crushed by England. This distinctive brand of Irish humor, noted in Confederate soldiers' letters, diaries and memoirs, lifted spirits in times of adversity and loss. Sergeant Major Newsom Edward Jenkins, Fourteenth North Carolina Infantry, Army of Northern Virginia, described the "clown and joker [of the regiment who] was [Private] Lyman Latham, whose father was of pure Scottish descent." This soldier perhaps still possessed telltale qualities of a Scottish accent like his sense of Celtic humor.

Significantly, no aspect of life, especially in the army, escaped the mockery and sharp wit of the Irish. As back in Ireland, the Sons of Erin routinely poked fun at anything and everything, including officers and government leaders, such as President Jefferson Davis. Like no other ethnic group of individuals in the Army of Northern Virginia, the Irish soldiers possessed the uncanny ability to find a grim humor in the worst situations, including on the battlefield.[148]

Embodying the characteristics of so many other Irish soldiers, Private William "Bill" Calhoun, Company B (Tom Green Rifles), was the "wag and wit" of the Fourth Texas, Hood's Texas Brigade. A fellow private described Calhoun as "the life of old Company B [and] was known to every man in the regiment….Naturally smart, witty, and full of repartee, he soon became a favorite both with officers and men. He possessed an amiable disposition, was kind-hearted and cheerful….Careless of dress, he moved with a swinging gait, which he appeared to cultivate for the amusement of his friends."[149] Reflecting his distinctive Celtic-Gaelic roots and with Ireland's patron saint in mind, Calhoun's favorite saying was, appropriately, "Holy Saint Patrick."[150]

Like Lee's infantry regiments, so the army's artillery was heavily represented by Irish and Scotch-Irish gunners, more than has been generally recognized by Civil War historians. An officer of the Rockbridge, Virginia, artillery, William Thomas Poague, never forgot the hard-fighting qualities and Celtic-Gaelic spirit of his Irish artillerymen. When a Federal shell smashed into a nearby pine tree, an Irish cannoneer named Tom Martin from Virginia yelled out, "By jabers! Abe Lincoln's at his old trade of making rails."[151] And when a fight erupted between the enlisted men of two rival Confederate batteries, a tough Irish officer named Lieutenant Baxter McCorkle, who was "a stalwart young fellow [waded into the melee and] knocked the brawlers right and left and soon quelled the disorders."[152]

As mentioned, General John Bell Hood's Texas Brigade, one of the army's best fighting units, also possessed its fair share of Irishmen in the ranks. During the showdown at Gettysburg, Kentucky-born General Jerome Bonaparte Robertson, the son of a Scottish immigrant who had led Kentucky volunteers during the Texas revolution, commanded the Texas Brigade. No city in Texas was more cosmopolitan and contained so many Irish as the port of Galveston, and the port's residents from Ireland served in the Texas Brigade. However, the Irish were scattered throughout the state, including in small towns from the central plains to the bayou country of east Texas.

Fated to be killed while leading the Texas Brigade's sweeping attack at

Gaines's Mill outside of Richmond on the Virginia peninsula, Captain Edwin "Ed" D. Ryan, a merchant from Waco in his mid-twenties, organized Company E (Lone Star Guards), Fourth Texas. As mentioned, Irish soldiers of regiments across the South possessed colorful personalities and daredevil qualities on the battlefield that often appeared in non-Irish soldiers' letters, diaries and postwar memoirs. Bill Calhoun was the very "life of old Company B," the Tom Green Rifles, Fourth Texas. Like so many other Irish soldiers, Calhoun was described as "naturally smart, witty, and full of repartee, [and] he soon became a favorite both with officers and men [and] He possessed an amiable disposition, was kindhearted and cheerful."[153]

These Texans revered the cherished legacies of their state's revolution, including the showdowns at the Alamo and San Jacinto, but they had no idea that there was a Gettysburg-Irish connection to the 1835–36 struggle for independence on Texas soil. One member of the New Orleans Greys, the finest combat unit of the Texas Revolution (partly because it included so many Irish volunteers from the Crescent City), was Joseph P. Riddle. As cruel fate would have it, he was executed along with hundreds of his comrades (recent volunteers who had arrived in Texas from the United States) on the most infamous Palm Sunday in Texas history, at Goliad. On that terrible day, General Antonio Lopez de Santa Anna's *soldados* executed around four hundred Americans in the greatest atrocity of the Texas uprising that depended on outside support. Riddle's grandfather James Riddle hailed from the rolling hills of Parish Rhea, County Donegal, north Ireland. James Riddle and other family members had planted deep roots in American soil during the early 1750s, finding freedoms that they had lacked in Ulster Province.[154]

WADING ACROSS THE POTOMAC RIVER

Crossing the Potomac River, the watery boundary between Virginia and Maryland, was symbolic for the Irish Rebels and their lofty nationalistic aspirations. In the ranks of the First Virginia, Pickett's Division, Lieutenant John Edward Dooley Jr., the bright student from Georgetown College, penned in his journal on June 25: "Late in the afternoon we reach the Potomac and being disappointed in our pontoons prepare to wade this mighty stream which separated us from our beloved Virginia soil. Terrible had been that march along the scorched and blazing plains of Virginia.

Angry was the glare of the sun during those fearful days of June…we now stand upon the banks of the Potomac and prepare to cross" the river.[155]

Of Irish descent, Lieutenant George Williamson Finley, Fifty-Sixth Virginia, Pickett's Division, described the peculiar appearance of Lee's high-spirited invaders, who were hardened veterans:

> *No two [were] dressed alike* [while] *Some of the them* [were] *bare footed* [and] *Many of them wearing butternut trousers* [that were] *captured Federal sky blue trousers boiled in walnut juice, and they varied in shade from a light tan to a dark brown….And calico shirts with wide suspenders and brown, gray, or black, wide-brimmed, slouch hats pinned up on the wide or rolled up in the front. Confederate infantry did not wear kepi caps like Yankees* [because] *it just wasn't dignified, and* [they were] *not going to keep the rain and the sun off the back of your head better than a wide-brimmed slouch hat* [and all in all] *Our boys looked like a pack of dirty, lean, gray, brown, hungry wolves."*[156]

Yet these young men and boys were ideal soldiers, possessing finely tuned combat capabilities (rather than looks that shocked the citizens of Maryland and Pennsylvania) that were well-suited and required for the Northern campaign's stern demands, because now "it is a race [north] between [Major General Joseph] Hooker and Lee, the first having the inside circle" and the advantage.[157]

But General Hooker's ambitious race to catch up to the Army of Northern Virginia was already coming to an end. Noted for his bombastic style and overconfidence that hid a host of weaknesses as an army commander, he was about to lose his job commanding the Army of the Potomac. An astute judge of character who was evolving into a brilliant war leader, President Lincoln had already seen enough of Hooker's boasting and bluster, which had worn thin after the recent defeat at Chancellorsville without significant results on the battlefield, where it counted.

Many of his subordinate generals had turned against the arrogant Hooker, steadily eroding his standing with Lincoln. The flamboyant Hooker, who had the dubious honor of having his name attached to the working girls of the many brothels of Washington, D.C., was finally replaced by Major General George Gordon Meade only days before the final showdown at Gettysburg. Lincoln had made a wise decision. Meticulously careful in his decision-making on the battlefield and a strict disciplinarian who demanded a great deal from his men, the prudent Meade was an ideal choice to command the Army of

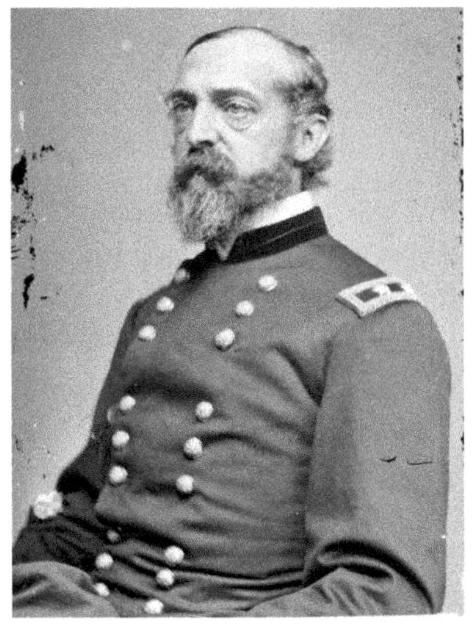

Major General George Gordon Meade proved highly capable in defending the high ground at Gettysburg, verifying President Abraham Lincoln's faith in the Army of the Potomac's newest commander. *Courtesy of the Library of Congress.*

the Potomac just in time for its greatest challenge to date.[158] Like Lee in regard to his relationship with Richmond's officials, including President Davis, Meade was not hampered by interference. He had been told by Lincoln's chief of staff, Henry "Old Brains" Halleck, that "your army is free to act as you may deem proper" for repelling Lee's invasion.[159]

After crossing the Potomac at Williamsport and Shepherdstown to leave Virginia soil behind with a chorus of wild cheers that echoed through the woodlands of early summer, Lee's troops entered Maryland in a festive mood. Confederate bands also enlivened spirits when they struck up the appropriate popular tune "My Maryland, My Maryland."[160] Symbolically, Irish soldiers were found in plentiful numbers in Lee's Maryland regiments. One teenage Maryland soldier, George Wilson Booth, described a Maryland Irish company earlier in the war: "They were mostly of Irish-American descent, sometimes unruly, by reason of imperfect handling, but were of the material that makes the best of soldiers" for the Confederacy.[161]

Most important for the arduous challenges of Lee's second invasion of the North, faithful Irish chaplains played their part in fueling the determination of the Sons of Erin for waging a holy war north of the Potomac. Lieutenant John Edward Dooley Jr., Montgomery Guard, First Virginia, Pickett's Division, described the situation just before the confident push into Pennsylvania: "Some of the parsons or chaplains are very zealous and persevering in assembling the soldiers to prayer; especially the chaplain of the eleventh Va. And the seventh [both of these Old Dominion regiments were part of General Kemper's Virginia Brigade like the First Virginia]. The latter is held in high esteem by all, whether members of religion or not [and] he is as bold as the bravest and is to be seen in the first and fiercest battles, consoling and assisting the wounded. Florence McCarthy of Richmond, chaplain of the 7th inf., is also distinguished for his preaching and zeal among the soldiers."[162]

Of course, dedicated Irish chaplains in blue also fulfilled identical roles. This was especially the case in regard to the Irish Brigade. For example, Father William Corby, Eighty-Eighth New York, and Ireland-born Father Thomas Mooney, Sixty-Ninth New York Volunteer Infantry of the Irish Brigade, baptized not only Irishmen but also cannon that were manned and defended by Emerald Islanders. Father Corby emphasized how the Irish Brigade "springs from a fearless race, whose valor has been tested in a war that was incessant for three hundred years, with the Danes and Normans, followed by contests, more or less fierce, for centuries, with England."[163]

A NEW LAND OF WONDER NORTH OF THE POTOMAC

After crossing the Potomac and marching through the unspoiled countryside of western Maryland like in September 1862, the reinvigorated Confederates pushed across the even more pristine Pennsylvania soil unabated, with high hopes and visions of success on the horizon. Lieutenant John Dooley Jr. described how "we advanced into Pennsylvania [and] the road becomes almost impassible, so slippery is the mud; whilst a cold, steady rain falls constantly upon our ranks. The wheat fields are every where nearly ripe for harvesting, and all around plenty appears to bless the fertile land."[164] From Richmond, which he loved, and still very much a city boy, Dooley marveled at the meticulousness of the well-manicured farmlands cultivated by "these Thrifty German Farmers" of Maryland and Pennsylvania.[165]

The fast-moving Confederates met no Yankee opposition of any sort, while the Army of the Potomac was still marching north across western Maryland from Washington, D.C. In part a legacy of its Quaker founding, Pennsylvania lacked a standing army tradition and a viable defensive force against Lee's invaders. And the common farmers of the largely German population of southeast Pennsylvania were content to cause no problems for the interlopers primarily because they wished to be left alone. Thoughts of unleashing a homespun brand of guerrilla warfare were practically non-existent. The welfare of crops remained the top priority among the Pennsylvanians. Instead, the Teutonic population continued to remain focused on the welfare of the bountiful farms rather than risk reprisals. Therefore, Lee's advance through the Keystone State resembled a military parade, reminding Mexican-American War veterans of the triumphant march through Mexico's luxurious central valley on the way to Mexico City.[166]

This was the first time that most of Lee's soldiers had ever set foot on Pennsylvania soil, and the experience of marching through the picturesque countryside of the Keystone State left them in wonder: a wake-up call and new awareness that bestowed a host of startling new realities never to be forgotten by the lower-class soldiers from the backwoods of the South. The vast majority of these mostly young lower-class fighting men, including conscripted soldiers, had no realistic chance of ever becoming part of the upper-class elite or living in a white-columned mansion in the future. What these young Southern farm boys and Emerald Islanders saw around them was simply astounding. Lee's men had long lived a hand-to-mouth existence in the war-ravaged Virginia now lacking in resources. Rich farmlands and fertile fields of wheat and other crops stretched to the horizon in every direction—a land of plenty. The smokehouses, food cellars and large red-painted barns of the largely German farmers of Pennsylvania were overflowing with provisions of all kinds. One concerned Confederate general even worried that "we will all get fat here."[167]

And the huge German barns, with sturdy stone foundations supporting magnificent wooden structures standing two and three stories tall, astounded Lee's men from the South's remote rural areas, which was the vast majority. Barns of this size were not seen in the South or in Ireland. In Ireland, the "barns are not a large feature of the Irish life [because] the mildness of the climate is such that merely a shed or shelter is sufficient for the animals."[168]

A legacy of Ireland's subjugation by England (and quite unlike the industrious German farmers of Pennsylvania) and working as tenant farmers on the landlord's property, many Scotch-Irish settlers continued to maintain a wise tradition of not displaying signs of surplus—like a large barn—to avoid indications of agricultural wealth and prosperity. This was a stealthy habit to keep the English military, landlord, tax collector or envious Anglo-Irish neighbors from undertaking attempts to confiscate meager savings and property.[169]

MARCHING EVER CLOSER TO GETTYSBURG

All the while, fate itself seemed to be steadily drawing the Army of Northern Virginia from the west and toward the Army of the Potomac that was marching from the south toward the small town of Gettysburg. John Dooley Jr. wrote in his journal, "Our Division (Pickett's) is the rearmost [division of Longstreet's First Corps], and we are left in the vicinity of Chambersburg, Pennsylvania, to cover the march of the main body advancing on Gettysburg [and we are] to be ready at a moment's warning to join the main army whenever the enemy might be found, for as yet we were ignorant of his position."[170]

Ironically, in approaching Gettysburg, Lee's Irish soldiers had no idea that they were about to fight and die on the fertile farmlands of Adams County that had been early settled by a good many Irish immigrants, mostly Scotch-Irish from Ulster Province. Nevertheless, as in sizeable Pennsylvania cities like Philadelphia, anti-Irish sentiment, especially against Irish Catholics (especially recent immigrants), had been an ugly feature of life in an increasingly intolerant Gettysburg in the 1850s, because of the rise of the Irish-hating Know-Nothings. Even the spirit of anti-abolitionism had been strong among the area's people, including among the Scotch-Irish. Ironically, when a fiery abolitionist woman of Irish descent attempted to speak of abolition's merits in 1845, Abby Kelly met a hostile reception among the people of Adams County, including in Gettysburg.[171]

At this time, some of these picturesque farms around Gettysburg were still owned by a good many Irish whose ancestors had decided not to push farther west like the vast majority of their countrymen, who had long ago followed the setting sun in search of new lands. And even those Irish who moved west from the Gettysburg area left behind their distinctive Irish names for farms, creeks and woodlots. Most of the first day's combat that swirled northwest of Gettysburg on July 1 took place on the farm of Edward McPherson, a Pennsylvania congressman at the war's beginning who was voted out of office by 1863.

Much of the first day's most bitter combat erupted around McPherson's Ridge, located before Seminary Ridge just outside of the market town where ten roads met to suddenly make Gettysburg of strategic importance. A Scotch-Irish congressman before the war and respected lawyer, Moses McClean, owned the prosperous farm. Because the Scotch-Irish, along with the Germans, had early on settled the Gettysburg area, Celtic-Gaelic names graced other farms and sites on the Gettysburg battlefield, such as the James McKnight farm and the James McAllister Mill (a former stop for escaped Maryland slaves journeying north on the Underground Railroad) on the west bank of Rock Creek.[172]

Lee's Gaelic-Celtic fighting men were not aware that they were about to enter the greatest battle ever fought on the North American continent, although they realized that a showdown on Northern soil was inevitable. Lieutenant Dooley wrote, "We know how straight into the very jaws of destruction and death leads this road of Gettysburg; and none of us are yet aware that a battle is before us; still there pervades our ranks a solemn feeling, as if some unforeseen danger was ever dropping darksome shadows over the road we unshrinkingly tread."[173]

Another undeniable reality—an Irish conundrum—was equally not fully understood by the Irish of the Army of Northern Virginia at this time. Indeed, neither "Confederate nor Federal Irishman could understand the position of the other. The northern zealot was shocked at a southern Irishman fighting against the land of liberty; the southern Celt failed to see how an Irishman who wished for the freedom of his native isle could fight against a people striving to secure their independence. They seemed perfectly able to level their guns against their fellow countrymen if they were arrayed on the 'wrong' side."[174]

The Famed Irish Brigade

At this time, Irish Rebels, mostly Protestant Scotch-Irish, almost certainly lusted for the opportunity to thoroughly whip the Irish, mostly Catholics, of the famed Irish Brigade. If so, then the showdown at Gettysburg might well provide that opportunity for Lee's Irish soldiers, as well as to demonstrate their superiority over their fellow countrymen in blue. Not unlike the Irish Confederates, but less so because they were mostly Protestant, the hard-fighting Irish Brigade (mostly Catholics) had long been long used as little more than cannon fodder because of its well-known combat prowess in some of the bloodiest battles of the war.

Known for their "Gaelic cheer" and green battle-flags like that of the Eighty-Eighth New York, whose flag was inscribed with the words "They shall not retreat from the clash of spears," these Irishmen in blue (more boys from the city than from the rural countryside, like most of Lee's Irishmen) had been slaughtered on the great killing fields of Antietam and Fredericksburg within only a relatively short period—the last few months of 1862. Indeed, the seemingly ill-fated troops of the Irish Brigade suffered the highest casualty rate of any Union brigade during

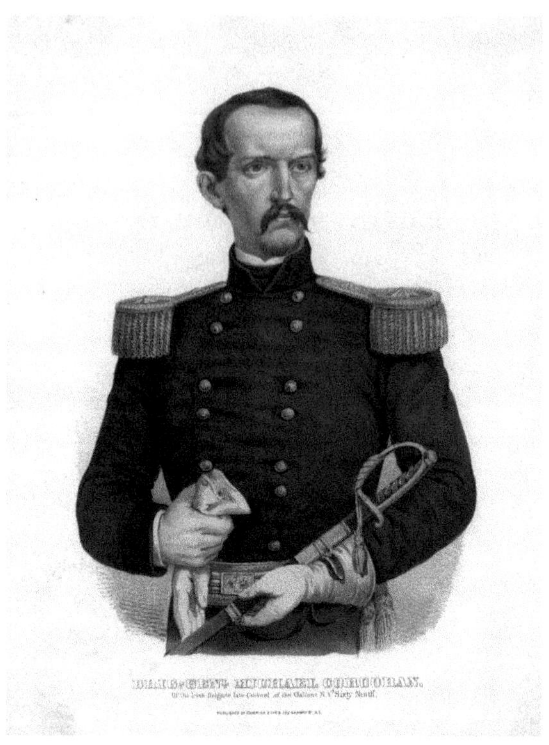

Born in County Sligo, Ireland, Michael Corcoran served as the first colonel of the hard-fighting Sixty-Ninth New York Volunteer Infantry at the battle of First Manassas. Destined for a brigadier general's rank, Corcoran died in December 1863. *Courtesy of the Library of Congress.*

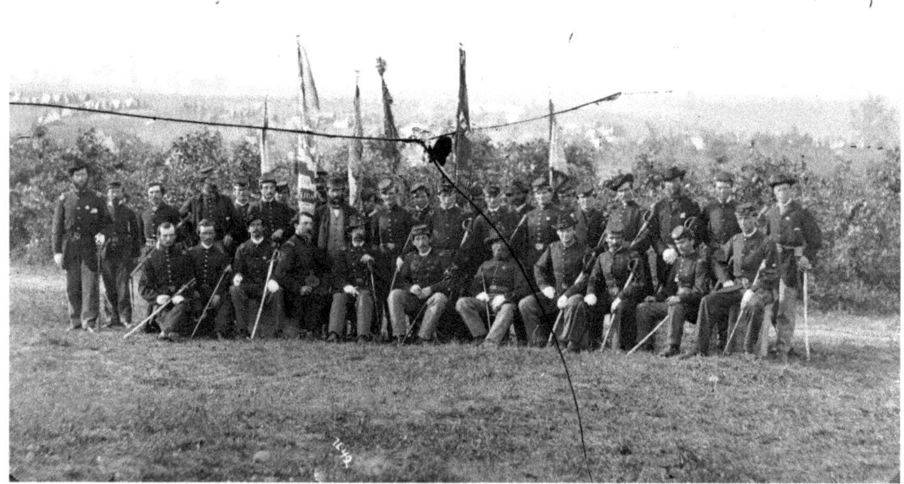

Ireland-born Lieutenant Colonel James J. Smith and other veteran officers of the Sixty-Ninth New York, Irish Brigade. The highly competent Smith first made his reputation as the hard-working adjutant of the Sixth-Ninth New York, Irish Brigade. *Courtesy of the Library of Congress.*

the four years of the war; large numbers of Irish found final burial places in trenches.

The Irish Brigade was now part of Major General Winfield Scott's Second Corps and under the command of Colonel Patrick Kelly, age forty-two. At this time, the Irish Brigade (Sixty-Ninth New York, Twenty-Eighth Massachusetts, Eighty-Eighth New York, Sixty-Third New York, and One Hundred and Sixteenth Pennsylvania) was officially designated as the Second Brigade, First Division, Second Corps. Father William Corby, standing atop a rocky outcropping, bestowed a general absolution in Latin upon the kneeing Irish Brigade soldiers just before they entered the raging battle. For many reasons, Corby was a guiding light and inspirational force to the Irish soldiers. Regardless if the men were north Ireland Protestants or Catholics from the midlands and the south, the dedicated Father Corby blessed them all. He bestowed the sacraments to dying young men and boys from the Green Isle, comforting them as much as possible before they died. Corby gently cradled their heads while preparing them for the next world, where there were no horrors of war. He held the hands of grizzled veterans while they cried tears, begged for mercy, and called for their mothers who they would never see again. Father Corby was by the side of a seemingly countless number of Irish Brigade men when they breathed their last and departed this world of suffering.

Colonel Kelly, from County Galway, was fated to be killed in the attack on Petersburg, Virginia, defenses on June 16, 1864, while leading the Irish Brigade into a storm of lead. Here, at the Wheatfield, and with Colonel Kelly leading the way, the battle-hardened veterans of the Irish Brigade attempted to stem the attackers that had been unleashed to break through the Cemetery Ridge defensive line, and lost heavily for confronting a victorious tide on this hot afternoon.

The Irish Brigade consisted mostly of Irishmen from the urban sprawl of New York City, thanks in large part to the Irish exodus to escape the Great Potato Famine of the 1840s. The hunger crisis had brought multitudes of impoverished Irish to primarily lower-class shantytowns and slum tenements (such as Sweeney's Shambles) of lower Manhattan, including the infamous Five Points. As mentioned, the Army of the Potomac's most ethnic unit had been originally led by the famed Young Irelander and nationalist General Thomas Francis Meagher during the major showdowns in the bloody year of 1862. Colonel Kelly now continued Meagher's legacy of solid leadership and leading the way.

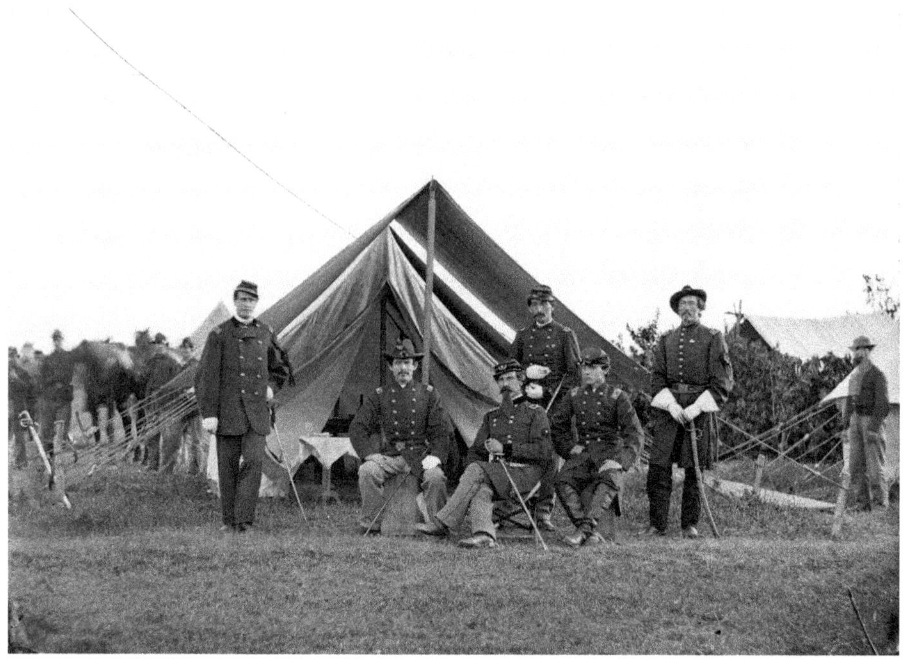

Brigadier General Robert Nugent and his staff of the Irish Brigade. Photograph taken in the District of Columbia. Nugent commanded the hard-fighting Irish of the Sixty-Ninth New York, Irish Brigade, during the 1862 Peninsula campaign. He was seriously wounded in the brigade's famous attack on the high ground at Fredericksburg. Nugent continued to suffer from complications of his old wound until his death in 1901. Courtesy *of the Library of Congress.*

As fate would have it, the Irish Brigade suffered more than did other brigades of the Army of Potomac, still it attacked with abandon, calling out its distinctive Gaelic war cries, including during the showdown in the Wheatfield. The men of the Irish Brigade had delivered as much punishment as they received throughout 1862. Early armed with .69-caliber smoothbore muskets, the Irish were especially effective at close-range in firing volleys that swept the enemy's ranks, which included Irish Rebels, with deadly loads of "buck & ball." In addition, the Irish relied heavily on the cold steel of the bayonet in the honored tradition of the famed "Wild Geese" exiles who had performed magnificently on the battlefields of Europe.

Hundreds of Irish soldiers were cut down while battling in both offensive and defensive roles under the beautiful battle flags of green. In the war's beginning—and like in regard to Confederate flags of units from Mobile and Charleston—the silk banner of the Sixty-Ninth New York had been blessed by the Ireland-born archbishop at St. Patrick's Cathedral on Mulberry Street in Manhattan. The marching song (an old Irish drinking song with roots in Limerick on the Shannon River) of the Irish Brigade was called, in Gaelic, "Garrai Eoin," better known as "Garry Owen." But, of course, the men of the Irish Brigade sang other popular Irish songs, including "The Colleen Bawn," "The Felons of Our Land," and "O'Connor's Bride."

As mentioned, Colonel Kelly was a worthy placement for Meagher, one of Ireland's foremost Catholic nationalists from Waterford in southeast Ireland who possessed an excellent Jesuit education. As mentioned, he had been exiled for his revolutionary leadership activities during the 1848 Irish uprising and for fanning the flames of Irish nationalism. For such reasons, Meagher had proved to be the perfect first leader for the mostly Catholic Irish soldiers of the most distinctively ethnic unit of the Army of the Potomac. Relying on the bayonet in a headlong assault and with green battle flags waving proudly above the charging formations, the Irish Brigade lost more than one thousand men in overrunning the Sunken Road at Antietam (the second phase of the September 17, 1862 battle in western Maryland) and then in attacking the formidable high ground of Marye's Heights at Fredericksburg less than three months later. The Irish Brigade lost more than four thousand men before the war's end, while fighting and dying not only for the Union but also for Ireland.[175]

A TRAGIC PARADOX

In a central paradox and tragedy of the Irish experience during the war years, Meagher's Irish Brigade, consisting of die-hard soldiers mostly from Boston, Philadelphia and New York City, was decimated severely at Fredericksburg in large part by their fellow countrymen of the Twenty-Fourth Georgia Infantry. The equally tough and highly motivated Georgia Irish defended the Sunken Road at the foot of Marye's Heights, bearing the brunt of the Second Corps' assaults over the open fields lying before the high ground. Here, behind a stone wall at the base of Marye's Heights, Irish Rebels from Gwinnett, Towns, Elbert, Hall, Banks and White Counties, Georgia, stood firm while cutting the Irish Brigade's attack to pieces.

These Peach State veterans were under the steady command of a native of County Antrim in north Ireland, Colonel Robert Emmet McMillan. His name reflected the revolutionary legacy of Irish patriot Robert Emmet.

A former state legislator who had organized the McMillan Guards from Habersham County, Georgia, McMillan relied on the solid leadership of his son Robert Emmet McMillan Jr., who served as the regimental major. By any measure, this was a formidable father-son Scotch-Irish leadership team that successfully met the Irish Brigade's assault on that bloody December day. Still another son of Scotch-Irish roots, Captain Garnett McMillian, commanded a seasoned company of the Twenty-Fourth Georgia. Leading the Georgia Brigade after its esteemed commander, Thomas Read Rootes Cobb, had been mortally wounded in the battle's beginning at Fredericksburg, McMillian allowed the Irishmen in blue to charge close to the Sunken Road. Then, he ordered his Georgia men to open fire after imploring them to aim low to ensure horrendous casualties among the Irish Brigade attackers surging across the brown, open fields of winter.

The row of guns of the Washington Artillery from New Orleans, which included a good many Louisiana Irish cannoneers, roared from atop the open hill behind them. Meanwhile, the veterans of the Twenty-Fourth Georgia, with the experienced soldiers of the Eighteenth Georgia on their right and another Peach State command, the Phillips Legion infantrymen (including a fair number of Irish officers and enlisted men), on its left, blasted away with lethal loads of "buck and ball" from smoothbore muskets. Feeling no sympathy for their fellow countrymen of the Irish Brigade and only wanting to stop them from reaching Marye's Heights, these Emerald Isle defenders especially took aim at the brave color-bearers who carried their flapping green banners into the din.

Even while shooting down their Green Isle countrymen with a heartless effectiveness that left a good many widows and orphans across the North, the Irish from Georgia felt a sense of admiration for their enemy amid the surreal horror of slaughter. They cheered the courage and discipline of the Irish Brigade's veterans in the sweeping attack, shouting words of praise for Irish bravery and waving slouch hats in tribute to Irish heroism.[176]

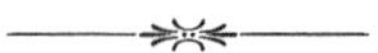

IN STILL ANOTHER BITTER and sad irony of the Civil War, Lieutenant John Edward Dooley Jr. described how the Irish Brigade "was almost totally annihilated at Fredericksburg [and] the field on which they fell was at the foot of Marye's hill, and was the property of Col. Marye, an officer of our brigade. In 1848 or '49 when [the Great] famine was inflicting such distress in Ireland, the whole crop of Corn raised upon this identical field had been sent in contribution for the relief of that starving and oppressed people."[177]

Indeed, sickened by the slaughter of so many Irish soldiers, including famine Irish, General Thomas Francis Meagher described the fate of his men in a sad letter that told of the extent of the tragedy. The Irish Brigade "has ceased to be a Brigade, and hardly exhibits the numerical strength which qualifies it for a higher designation than that of a Colonel's command."[178]

As mentioned, brave Sergeant Richard Rowland Kirkland, a young Scotch-Irish soldier of Kershaw's South Carolina Brigade, went over the body-strewn field and assisted the wounded Federals, including Irish Brigade soldiers. From his load of canteens, he gave sips of water to many of the seemingly countless fallen Yankees, whose burning thirst had tortured them hour after hour until the arrival of the "Angel of Marye's Heights" in a gray uniform.[179]

IRISH TIGERS FROM LOUISIANA

A good many Louisiana Irish marched into Pennsylvania in the hopes of reversing the war's fortunes before time ran out for the Confederacy. General Meagher and his Irish Brigade soldiers, mostly northeastern men, were not aware that the largest number of equally determined Irish counterparts now serving in the Army of Northern Virginia hailed from the Crescent City. New Orleans contained the largest number of pre-famine Irish, who had migrated to the South from across Ireland. The South's largest city—known as the Crescent City because of its shape along the Mississippi River—New Orleans was four times larger than the Confederacy's capital of Richmond. This antebellum-period demographic translated into the fact that thousands of Irish fighting men served in Lee's Louisiana Regiments, and a large number of them invaded Pennsylvania soil in numerous Pelican State regiments.

By 1860, the Irish population of New Orleans stood at around twenty-five thousand, which was almost 17 percent of the city's total white population. By this time, many Emerald Islanders had gained middle-class status in contrast to the recent arrivals from Ireland. As in the case of New York City, Boston and Philadelphia (whose residents filled the Irish Brigade's ranks), a flood of Irish immigrants had poured into New Orleans because of the potato famine of the mid-1840s.

To a greater extent than for Irishmen living in cities in the northeast, a third of the Irish in New Orleans had worked in skilled and semiskilled occupations, paving the way for their rise to middle-class status. These demographic realities helped to guarantee that the largest number of Irish in the Army of Northern Virginia hailed from New Orleans. The South's most cosmopolitan urban center included the lower-class shantytown known as the "Irish Channel" because of its distinctive ethnic composition and character.

Indeed, no state or city provided more Irish soldiers to Lee's Army and the Confederacy than did the Pelican State and the Crescent City. Therefore, the Irish of New Orleans celebrated St. Patrick's Day with a unique mixture of typical Celtic-Gaelic enthusiasm and reverence, while promoting Southern and Irish nationalism.[180]

Among the most elite fighting men of the Confederacy, the Louisiana Tigers—a collective name for a number of Louisiana Confederate units (originally only a single volunteer company of the name from New Orleans)—had garnered a widespread reputation. The First and Second Louisiana Brigades served as a core unit of the Louisiana Tigers, who early on gained a reputation for ferocity on and off the battlefield. These Louisiana Irish were also known as expert "Yankee-slayers" without peers, and for ample good reason. As could be expected, a large percentage of these Yankee-slayers—who also wanted "to chop the Yankees into sausage-meat"—were Irish soldiers.[181]

The hard-fighting Sixth Louisiana Infantry, General Harry Thompson Hays's First Louisiana Brigade, consisted almost exclusively of Irish Catholics, mostly common laborers from New Orleans. This command was so thoroughly Celtic-Gaelic that it was known as "the South's Irish Brigade" because so many of its members hailed from the rough Irish neighborhoods of New Orleans. General Hays was of Scotch-Irish Protestant descent, but he was in fact a die-hard Catholic who graduated from Baltimore's St. Mary's College. At Gettysburg, he led a large percentage of Irish Catholics from New Orleans with distinction during some of the hardest fighting of the war. Seven of the regiment's ten companies hailed from New Orleans. These diehard fighting men served in Irish companies of the Sixth Louisiana, such as the Calhoun Guards (Company B) and the Irish Brigade (Companies I and F). The latter two companies drew upon the Irish Brigade of exiles, known as the "Wild Geese," who had fought with distinction for France and Spain on Europe's battlefields to win glory and fame.

This well-known "Irish regiment" won distinction during the nightmarish showdown at Gettysburg despite losing nearly 50 percent at Antietam on the war's bloodiest single day less than ten months before. Half of the regiment was composed of men born in Ireland, and the other half were Irish Americans or the sons of Irish immigrants. These Louisiana Irish were a comparable counterpart to, and a mirror image of, the New York and Massachusetts regiments of Colonel Kelly's Irish Brigade at Gettysburg. These Emerald Islanders from Louisiana fought in the tactical offensive or in vital rearguard situations as enthusiastically as they celebrated St. Patrick's Day, earning a lofty reputation for combat prowess.[182]

The Irish "Tigers" were heavily represented in other Louisiana regiments of Hays's Brigade. Many of these confident Emerald Islanders had marched to war with hatbands proclaiming, "Tiger in Search of Abe" Lincoln, and the lust to kill the president was high. The Louisiana Tigers earned an unparalleled reputation for a determination to "follow their officers to the death" regardless of the odds or battlefield situation. The Irish Volunteers (Company F) and the Sarsfield Rangers (Company C) were part of the Seventh Louisiana Infantry (more than one-third of which was Ireland-born), while the Emerald Guards (Company E) served with the Ninth Louisiana Infantry. The Irishmen of the Emmet Guards—named after young Robert Emmet--served as members of Company D, First Louisiana Infantry, which also included the Montgomery Guards (Company E). In addition, other companies in these fine Pelican State regiments, whose members wore distinctive Pelican buttons, were entirely Irish and compiled distinguished combat records.[183]

One secret that explained the superior combat prowess of the Louisiana Rebels, who had early on earned the sobriquet "Lee's Tigers," was the guiding hand of inspirational men of God. Chaplain James B. Sheeran was one of the spiritual leaders who reinforced the fighting spirit of the Louisiana Irish and helped to create a moral soldiery, despite their reputations as hell-raisers. Serving as the Fourteenth Louisiana chaplain, this former priest from New Orleans instilled faith in Lee's Louisianans, both Protestant and Catholic, during the most crucial years of the war. Sheeran, born at Temple Mehill, County Longford, was a true fighting chaplain and holy warrior. He served on the front lines, ignoring danger to faithfully administer to his Southern boys. With all his heart and soul, and for reasons that he always found to have been moral, he hated "Lincoln's bandits," "hirelings" and the "unfortunate subjects of King Abe," in his own words that revealed his contempt.

From the beginning, Father Sheeran was determined to create holy warriors who would reap victory for God and country in a decisive showdown like Gettysburg. He had long basked in the "opportunity of preparing all Catholic soldiers of our Brig. [Hays] to meet their God as well as to meet their foe."[184] He was proud of this hard-fighting moral soldiery from the Emerald Isle because they fought with their hearts for righteous reasons, including in the name of God. He described his sheer joy when often hearing "the sturdy voices of many of our Catholic soldiers united in reciting the rosary of our dear Lady," the Virgin Mary.[185]

As this faithful man of God from Ireland saw firsthand on the front lines while wearing a Confederate uniform as Yankee bullets whizzed around him, "I had learned by personal observation that no men fight more bravely than Catholics who approach the sacraments before battle" against the hated Yankees.[186] The Ireland-born chaplain marveled at how some Celtic-Gaelic soldiers retained every bit of their Irishness and the old ways of the Emerald Isle, causing him to admit how "you would think he left there [Ireland] yesterday."[187]

Like his equally determined followers, Sheeran was convinced that "the North had no right to force the South to remain in the Union as England had no right to force Ireland into a union with her."[188] It was well that Father Sheeran, who never stopped praying for Confederate victory, had prepared his Louisiana Rebels, both Catholic and Protestant, for hard fighting and, eventually, for meeting their Maker, because they became key players in the battle of Gettysburg and paid a high price in consequence.

THE ACCIDENTAL BATTLE ERUPTS AT GETTYSBURG ON JULY 1

Having no idea of the size of the opponent before him or his exact location by the end of June 1863, in part because he lacked sufficient cavalry to perform intelligence-gathering missions, Lee was caught by surprise by the sudden appearance of advance elements of the Army of the Potomac that had not only moved faster than anticipated but also with more aggressiveness than expected. The experienced troopers of the well-armed Union cavalry division under Brigadier General John Buford had gained good defensive positions just west and northwest of Gettysburg by the hot Wednesday morning of July 1. Here, around 7:30 a.m., they clashed with advance elements of the troops of Major General Henry Heth's Division, of Lieutenant General Ambrose Powell Hill's Third Corps, which advanced from the west before the army.

Blasting away with fast-firing, breech-loading carbines in the blazing heat that felt like South Carolina instead of Pennsylvania, Buford's troopers bought precious time while Major General George Gordon Meade's troops continued to march north toward Gettysburg from western Maryland. Swiftly marching bluecoat infantrymen of the I Corps, including the crack Iron Brigade, which contained excellent units like the Twenty-Fourth Michigan Volunteer Infantry, bolstered the dismounted cavalrymen in timely fashion. The I Corps troops strengthened the desperate defensive stands of the fast-firing horsemen, who saw their finest day in their brilliant delaying tactics, buying precious time for more units of the Army of the Potomac to arrive on the battlefield.

Under the command of the capable Major General John F. Reynolds, the senior commander on the field before he was killed on the morning of July 1, the I Corps' troops had reached the field in the nick of time. During the combat that continued to intensify northwest of Gettysburg, an Irish private of the Iron Brigade named Patrick Maloney, Second Wisconsin Volunteer Infantry, captured the first general of the Army of Northern Virginia taken in battle, diminutive, but feisty, Brigadier General James J. Archer. Ironically, General Lee, who belatedly reached the battlefield after riding east down the Chambersburg Road that entered Gettysburg from the northwest, suddenly found himself involved in an escalating battle that he neither planned nor desired at this time, because his army was not concentrated. All the while, the battle continued to wage fiercely and then spiral out of control with a life of its own, as if destiny had already charted its course.

But General Lee's luck finally began to change when fast-moving developments suddenly turned in his favor. The arrival of the first troops of the Second Corps fully committed Lee to the battle because of the new advantageous tactical opportunities presented to him, despite the absence of Lieutenant General James Longstreet's First Corps, which was still marching on the road to Gettysburg from the west, bringing up the army's rear. Hit simultaneously by howling Rebel attackers from the west and the newly arrived Second Corps, which had been redirected by Lee to march south and then launch assaults from the north, the First and Eleventh Corps were hurled rearward and toward Gettysburg.

However, after fleeing through the streets of a chaotic Gettysburg, the first hard-hit survivors of Meade's foremost units gamely took good defensive positions on Cemetery Hill (the northern end of Cemetery Ridge) and on the densely wooded Culp's Hill to the east. These twin elevations eventually anchored Meade's northern, or right, flank after the defensive line was extended south down Cemetery Ridge by the arrival of additional Union command from western Maryland.

Here, Gettysburg's cemetery was perched on the high ground of the appropriately named Cemetery Hill. The Second Corps' commander, Lieutenant General Richard "Dick" Stoddert Ewell, a Mexican-American War veteran who had a leg recently amputated, had replaced Stonewall Jackson, who had been cut down by friendly fire at Chancellorsville and was truly irreplaceable. No longer the same man as before the amputation and a recent marriage, Ewell was not up to the challenge of taking the high ground at the northern end of Cemetery Ridge and Culp's Hill.

For a variety of reasons that are still debated today, General Ewell failed to mount the offensive effort necessary to overrun the two key high-ground positions (Culp's Hill and Cemetery Hill) late on July 1. Ewell's failure to gain the tactical opportunity allowed Meade's initial elements to gain invaluable time and solidify its excellent defensive positions on the high ground. Lee's directives for Ewell to take the strategic high ground at the northern end of Cemetery Ridge were left unfulfilled. But to be fair to the much-criticized General Ewell, Lee's directives were not as forceful as they should have been under the circumstances, and the Federal position at East Cemetery Hill, bolstered by artillery, was strong at this time.

This missed opportunity had been created by the amazing extent of the Rebels' success on July 1, and it was a golden one that would not come again on the battle-line's northern end. General Hays's Louisiana Tigers, including a large number of seasoned Irish fighting men, played key roles in the first day's success. With fixed bayonets sparkling in the July sunshine and with well-placed shots from trusty muskets, Emerald Islanders from Louisiana were among the attackers who had hurled back the Yankees from the north and overran the town. The hard-hit survivors of the First and Eleventh Corps had fled down Gettysburg's narrow streets lined with rows of brick and wooden houses with the Irish of Louisiana in close pursuit. Losses were relatively light for the Irish Rebels during their sparkling success. Irish Confederate sharpshooters hidden in houses had found plenty of blue-uniformed targets, inflicting higher losses among the fleeing Federals, who finally gained safety on the northern end of Cemetery Ridge. But the Louisiana attackers suffered less damage (at least six to one, in General Hays's estimation) than the Yankees during the successful offensive effort.

Nothing had been able to slow the sweeping attack of Hays's Louisiana Brigade, verifying its widespread renown as the hard-fighting "Louisiana Tigers" and "Lee's Tigers." During the close-range combat that initially raged in the confined urban environment of the town on July 1, between four thousand and five thousand Yankees were captured, and approximately five thousand Federals became casualties. The elated victors hurriedly stripped parts of uniforms, equipment and shoes from the bodies of the Union dead who lay inside the town's environs. Once again, the U.S. government became the best supplier for Lee's men, who now wore parts of blue uniforms and equipment that advertised the extent of their success on the first day.

Born in Ireland, Captain Michael O'Connor, age thirty-seven and leading his veteran company of the Sixth Louisiana, wrote with pride, "We drove them back and captured the town" by 5:00 p.m. But as mentioned, the opportunity to complete the victory was not fully exploited. Federal infantrymen, with ample artillery to support them, rallied and were positioned on the commanding heights of Cemetery Hill. Confederate momentum had been expended and the opportunities lost by the arrival of darkness on July 1. Seasoned leadership on the north, especially General Ewell, had failed to launch the much-needed effort to capture the all-important high ground of Cemetery Hill before it shortly became impregnable.[189]

Like other veteran leaders of the Second Corps (Stonewall Jackson's old command) and seasoned Irishmen—from lowly privates to officers—in the ranks, General Hays realized that the tactical opportunity on the north should be exploited in full. He therefore implored Ewell to unleash his soldiers one last time in an attempt to carry the strategic high ground on the north. Despite knowing that the large numbers of Sons of Erin of his Second Corps would never cease fighting until the final victory was won, General Ewell failed to unleash one final offensive effort at the end of July 1. Instead of launching the tactical offensive to carry the high ground and push the Federals off their perch, he had only marveled at the fighting spirit of Hays's men. He asked if the Irish and their comrades of the Louisiana regiments "never get a bellyful of fighting."[190]

But in truth, and as mentioned, Ewell was not entirely to blame for the missed opportunity for striking the Army of the Potomac's defensive line, which had belatedly taken shape on the strategic high ground at the northern end of Cemetery Ridge. Ewell's men, stained with sweat and covered in dust, were exhausted after battling and chasing the Yankees on one of the hottest days of the year. As if suddenly no longer the commander who had won so many sparkling successes in Virginia, and physically worn down by the day's exertions and a lingering illness, General Lee himself displayed a lack of decisiveness that also ensured a missed opportunity. Delegating too much authority to the new commander of the Second Corps, he had allowed Ewell, who was not experienced in leading an entire corps in battle, to do what he thought best under the circumstances.

All in all, this was a fatal delegation and a lack of communication destined to come back to haunt Lee and his army for the next two days. In the end, General Ewell's greatest mistake was in not taking the steps necessary for capturing Culp's Hill, where the greatest tactical opportunity existed (Cemetery Hill was too formidable). Unfortunately for Lee and his army, both high-ground positions were about to become stronger with the arrival of additional Federal reinforcements, until they became virtually impregnable. Consequently, the golden opportunities that had been presented on July 1 would never be exploited by these battle-hardened veterans, setting the stage for Lee's greater offensive efforts in the next two days to hurl the Yankees off their perches anchored on Cemetery Ridge.[191]

LEE AGAIN TAKES THE OFFENSIVE ON THURSDAY, JULY 2

To exploit the gains made on July 1, Lee was determined to maintain the tactical offensive in order to deliver a decisive blow to the battered Army of the Potomac. He had decided to turn the Army of the Potomac's left with the veterans of his best corps, General "Old Pete" Longstreet's First Corps, which was not available unlike on the first day. However, Longstreet did not agree with his superior's final decision about the wisdom of unleashing the offensive on July 2. The defensive-minded Longstreet, a stubborn contrarian at Gettysburg, thought differently when Lee pointed to Cemetery Hill during their open air conference on parallel Seminary Ridge and emphasized in no uncertain terms, "If the enemy is there tomorrow, we must attack him."[192]

Striking Meade's vulnerable left flank called for, first, a wide flank march of Longstreet's First Corps to the south, which had been ordered by Lee to begin early on July 2. However, Longstreet encountered a number of unexpected complications and problems. Even more, he had earlier made the mistake of deciding to await the arrival of his rearmost Alabama brigade before embarking on the lengthy march south that began belatedly not long

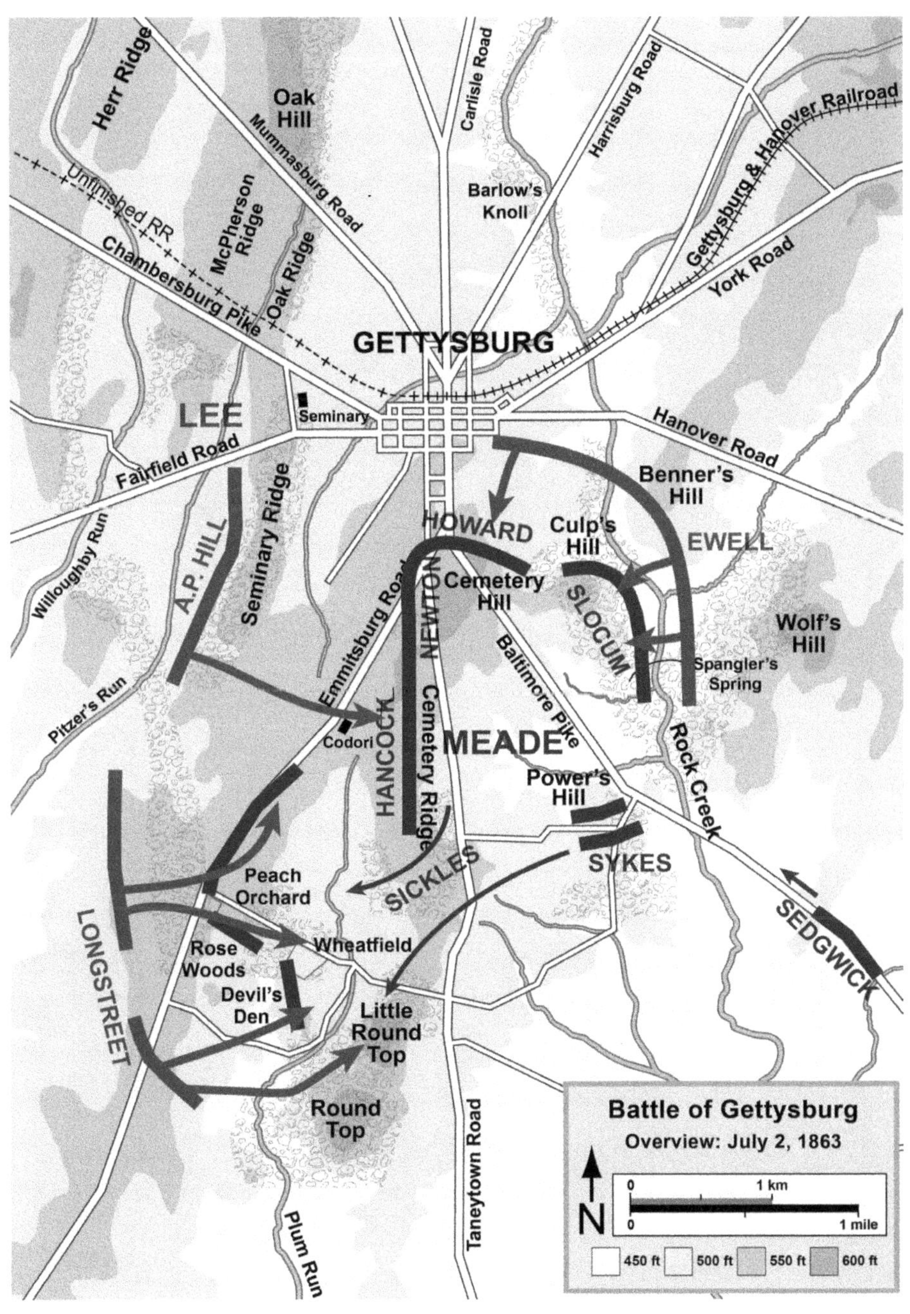
Battle of Gettysburg
Overview: July 2, 1863
GETTYSBURG
Herr Ridge
Oak Hill
Mummasburg Road
Carlisle Road
Harrisburg Road
Gettysburg & Hanover Railroad
Barlow's Knoll
Unfinished RR
McPherson Ridge
Oak Ridge
Chambersburg Pike
York Road
LEE
Seminary
Fairfield Road
Hanover Road
Benner's Hill
Seminary Ridge
A.P. HILL
Willoughby Run
HOWARD
Culp's Hill
EWELL
Cemetery Hill
NEWTON
SLOCUM
Wolf's Hill
Emmitsburg Road
Baltimore Pike
Spangler's Spring
Pitzer's Run
Codori
HANCOCK
Cemetery Ridge
MEADE
Rock Creek
Power's Hill
SYKES
SICKLES
Peach Orchard
SEDGWICK
LONGSTREET
Rose Woods
Wheatfield
Devil's Den
Little Round Top
Round Top
Taneytown Road
Plum Run
N
0
1 km
1 mile
450 ft
500 ft
550 ft
600 ft

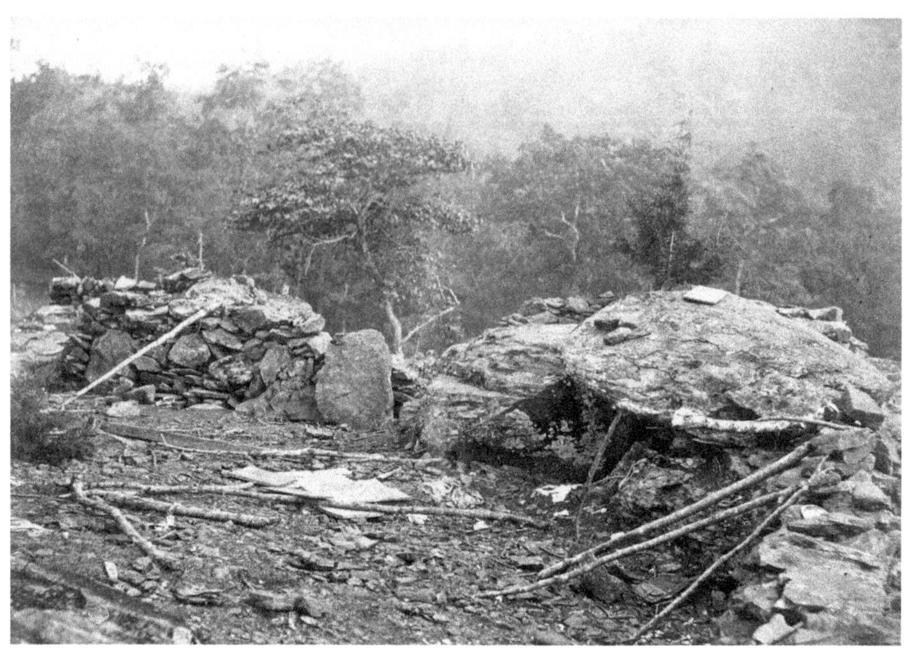

Federal breastworks located on the southern crest of the strategic high ground at the southern end of the battle-line on Little Round Top. *Courtesy of the Library of Congress.*

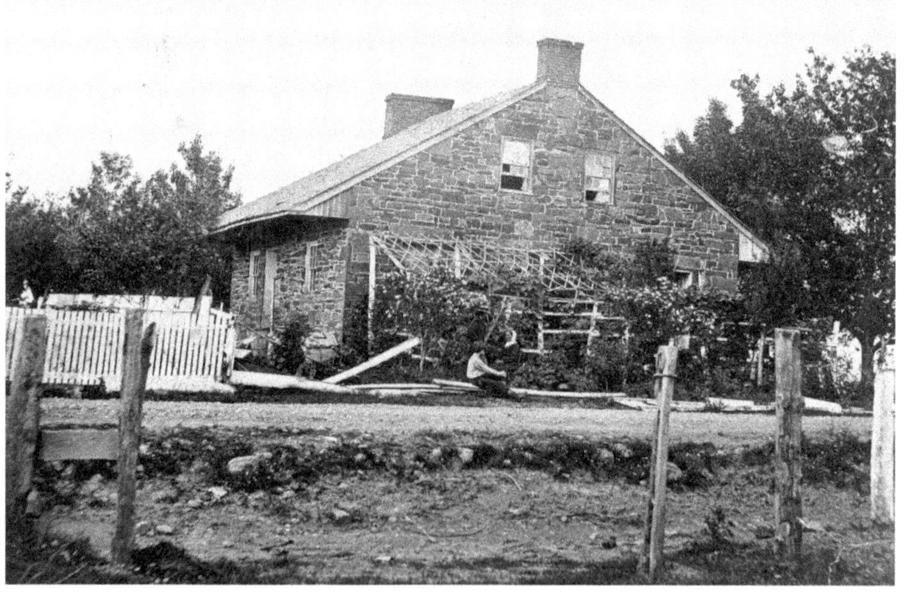

General Lee's headquarters at the Widow Mary Thompson House, located on Seminary Ridge along the Chambersburg Pike. *Courtesy of the Library of Congress.*

after noon with the two divisions of his First Corps. Longstreet's objective was to gain an advanced and the most tactically favorable position along the Emmitsburg Road in order to advance his nearly fifteen thousand troops northeast (toward Gettysburg) and parallel to the dusty road, then hit Meade's left flank on the south and well below Cemetery Hill. Relying on his well-honed tactical skills for which he was famous, Lee had correctly reasoned that Meade's left hung in midair, which made it ripe for inflicting a decisive blow.

Because of the presence of a mere handful of Union signalmen atop Little Round Top, the first elevation after Cemetery Ridge gradually descended south to a low point just north of the rocky hill, Longstreet's troops were exposed if they marched across an open rise just east of the Black Horse Tavern and northwest of Little Round Top. Therefore, Longstreet was forced to take the time-consuming step of backtracking his troops to ensure the concealment of a resumed march south, costing precious time exactly when time was of the essence. Therefore, Longstreet's First Corps was not in the anticipated advanced position to launch its flank assault until late in the afternoon. This was a costly delay, because by midmorning on July 2 (the most crucial day of the three-day battle of Gettysburg), all of the Army of the Potomac's corps had arrived on the field, except the Sixth Corps, and hurriedly took defensive positions.

To Turn the Union Army's Left Flank

On the far south of Longstreet's battle line, Major General John Bell Hood's Division, consisting of four veteran brigades, was ordered to begin the attack in echelon, as planned by Lee. With his usual optimism, the ever-aggressive commander in chief envisioned the turning of Meade's left flank with a sweeping attack as at Chancellorsville, when Stonewall Jackson had rolled up the right flank of the Army of the Potomac to win one of Lee's greatest victories. At this time, the aggressive Hood was one of the youngest and most promising stars of the Army of Northern Virginia. In fact, he might well have been Lee's finest division commander by this time.

Ironically, Hood's father, John W. Hood, had studied medicine at the Philadelphia Medical Institute in the all-important city that Lee would almost certainly capture if the Army of the Potomac could be destroyed at Gettysburg. John W. Hood had studied medicine under his mentor, Dr. John

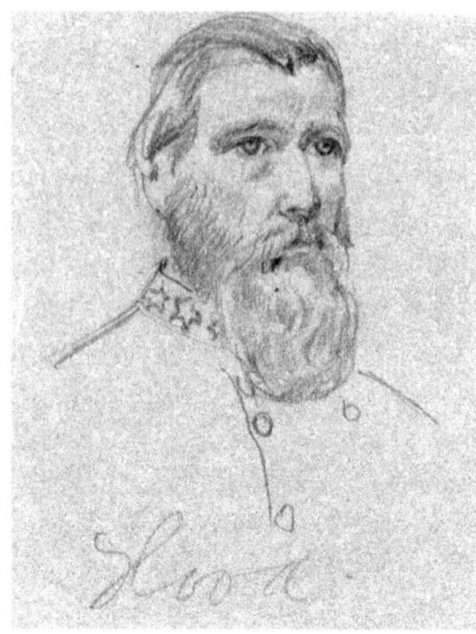

General John Bell Hood, perhaps the finest young division commander of the Army of Northern Virginia by the time of the Gettysburg Campaign. *Courtesy of the Library of Congress.*

Bell, and gained a lifelong admiration for the Ireland-born Dr. Bell. In fact, he bestowed his son with the Irish doctor's last name.[193]

As mentioned, Longstreet was reluctant to stake everything on still another offensive effort against the high ground defended by veteran Federal infantrymen, because he feared a tactical repeat of the suicidal assaults on Malvern Hill. He therefore most of all desired to outmaneuver the Union left flank by marching farther south, around the two Round Tops, instead of striking the high ground head-on. He understood how Lee's past victories, based on bold offensive tactics, had been too costly for an army already handicapped by limited manpower. Above all else, Longstreet fully realized the terrible attrition that was slowly destroying the Army of Northern Virginia: "even victories [including most recently at Chancellorsville, where the veteran officer corps had been decimated] such as these were consuming us, and would eventually destroy us."[194]

Of course, this no-win situation for the Confederacy was also the reason that Lee, especially with his fighting blood up after having gained "a taste of victory" on the previous day, hoped to deliver a knockout punch to end the Army of the Potomac's existence as quickly as possible, before this increasingly bloody war of attrition destroyed his own army because of the South's limited manpower. Quite simply, on July 2, Lee was going for broke by unleashing his finest corps to strike the Union left flank with a powerful blow and turn it, because this was a tactical opportunity that might never come again for the Army of Northern Virginia, or so he believed.[195]

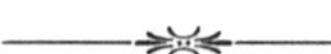

BUT LEE'S AMBITIOUS OFFENSIVE plan was upset more by accident than by his enemy's design. As fate would have it, Major General Daniel E. Sickles had advanced west with his entire Third Corps without orders

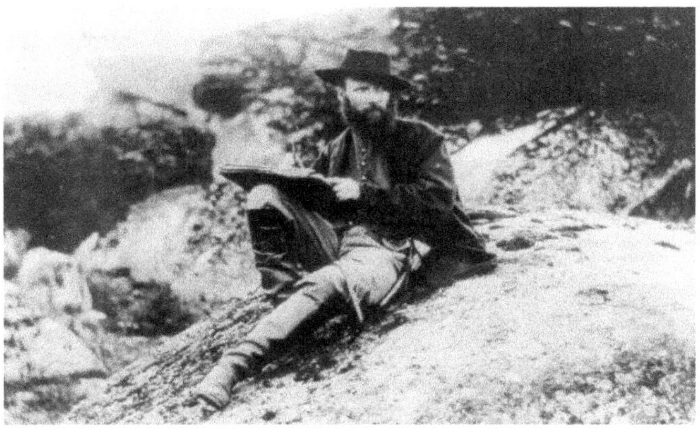

Alfred Waud produced some of the finest sketches of Civil War scenes, including battles. Waud, the finest artist for *Harper's Weekly*, was photographed making a sketch while sitting atop a boulder at the Devil's Den. *Courtesy of the Library of Congress.*

from Meade's main defensive line on Cemetery Ridge. He had then taken a defensive position on the high ground of the Peach Orchard and the Emmitsburg Road Ridge that lay between Seminary and Cemetery Ridges because it was more elevated than his assigned position, which dipped to a low point just north of Little Round Top. Therefore, more than ten thousand Union troops and seemingly countless artillery pieces of the formidable Third Corps now blocked the planned advance of Longstreet's lead division, under Major General Lafayette McLaws, northeast up and parallel to the Emmitsburg Road.

Of Scotch-Irish descent and possessing a feisty fighting spirit, McLaws had been earlier told by Longstreet that nothing would block his advance northeast to strike and turn the Union left flank. Therefore, McLaws had been led to believe that he would be presented with an easy avenue over the open fields to achieve victory. Instead, thanks to General Sickles's unauthorized move forward, or west, to the next high ground (Emittsburg Road Ridge), Longstreet was now presented with an even better tactical opportunity to turn Meade's left flank, because Sickles's advanced position was vulnerable in having been relocated so far before Meade's line and had been spread too thin to cover too much ground.

General Meade's defensive line on Cemetery Ridge was now in danger, because the Third Corps was spread along such a wide front and vulnerable when positioned so far ahead of the rest of the army. Therefore, to counter the blocking position of the Third Corps, including good defensive positions aligned on the high ground of the Peach Orchard and the Emmitsburg Road Ridge, the four brigades of Hood's Division were ordered to hurriedly march south in search of a better tactical opportunity to turn Meade's left flank farther south beyond Lee's existing right.[196]

A Talented Irish Battery Commander, James Reilly

Hood's foremost artilleryman of his crack division of Longstreet's First Corps was Ireland-born Captain James Reilly. This talented Irishman always seemed to rise to the challenge, especially in crisis situations. He commanded the six guns of the Rowan Artillery, which was part of the divisional artillery battalion, from North Carolina. The capable Reilly had long led the Rowan Artillery with consummate skill based on a good many years of solid experience. He hailed from the market town of Ballydonaugh, near Athlone, County Westmeath, which was located in the fertile central plains of Ireland. Reilly hailed from this ancient land where Gaelic was still spoken with a musical-like grace and the old folkways were cherished by the common people like the holy shroud of St. Patrick.

Reilly had run away from home at age sixteen to join the British army because of his burning desire to see adventure and wear a scarlet uniform. But the young man who followed his dreams was retrieved by members of his distraught family, ending his wanderlust—but only briefly. If nothing else, Reilly was a very determined young man with a strong will.

With his wanderlust getting the better of him once again, the hard-headed "Jimmy" Reilly attempted to enlist at age eighteen. This time, he succeeded in joining the British army, making his dream come true by stubborn persistence. However, Reilly was still not satisfied. He later emigrated to America to start anew, but his desire for embarking upon a military career never left him. At the first opportunity, with the Mexican-American War drawing near and tiring of his occupation as a common laborer (the typical fate of so many Irish immigrants in America), Reilly joined the U.S. Army in New York in August 1845. War was on the horizon, primarily over the annexation of Texas, which Mexico refused to consider lost after Anglo-Celtic settlers had declared independence on March 2, 1836, when the Alamo garrison had been besieged and doomed to annihilation in only four days. The two neighboring republics possessed vastly different cultures, races and heritage that served as a central foundation for open warfare. Young men, especially Irish immigrants hoping to escape their mundane lives in lowly places, began to enlist and fight for their country in 1846. Reilly served with distinction in General Winfield Scott's Army on the march of around 250 miles from the gulf coast at Vera Cruz to Mexico City, which was located in the Central Valley of Mexico.

During the Civil War years, and despite being a devout Catholic who revered St. Patrick, Reilly was an independent-minded and unorthodox Emerald Islander, even in a revolutionary Southern army where unorthodoxy was prevalent. As could be expected, however, the Irishman's penchant for unconventionality occasionally found him in trouble with his superiors, especially West Pointers. He was fond of swearing with vigor in his thick Irish brogue, which rose in eloquence and to impressive heights on the battlefield, especially in crisis situations. During the heat of combat, he also often used the phrase "in the name of St. Patrick an' all the ither hoully saints." Nevertheless, and most important, Reilly was widely respected by his superiors and the North Carolina artillerymen who served under him. He was a natural leader and competent officer who proved invaluable in the dramatic showdown on July 2, 1863.[197]

Reilly's Mexican-American War experience proved invaluable in the fight for possession of the strategic high ground. Ironically, during the push of Scott's Army to Mexico City and deeper into the heart of Mexico, and while winning a series of 1847 battles along the way, Reilly had served in the crack U.S. artillery unit commanded by Lieutenant Henry Jackson Hunt, a gifted West Pointer (class of 1839). As fate would have it, the Michigan-born Hunt was now Meade's highly capable chief of artillery and a brigadier general of outstanding ability. Hunt had skillfully deployed and aligned his batteries across the high ground in transforming Cemetery Ridge into an extremely strong position.[198]

Joining the exodus of Southerners who had worn the blue before the war, the Irishman had resigned from the U.S. Army on the eve of North Carolina's belated secession. He joined North Carolina state service in his first revolution against centralized authority, which was something well known to his Irish ancestors. Reilly then took command of the Rowan Artillery, which contained a fair number of North Carolina Irish and Scotch-Irish gunners, including officers.[199]

The elite fighting men of the Texas Brigade, Hood's Division, Longstreet's First Corps, had long been ably supported by Reilly's North Carolina gunners. One Texas soldier, John W. Stevens, Company K, Fifth Texas, recalled, "as we were forming Gens. Longstreet, Hood and Pickett were all sitting on their horses just in front of us [the Texas Brigade, Hood's Division and] Riley's [sic] battery had just unlimbered and was firing very rapidly upon the enemy. These generals were directing the fire of Riley's [sic] guns, all of which lead our men to the conclusion that we are very near to the infantry's line" of blue.[200]

In capably supporting the Lone Star State soldiers with accurate long-range fire, the performance of the Irish captain was one secret of the outstanding battlefield success of Hood's Texas Brigade over an extended period. Its reputation for combat prowess was unsurpassed in the Army of Northern Virginia by 1863.

One Texas Brigade soldier who referred to the talented Irish artillery officer as "Old Tarantula" because of his age and hot temper, Valerius "Val" Cincinnatus C. Giles, Company B (Tom Green Rifles), Fourth Texas, paid a well-deserved compliment to the grisly Irishman, who swore as hard as he fought Yankees: "Attached to the Texas Brigade was a fine battery of six Napoleon guns, commanded by Captain Riley [sic]. Riley had been an artillery sergeant in the old [United States] Army....He was an Irishman, rough, gruff, grizzly, and brave. He loved his profession and knew his business."[201]

With half a dozen guns positioned on high ground on the far right, or south, near the crest of the Emmitsburg Ridge, which ran roughly parallel to Cemetery Ridge, Reilly's guns were aligned in a good position to provide excellent support for the upcoming attack of Hood's troops on Meade's left flank during the upcoming bid to capture Little Round Top.[202]

ATTACKING UP THE SLOPES OF LITTLE ROUND TOP

Now positioned on the far south below the rawboned soldiers of the Texas Brigade, the Alabama Brigade of five veteran regiments was under the command of Brigadier General Evander McIver Law. The young general's middle name reflected his Scotch-Irish antecedents, as did his sharp facial features, which were a trademark of the common people of Ulster Province, north Ireland. Like his division commander, General John Bell Hood, who Lee and Longstreet depended upon this afternoon to strike a stunning blow, Law's star was also on the rise in the Army of Northern Virginia. Law's five Alabama regiments were positioned on the southern end of Longstreet's sprawling battle line, which extended in a north–south orientation.

Commanding the Fifteenth Alabama, Law's Brigade, young Colonel William Calvin Oates, also of Scotch-Irish heritage and with a well-deserved reputation on the rise like Law's, targeted the high ground for capture. Big Round Top was located just south of Little Round Top, its twin that was now beyond the left flank of Meade's Army, and hence a waiting opportunity for Longstreet's Confederates. The boulder-strewn elevation known as Little Round Top, at the lower end of Cemetery Ridge, was about to be occupied and held by Colonel Strong Vincent's Third Brigade, First Division, Fifth Corps under Major General George Sykes. Vincent and his brigade had arrived in the nick of time to take defensive positions across the western and southern slope of Little Round Top. The fine brigade of veterans included the Twentieth Maine Volunteer Infantry, which anchored the brigade's left flank on the far south. After scaling the imposing heights of Big Round Top, heavily wooded and boulder-strewn, while battling and chasing the Union army's best sharpshooters (Colonel Hiram Berdan's Sharpshooters) up the slope, Oates and his breathless Alabama boys, covered in sweat, rested on the commanding crest. They had fought hard and executed an exhaustive climb up the wooded slope on one of the hottest days of the year and suffered in consequence.

Big Round Top's boulder-studded crest completely dominated Little Round Top, which was open on its western face and positioned on lower ground just to the north of its towering twin. Moving swiftly off the high ground after having rested atop Big Round Top's crest to catch their breath in the searing afternoon heat, Oates and his men of the Fifteenth Alabama then advanced north. With fixed bayonets, they moved downhill through the dense forest of hardwood trees that covered the northern slope of Big Round Top like a green shroud.

Here, on the southern slope of Little Round Top, the stage was now set for the dramatic showdown between Colonel Oates and Joshua Lawrence Chamberlain, who commanded the rough-hewn fighting men of the Twentieth Maine. At the last minute, these hardy Maine soldiers, including woodsmen and lumberjacks, had taken a good defensive position on Little Round Top's southern slope at the southern end, or left flank, of Vincent's brigade—the extreme left flank of the overly extended defensive line of the Army of the Potomac.

Oates's elite group of fighting men, Company K, known as the Eufaula City Guard and the Eufaula Zouaves, Fifteenth Alabama, consisted of veteran Irish soldiers. These Sons of Erin were mostly common laborers and recent immigrants from the Chattahoochee River country of Barbour, Dale and Henry Counties. Eager to meet the Yankees in the heady days of the war's beginning, they had enlisted at Eufaula, Barbour County, Alabama. Led by teenage Irish Captain William J. Bethune, who was a highly respected officer despite his youth and lack of a formal military education, Company

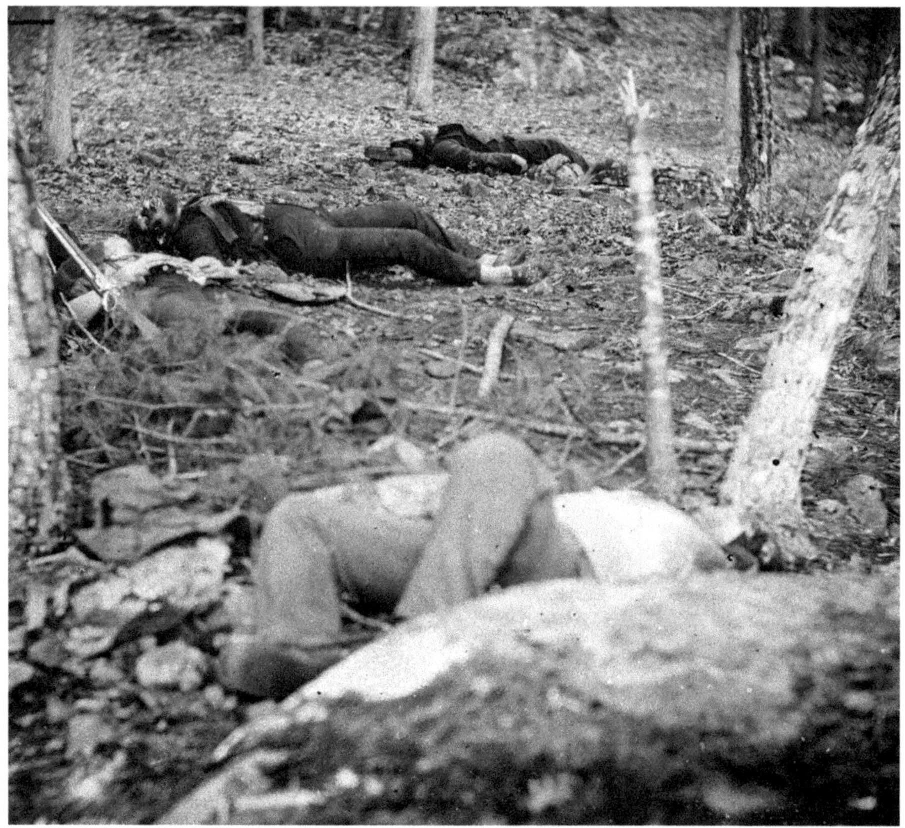

Killed on the afternoon of July 2, 1863, soldier dead at the northwestern base of Big Round Top. *Courtesy of the Library of Congress.*

K included mostly young Celtic-Gaelic soldiers, like the popular drummer boy Patrick F. "Pat" Brannon, age thirteen. Like so many other impoverished Irish who had been forced to emigrate during the Great Potato Famine, his Catholic family had fled Ireland. Patrick's older brother Private Thomas Brannon had been killed during Longstreet's sweeping attack that reaped a dramatic success for Lee and the Army of Northern Virginia at Second Manassas during the previous August.[203]

After surging down the timbered northern slope of Big Round Top, Oates and his men were surprised to suddenly receive a close-range volley that erupted from hidden positions strewn across the southern slope of Little Round Top. Here, the blue ranks of the Twentieth Maine, which included a number of Ireland-born soldiers, were aligned in excellent defensive position in the dense summer foliage of the shadowy oak and hickory woodlands on the high ground overlooking the wooded "saddle" between the two Round Tops. Despite losing a number of good soldiers in the first volley that had so suddenly exploded from the Twentieth Maine's ranks, the resourceful Fifteenth Alabama soldiers, ignoring their weariness and sore feet from a host of stern physical challenges, including a long march to reach the battlefield, since the day's beginning, gamely fought back against the well-positioned Maine men.

Demonstrating tactical flexibility and a determination to maintain momentum in a confusing battlefield situation, Oates continued to exploit the initiative, refusing to relinquish ground and forsake the struggle for possession of the rocky hilltop. With sword and revolver in hand, he led repeated assaults up the southern slope covered with clouds of sulfurous smoke that hid the thin line of Maine soldiers, who busily loaded and fired from behind the cover of rocks and logs. Some of Oates's best Irish soldiers were fatally cut down in the slugfest at close range, including Private A.P. "Sandy" McMillan, age twenty-two.

After vicious combat at the apex of his assault while going for broke, Oates was determined to turn the Twentieth Maine's left flank. However, too many Alabama men had been killed and wounded by this time to succeed in the crucial mission of turning the flank of Vincent's Brigade, which was relatively fresh and in better shape than the Alabama boys. The Irish leader of Company K, Captain Bethune, was shot in the face and went down on the timbered slope now littered with bodies in butternut and gray. But Bethune survived the nightmarish combat at the southern end of the two armies' battle line on the far south, where the struggle for possession of Little Round Top raged furiously for an extended period.

After the fall of the popular Captain Bethune, the Emerald Islanders of Company K, Fifteenth Alabama, continued to attack up the body-strewn slope with Celtic-Gaelic war cries in an all-out effort to hurl the stubborn Maine soldiers off the strategic high ground. The Sons of Erin of Company K were now led by their most inspirational leader, never-say-die Sergeant Patrick O'Connor, who was every inch a fighter. A former tinner who had evidently acquired this artisan skill in America rather than in Ireland, O'Connor was known for his dynamic leadership in key battlefield situations, and these well-honed talents were fully displayed at Gettysburg. O'Connor once again bravely led the Alabamians, yelling and firing in a desperate attempt to turn the left flank of Chamberlain's Twentieth Maine.

Literally the heart and soul of the tough Irish fighters of Company K, O'Connor, age twenty-three, led by example, encouraging his men in repeated charges up the southern slope of Little Round Top. He survived this afternoon but was fated to be killed in 1864. O'Connor inspired not only his Company K Irish in repeated charges up the southern slope of this rocky hill that had become a hell on earth for the Irish attackers but also the men of the other Fifteenth Alabama companies. Driven by a fanatical desire to push the last Maine soldier off the high ground at any cost in order to turn the left flank of Vincent's brigade, O'Connor's courage in the heat of combat was a sight to behold, and his Sons of Erin followed his bold example in charging up the timbered slope.

O'Connor was in the midst of the savage hand-to-hand combat with the Maine soldiers on the embattled southern slope of Little Round Top. When a Maine soldier attempted to wrestle the Fifteenth Alabama's colors from the flag-bearer, O'Connor thrust his bayonet into the head of the unfortunate man, who met his Maker at Little Round Top. But the Alabamians' efforts and heroics in attempting to hurl the Maine soldiers off the southern end of Little Round Top were simply not enough to win the day. Despite very nearly pushing the Maine regiment off its commanding perch by turning the regiment's left flank after some of the most savage combat at Gettysburg, the repeated assaults of the Fifteenth Alabama were repulsed at a fearful cost in young lives. Quite simply, some of the best and brightest of the crack Alabama regiment had been cut down by bayonet thrusts, musket-butts, and well-aimed shots.[204]

STILL ANOTHER FLANK ON LITTLE ROUND TOP TARGETED

As Oates and his Fifteenth Alabama soldiers had learned after their fanatical offensive efforts to carry the strategic high ground, Little Round Top proved to be the most formidable of all objectives for any of Lee's attackers on July 2. While Oates and his Fifteenth Alabama charged up the southern slope to grapple with the Twentieth Maine's tough defenders who could not be swept aside, Hood's Texas and Alabama solders of the Texas Brigade launched repeated assaults up the open, rocky western slope of Little Round Top just to the north. Here, Vincent's line of blue extended north along the open and rocky western slope. These seasoned soldiers in the northern sector (equally as important as the high ground of the southern sector) possessed the same vital mission as Colonel Oates and his Alabama boys: turning the left flank of the Army of the Potomac on the most important day of decision at Gettysburg: July 2.[205]

These hard-fighting Texans, the elite combat troops of Lee's army, included a good many Irish and Scotch-Irish soldiers who were exactly the kind of never-say-die fighting men needed if Little Round Top was to be captured this afternoon when so much was at stake: a lethal combination that was no accident or coincidence in terms of explaining why these were the best combat men of Lee's army and why they came so close to winning it all on the decisive second day at Gettysburg. The Texas Brigade was now led by Kentucky-born Brigadier General Jerome Bonaparte Robertson, a Texas revolutionary war veteran who had played a role in creating Lee's best fighting men. Symbolically, the Texas general's father was a Celtic immigrant from Scotland.

Boding well for Southern fortunes, the Texans matched the Alabamians in the intensity and ferocity of their attack. Carrying the colorful battle flag of the Fifth Texas, Irishman T.W. Fitzgerald led the way up the rocky western slope of Little Round Top while encouraging the Fifth Texas troops onward into the hail of lead. During repeated assaults up the body-strewn slope, the Fifth Texas attacked to the right of the Fourth Texas and to the left of the Fourth Alabama. Fitzgerald's heroism encouraged the determined attackers ever higher up the western slope and closer to the strategic crest. The regimental commander wrote how the brave Irishman "pressed gallantly forward, and was badly wounded far in front."[206]

Lieutenant Colonel Kindallis "King" Bryan, who had first marched off to war in command of the Liberty Invincibles (Company F, Fifth Texas), was one of the dynamic Fifth Texas leaders who led their troops up Little Round Top on the north. After regiment commander Colonel Robert M. Powell was cut down early in the assault, the capable Bryan filled the gap in splendid fashion, encouraging his Lone Star State troops up the bloody western slope of Little Round Top.

Bryan was an overachieving grandson of Irish Catholic immigrant Christopher Kindallis O'Bryan, who had migrated from County Clare, Ireland, to America in the 1760s. Like so many other Irish who fought for America as if they were battling the English for possession of the Emerald Isle, Christopher O'Bryan had then served in the Continental line under General George Washington. This lover of liberty had even named one of his sons George Washington O'Bryan after he had married the woman of his dreams in 1776. Serving along with his three brothers when he was only a teenager, Colonel Bryan had seen action in the Texas Revolution, being one of the first volunteers of the struggle to win Texas from the Republic of Mexico.

The promising lieutenant colonel, a large rancher and cattleman from the prairies of Liberty County, Texas, demonstrated inspired leadership on the afternoon of July 2, when it was most needed by the Army of Northern Virginia. Like his followers during the attacks on Little Round Top, "King" Bryan sought to revive the glory of the Battle of San Jacinto—the decisive April 21, 1836 battle that won Texas independence—by capturing Little Round Top's strategic crest at the head of his Fifth Texas attackers. He therefore continued to lead a good many soldiers of Irish descent—like Private Peter Mallory, who was destined to be killed in 1864—and other hardened veterans of the "Bloody Fifth" in the ranks surging up the boulder-strewn slope. Like so many other Lone Star State men on this day of destiny, Kindallis (a Gaelic word meaning "ruler of the valley") Bryan was shortly cut down by the heavy fire pouring down from the high ground of Little Round Top.[207]

But despite fanatical efforts, the formidable defensive position of Vincent's troops on Little Round Top continued to hold firm, despite the accurate fire of the booming guns of Ireland-born Captain Reilly. The North Carolina cannon of the Irishman had unleashed more than 850 rounds to support the Texans' all-out offensive effort to capture Little Round Top.[208]

Of Irish descent, Private Rufus King Felder, Fifth Texas, described the no-win situation in a bitter letter that revealed the tragedy of battling against a cruel fate and some incredibly tough Yankees: General "Meade…took position of a high mountain [and] made it impregnable [and therefore] [i]t seemed like madness in Lee to have attempted to carry the heights by storm [and the Texas Brigade] had the highest portion of the peak [of Little Round Top] to charge [and up] an almost perpendicular peak at the top of which the enemy had fortified to make it impossible to take had the enemy been armed with rocks."[209]

However, a remarkable success was nearly achieved by the Fourth Texas in the last offensive thrust of the day. What the Texas and Alabama attackers had not anticipated when on the verge of success in turning the weak right flank, on the far north, of Vincent's Brigade was the arrival of reinforcements under a gifted Irish colonel, Patrick Henry O'Rorke, at the last minute. The tragedy of the bitter civil war among the Irish people in America was about to have a dramatic impact on the vicious struggle for possession of Little Round Top.

O'Rorke was born in County Cavan, Ulster Province, in late March 1836. The family had emigrated and eventually settled down in a large

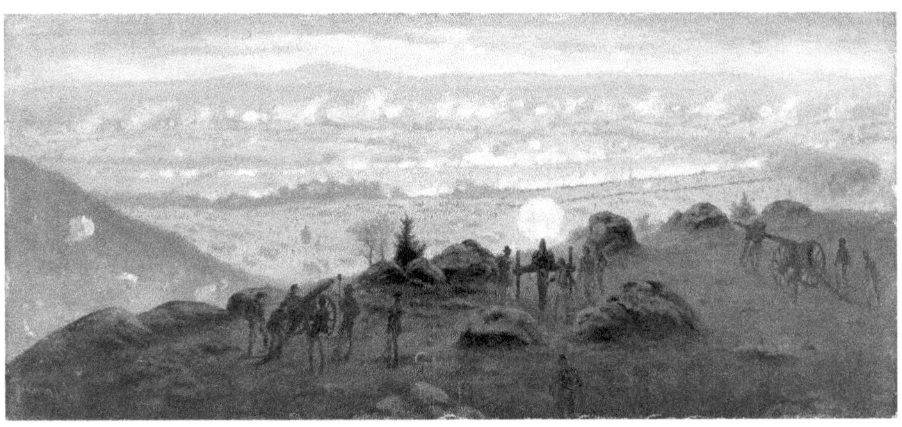

Union guns firing from the commanding perch on the rocky summit of Little Round Top on July 3, 1863. A painting based on a wartime sketch by New York City–born Edwin Forbes. *Courtesy of the Library of Congress.*

Irish community, "Little Dublin," in Rochester, New York. Instead of remaining a lowly marble cutter like his brothers in a dreary menial job without opportunities for upward mobility, O'Rorke aspired much higher in life. He eventually gained entry to West Point and embraced an almost impossible opportunity for an Irish immigrant. O'Rorke departed the military academy as not only the first in his class (1861), but also as only the second Ireland-born cadet to have graduated from the prestigious academy. He became a model officer who led by example. O'Rorke demonstrated outstanding ability, initiative, and aggressiveness, especially in crisis situations, while battling on behalf of what he believed was the "holy cause" of saving the Union.

With his order for his New Yorkers to advance down the western slope in his "rich Irish voice," this young Catholic officer saved the day on the collapsing right flank of Vincent's brigade on Little Round Top at the last minute. Just as the crumbling flank of the 16th Michigan (Vincent's northernmost regiment and right flank) was turned primarily by the veteran attackers of the 4th Texas, Colonel O'Rorke met the surging Rebels with his newly arrived 140th New York Volunteer Infantry.

Arriving at exactly the right time and place at the key moment at the northern end of the battle line spanning the western slope of Little Round Top, the New York regiment contained large numbers of Irish soldiers, especially from Rochester, New York. The timely attack down the rocky hill hurled the Texans, who were weary and low on rounds in cartridge-boxes, back down the slope when on the verge of a decisive success, but not before O'Rorke was fatally cut down. Most important, the Irishman's aggressive actions and bold tactics in the face of the Texans' onslaught in a true crisis situation had ensured that Little Round Top remained in Union hands for the day's remainder. Clearly, Colonel O'Rorke had made a timely contribution as important, if not more so, than Colonel Chamberlain's earlier actions to the south.[210]

BARKSDALE'S MISSISSIPPIANS UNLEASHED

While Ireland-born Colonel O'Rorke was destined to save the day on the embattled northern flank at Little Round Top, Longstreet belatedly unleashed his planned echelon assaults on Hood's left just on the north. Northwest of Little Round Top, along the Emmitsburg Road, before the high ground of the Peach Orchard (located on the Emmitsburg Road Ridge), which was situated on the property of farmer Joseph Sherfy, General William Barksdale's Mississippi Brigade, McLaws's Division, was ready to surge forward according to Lee's plan that had gone awry.

These veteran Mississippians of four regiments (Thirteenth, Seventeenth, Eighteenth, and Twenty-First Mississippi) were positioned before the Peach Orchard just north of Hood's Division. They had anxiously listened to the heavy firing from the attacking Texas and Alabama troops at Little Round Top to the southeast, watching the clouds of sulfurous smoke rising into a clear summer sky. Barksdale's nervous men waited for the signal to attack after General Joseph Kershaw's South Carolina Brigade, situated just south of the Mississippians, advanced east over the parched open fields of a dry summer just south of the Wheatfield Road. McLaws's troops pushed off in echelon to exploit the weaknesses of defending forces before them because of the eagerly anticipated rush of reinforcing Federal troops southward to face the threat of the attackers of Hood's Division, which Lee believed would open the door to greater tactical opportunities for McLaws.

A good many Irish soldiers now filled the surging ranks of the crack Mississippi Brigade, especially in the unit's best regiment, Colonel Benjamin Givens Humphreys's Twenty-First Mississippi. One secret of the Twenty-First Mississippi's success was its hard-fighting and capable Irish soldiers, including officers. The ranks of Company B (Jefferson Davis Guards) included Emerald Isle soldiers named Duffy, Gallagher, O'Brien, Murphy, Nugent, O'Connor, O'Leary, Ryan and Shenehan.

Even larger numbers of Irish served in Company E (Hurricane Rifles) under Captain Isaac D. Stamps, who was about to fall mortally wounded in the assault. The Hurricane Rifles included dedicated Emerald Islanders from the Kinney, McNeely, McMorris, McGraw and McCulloch clans, to name a few of the Celtic-Gaelic warriors, who had long made this a fine combat unit of the hard-hitting regiment. Irish soldiers were also heavily represented in the ranks of Company L, Twenty-First Mississippi, which was officially known as the Vicksburg Confederates. The soldiers hailed from the besieged port city of Vicksburg, Mississippi, which was located on the east bank overlooking the "Father of Waters." This key to the Mississippi River was destined to surrender to the forces of General Ulysses S. Grant in only two days on the Fourth of July 1863.

Among other clans of related Celtic-Gaelic soldiers, the men of the Conney, Fitzgerald, Donnelly, Gleeson, Sweeney and Fogarty kinship groups of Company L also served in Barksdale's Magnolia State Brigade. Fueling their motivation and resolve to do or die on this afternoon to compensate for the disturbing course of events that resulted in a new low point for Confederate fortunes in the Magnolia State, these Mississippi boys knew that even now the beloved Mississippi River town of their homes and families was under siege by Grant's massive army. Most of all, they realized that the relentless Grant, who had proved that he was one of Lincoln's best commanders, had tightened the noose around Vicksburg to slowly choke out the life of this vital port. Its death was now only a matter of time.[211]

BY ANY MEASURE, GENERAL Barksdale's attack was amazing on the afternoon of July 2, when everything hung in the balance. Quite simply, the Mississippi Brigade achieved an unparalleled level of success achieved by no other troops at Gettysburg. At the Abraham Trostle house along Plum Run that slowly trickled south just before Cemetery Ridge, the Ninth Massachusetts Battery was virtually destroyed by the hard-charging Mississippians after they had crashed through the Peach Orchard salient of the Third Corps. But in the end, and despite great initial success of smashing through multiple Union lines and capturing quite a few artillery pieces in a magnificent attack that continued all the way to nearly the end of the day, Barksdale's steamrolling assault and those of the other attacking three brigades of McLaws's Division had been repulsed, with bloody results and broken dreams.

For ample good reason, General McLaws, a scholarly warrior of Scottish descent, was bitter about how so much had gone wrong with the overly ambitious offensive plan. And things had continued to go wrong for most of the day. In a July 7, 1863 letter, an embittered McLaws wrote with disgust how the "loss in my Division was near twenty four hundred, the heaviest of the war, and many of the most valuable officers in the whole service have been killed. Thus ended the battle of the Peach Orchard....I think the attack was unnecessary and the whole plan of battle a very bad one."[212]

Ironically, as a strange fate and the unpredictable contours of history would have it, General McLaws had led a crack division of Longstreet's Corps at Gettysburg on a day of decision only because of the destructive power of a tropical hurricane long ago. His Celtic descendants had been returning to their native Scotland from St. Domingue (the most prosperous

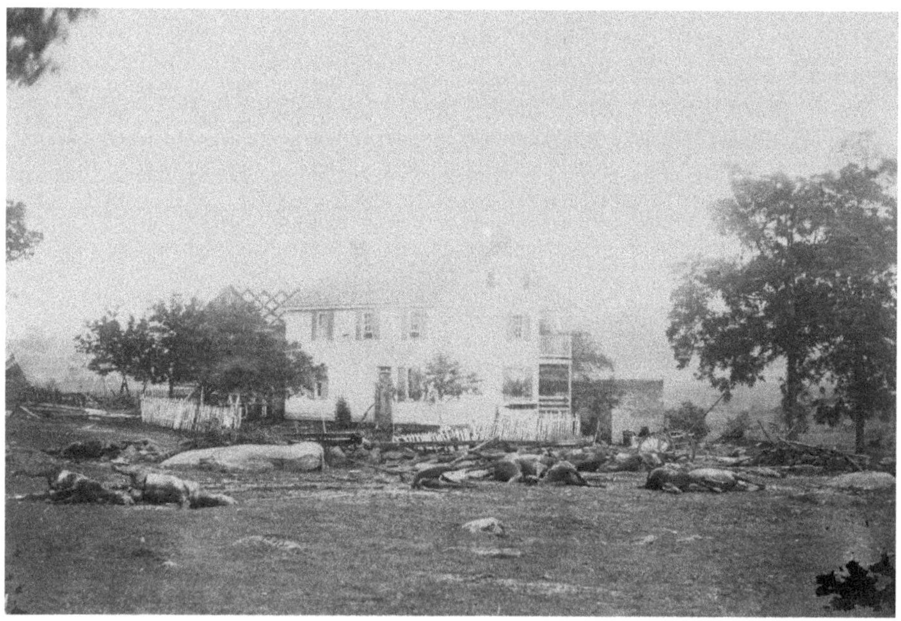

Decimated Ninth Massachusetts Battery at the Abraham Trostle House along Plum Run, just before the foot of Cemetery Ridge. Timothy H. O'Sullivan, a young Irish apprentice at Mathew Brady's photography shop in New York City, took this photo on July 6, 1863. O'Sullivan may have been born in Ireland around 1840 before migrating to New York City. The fact that an Irish photographer took photos of Irish dead at Gettysburg was symbolic of a central paradox of the Irish experience during the Civil War, especially in regard to the three days at Gettysburg: Irish in blue and gray battling each other in a bloody fratricidal conflict to determine America's destiny. *Courtesy of the Library of Congress.*

French colony thanks to sugar cultivation and slavery which is today's Haiti) when a hurricane had caused their sailing ship to wreck off the Georgia coast in the summer of 1783. The McLaws family then decided to set down roots in Georgia, where Lafayette McLaws found himself eventually caught up in the secession movement—an ill-fated cause that changed his life and fortunes forever.[213]

Attacking East Cemetery Hill in the Humid Darkness

While Lee's assaults on the Union left had struck with a fury seldom seen in this war but nevertheless met with bloody frustration in each case, Confederates facing Meade's right on the north remained stationary throughout the intense combat that raged on the afternoon of the second day. Late on the evening of July 2 and near twilight, the veterans of Ewell's Second Corps prepared to finally strike the Federal right after the repulse of Longstreet's First Corps attackers on the far south and because of the absence of a decisive success. Orders for the Confederates on the far north to attack came only belatedly, however.

This tardiness of the Southern offensive effort on the north allowed the Federals ample time to strengthen the strategic high ground of East Cemetery Hill, located just southeast of Gettysburg, which was bristling with a sizable number of Union artillery pieces. Manned by veterans, these guns were well placed atop the commanding crest and protected with earthen lunettes that stood along the dominant summit overlooking a wide area of open fields and pastures: a grim killing field to any attackers who dared to attack the high ground. Clearly, it would take a superior offensive effort to overwhelm this formidable elevated position crowned with so many Union guns in excellent firing positions, manned by veterans and supported by bluecoat infantry. Nevertheless, East Cemetery Hill had to be taken for Lee to fulfill his ambitions of achieving a decisive success.

Finally unleashed just before 8:00 p.m. on July 2 and not long before the long-awaited arrival of the red Pennsylvania sunset that promised to cool the day's blistering heat, Hays's Louisiana Rebels, consisting of more Irish fighting men than any other brigade of Lee's army, advanced with the conviction to "do it or die," in the words of one determined Louisianan. General Hays now orchestrated a two-brigade assault, with his battle-hardened Louisiana troops on the right and a North Carolina brigade on the left, in the twilight of the bloodiest day at Gettysburg. He hoped that this much-belated attack would overwhelm Meade's northern, or right, flank to unhinge Meade's entire battle line along lengthy Cemetery Ridge and decisively win this increasingly costly battle, which had lasted longer than anyone had imagined on July 1.

Consequently, the Louisiana Irish, who were part of "the infallible La Tigers," including Ireland-born Lieutenant Edward Owens of the Emerald Guards, Company F, Ninth Louisiana, finally struck a blow, after additional opportunities had slipped away. They should have attacked earlier in a coordinated assault with the attackers to the south when they had first heard firing from Longstreet's assault.

Most important, these veterans were known for their hard-hitting style; it had made the Louisiana Tigers such legendary fighting men by this time. A former grocer from New Orleans and former sergeant of the Irish of Montgomery Guards, Company E, First Louisiana, Colonel Michael Nolan, was one of the first to fall in the attack. The blue-eyed and fair-haired officer who led the First Louisiana Infantry was born in County Tipperary, Ireland, in 1821. He fell at the head of his men when shot down by a bluecoat of a lengthy skirmish line positioned before the main defensive line on East Cemetery Hill.

Colonel Nolan was an excellent commander in his early forties. His loss was a bad omen, occurring barely before the assault had begun against formidable East Cemetery Hill. But other dependable Irish officers and seasoned noncommissioned officers quickly filled the gap, compensating for Nolan's early fall. During the attack, they demonstrated their value to their men and units in an emergency situation. Lieutenant Colonel James Nelligan, a fast-talking auctioneer from New Orleans and the former commander of the Irish of the Emmet Guards, Company D, First Louisiana Infantry, was one veteran officer who continued to encourage his boys forward toward the formidable high ground of East Cemetery Hill in a bid to gain the hilltop and secure possession of the strategic Baltimore Road.

In a hurry to greet the attackers in the most appropriate manner in an emergency situation, Union gunners of Captain R. Bruce Rickett's First Pennsylvania Light Artillery (Combined Batteries F and G of the Third Volunteer Artillery Brigade, Artillery Reserve) positioned atop the hill depressed cannon barrels to rake the attackers with an unmerciful fire that swept down the slope. With fixed bayonets and "Rebel yells," the Louisiana Rebels swarmed farther up the slope and then over the first Union defensive

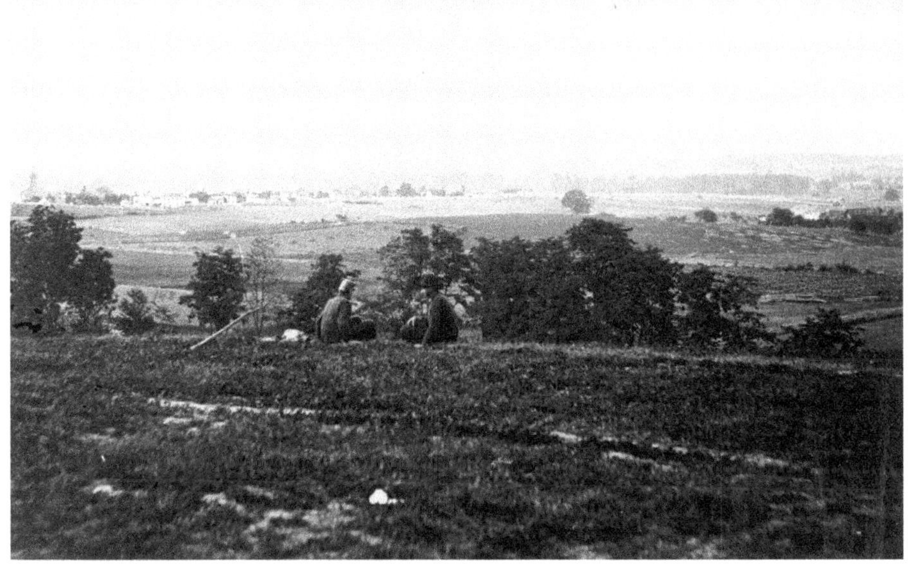

Louisiana Tigers attacked the strong defenses of East Cemetery Hill. Photograph taken in July 1863. *Courtesy of the Library of Congress.*

position situated along a stone wall located at the foot of East Cemetery Hill. Here, after bitter hand-to-hand combat between desperate men swinging musket butts and jabbing with bayonets, they pushed aside the Yankees, mostly New York and Ohio soldiers of Brigadier General Adelbert Ames's Second Brigade, First Division, Eleventh Corps, from behind a strong position along a stone wall. But the price of this tactical success was frightfully high for the attackers.

Elated Pelican State Rebels, including Emerald Islanders, shouted "We are the Louisiana Tigers!" To escape the fierce attackers, the hard-hit survivors in blue headed up the steep slope leading to the crest of East Cemetery Hill after having taken a severe beating. Then, continuing to exploit their momentum and the initiative, the howling Louisiana Tigers continued their attack up the steep slope.

With a cheer, they overcame additional resisting bluecoats on the high ground below the smoke-covered crest aligned with Union artillery pieces. After some of the most savage combat at Gettysburg, the mostly Irish from the Pelican State finally swarmed over the strategic crest of East Cemetery Hill. They captured a row of cannon and four battle flags, as well as dozens of prisoners, in the darkness. The six three-inch guns of Captain Rickett's Pennsylvania battery, situated just east of the Baltimore Road and the nearest Union guns to the Cemetery Gatehouse just to the rear, were overrun by the howling Rebels.

Irishmen of the Ninth Louisiana, consisting of men from northern and central Louisiana, took possession of the guns of the Pennsylvania battery after bayoneting cannoneers and knocking gunners down with musket butts in a flurry of vicious combat. The Sons of Erin of the Jackson Greys (Jackson Parish, northwest of Baton Rouge, Louisiana) and the Milliken Bend Guards (Madison Parish, located just across the Mississippi River from the bastion of Vicksburg, Mississippi) led the way in overrunning the battery and achieving a remarkable success in capturing the strategic crest of East Cemetery Hill. The Louisiana Rebels also overran the guns of Captain Michael Wiedrich's Battery I, First New York Light Artillery, positioned just north of Rickett's Battery. The First New York Light Artillery included many German artillerymen who bravely fought and died for their adopted country like some Teutonic Rebels (in far less numbers than the Irish) in the ranks.

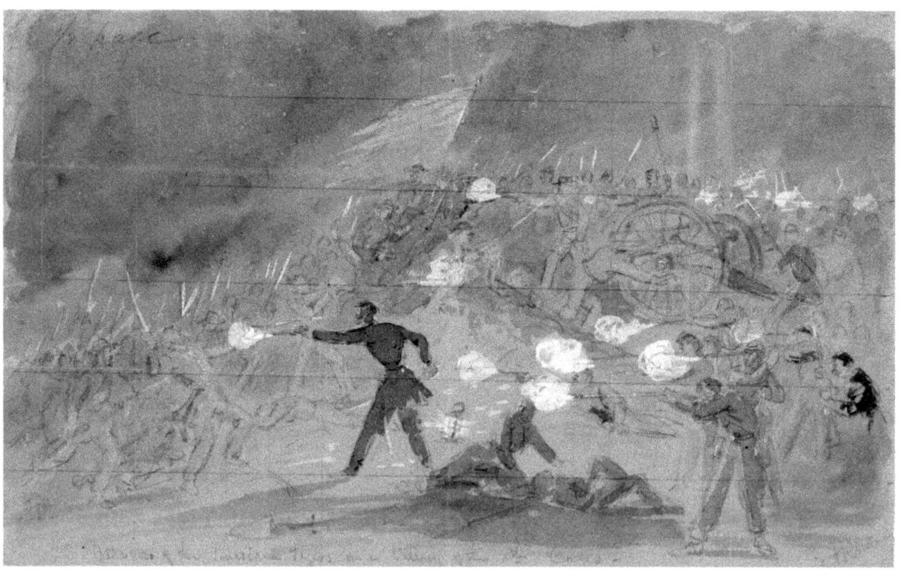

Louisiana Tigers overrunning guns of the Eleventh Corps, Army of the Potomac. *Courtesy of the Library of Congress.*

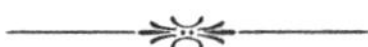

With their fighting blood up during one of the most dramatic assaults of the war, the Louisianans, along with Tar Heels of Colonel Isaac Erwin Avery's Brigade, Major General Jubal A. Early Division, Ewell's Second Corps, including the crack Sixth North Carolina, secured the strategic crest with fixed bayonets and a triumphant shout that echoed through the darkness. After a desperate rush up the slope, the Louisiana and North Carolina boys captured the northern and northeastern face of East Cemetery Hill after the last fiercely resisting Union infantrymen of the Eleventh Corps were cut down or hurled aside. The onrushing Rebels captured nearly half a dozen colorful Union flags and battery guidons during the melee atop the high ground. By this time, the strategic crest of East Cemetery Hill had been transformed into a hellish, body-strewn place on which Confederate flags, planted on earthen artillery lunettes, now flew in triumph. But more important, the Louisiana Rebels gained possession of the high-ground position at the northern end of Meade's battle line in their dramatic capture of the strategic crest of East Cemetery Ridge.

Here, on the smoke-laced crest among the captured artillery lunettes, the exhausted victors caught their breath. Most of all, they awaited much-needed assistance in the haunting blackness among the dead and wounded Union soldiers, including fallen Yankees pleading for help and water, to solidify their dramatic gains of capturing the strategic high ground.

Clearly, this was one of the finest hours of the hard-fighting Irish of the Louisiana Tigers, who had once again lived up to their lofty reputation. More significantly, the fate of the Battle of Gettysburg now hung in the balance, because this was strategic high ground upon which the dusty Baltimore Pike ran east to the all-important port city. If reinforcements came to the assistance of the victors, as fully expected at this time, a decisive victory would be won for General Lee and his army.

A Cruel Fate Intervenes

Sweaty and streaked with black powder, the victorious Louisianans rested on the crest after reloading muskets. Here, they awaited the reinforcements that they knew were absolutely necessary to solidify their significant tactical gains after having suffered heavy losses in charging up the steep slope. However, as a cruel fate would have it, the Pelican State soldiers waited in the darkness for reinforcements that would never come at a time they were most needed to exploit their extensive gains for a successful turning of Meade's right flank.

But instead of Confederates arriving out of the darkness to the victors' aid, the triumphant Louisiana Rebels were suddenly swept with a volley that erupted from the blackness. They then came under the onslaught of sizable Union reinforcements determined to push the Louisianans off the strategic crest at bayonet point. The hard-hitting "Gibraltar Brigade" had been dispatched by the ever-vigilant Major General Winfield Scott Hancock, who led the Second Corps with consummate skill. He made the right tactical decision in time, having ordered sizable reinforcements forward on the double to recapture the hill's strategic crest. These counterattacking Federals eventually hurled back the surviving Louisiana soldiers, who had long waited in vain for the promised reinforcements to exploit their gains in holding the vital crest of East Cemetery Hill that had been won with so much sacrifice.

Late in the night, the Louisiana Rebels, including so many Irish fighting men, had no choice but to abandon the captured artillery pieces and retire down the steep northern slope of East Cemetery Hill. They left behind some of the best and brightest Irishmen of Hays's Brigade, including many very good soldiers who had been hit. Some Emerald Islanders who had been cut down included Private John Carroll and Sergeants Thomas Casey and Patrick McGuinn, all of the Sixth Louisiana. Irishmen of the Seventh Louisiana killed in the attack included dependable Private Jerry Lynch. Also in the Seventh Louisiana's ranks, Privates Patrick Gaffney, William Henry Harris and Thomas McCarty were mortally wounded. The Ninth Louisiana lost good Irish soldiers when Privates John C. Calhoun and John H. McClannahan and Corporal Milledge Magee fell in the effort to fulfill an ambitious dream that never became reality.[214]

By the narrowest of margins, the Louisiana Irish came ever so close to changing the course of the Battle of Gettysburg and the fortunes of war by capturing strategic East Cemetery Hill and turning the northern flank of the Army of the Potomac. As fate would have it, the lost opportunity of the Louisiana Irish soldiers late on July 2 guaranteed that Lee would have to try again on the following day to overwhelm his opponent, who was well positioned on the high ground, to win decisive victory, but this time with far more attackers than ever before.[215]

Likewise, there would have been no Pickett's Charge on July 3 had the Texas and Alabama troops of General John Bell Hood's Division captured Little Round Top and turned Meade's left flank on the far south. Irish Confederates and the sons, grandsons and great-grandsons of Irish immigrants, Protestant and Catholic (but mostly the former), had performed heroically on the bloody afternoon of July 2. At the war's beginning, the optimistic and carefree members of the Irish companies had gathered in Texas and Louisiana to crush the Yankees with the same enthusiasm as when their forefathers of Celtic-Gaelic clans had united to confront the English invaders of their Ireland homeland. But visions of achieving decisive victory had been crushed on bloody July 2.[216]

ASSAULTING CULP'S HILL

In addition, the attacks of Major General Edward Johnson's Division, Ewell's Second Corps, on the heavily wooded, rocky Culp's Hill, situated just northeast of East Cemetery Hill, were equally frustrated on July 2. As during the Confederate attacks on Little Round Top and East Cemetery Hill, the Rebel assaults included an even a larger number of Louisiana Irish. Emerald Islanders of the First Louisiana Infantry, including Irish companies like the Emmet and Montgomery Guards and the Orleans Light Guards, hit hard but could not overcome the stubborn defenders of Culp's Hill. Despite the best efforts of the New Orleans Irish and courageous Irish leaders, Culp's Hill continued to remain securely in Union hands.[217]

Late in the night on the second day, the resurgent Confederates once again hurled attacks up the slope, covered in dense timber and boulders, of Culp's Hill. Beginning in the early-morning hours of July 3, the Stonewall Brigade launched four successive assaults. However, no permanent gain could be achieved on the high ground now held by too many veteran Yankees, who defended home soil with a tenacity not often seen in Virginia.

Clearly, attacking the high ground at both ends of Meade's sprawling battle line, anchored on dominant high ground, had proved to be an especially lethal proposition for Lee's troops on July 2. Consisting mostly of common laborers from the Shenandoah Valley and certainly the most colorful company of the Thirty-Third Virginia, the ranks of the Emerald Guard (Company E) were decimated in charging up Culp's Hill. The Irishmen lost their captain, who was encouraging his men up the bullet-swept slope, and most of Company E's members went down in the murderous explosions of musketry. Many captured Sons of Erin were now bound for prison camps across the North, where they eventually found final resting places in the North. Fighting for nearly five hours was not enough to secure victory for the Irish of the Emerald Guard and the other Irishmen who attacked Culp's Hill with bravado and flags flying. Clearly, rising splendidly to the challenge, the veteran soldiers of the Army of the Potomac, which included large numbers of Irish, were having their finest day on July 2, and this trend was destined to continue unabated on July 3.

The relatively few survivors of the hard-hit company (G) known as the Virginia Hibernians, Stonewall Brigade, finally retired for the last time through the bullet-scarred trees and down the bloody slope of Culp's Hill. Now short on ammunition, water and stamina, these crack Hibernians were members of the color company of the Twenty-Seventh Virginia. Verifying their elite status in the bloody assaults at the hill, these men faithfully guarded the regimental banner with their lives to keep it out of Yankee hands.

Mortally wounded in the living nightmare that was the bloody Battle of Gettysburg, Captain John Payne Welsh commanded the company of small farmers and mountaineers from Alleghany County in the Blue Ridge Mountains just west of Lexington. Born in Rockbridge County, Virginia, Welsh was the promising son of Scotch-Irish immigrants from the green hills of north Ireland. The captain's brother James Welsh braved Rebel shells and bullets while serving in an Illinois regiment in the western theater. Captain John Payne Welsh's luck ran out at Culp's Hill when he fell with a nasty hip wound. He lingered until July 15, 1863, when the seasoned captain of the Irish Rebels of the Virginia Hibernians died.[218]

An unknown number of Irish Confederates died in the assaults at the southern and northern ends of the sprawling battle line during repeated attempts in vain to turn the flanks of the Army of the Potomac. But decisive victory was not forthcoming to Lee and his men on July 2 despite their best offensive efforts and high losses. Therefore, Lee decided to continue his desperate offensive efforts on the following day in the hopes of securing the dramatic victory that would decide the destiny of two republics that actually had more similarities than differences.

Under the circumstances, an increasingly desperate Lee was going for broke on the third day at Gettysburg. He was still convinced that he could reap a decisive success if he continued to unleash the tactical offensive against the high-ground positions. Lee understood that the Army of Northern Virginia and the South were running out of time in this war of attrition. Victory had to be won on Northern soil. Quite simply, it was now or never for the Confederacy.

But the frightful price in lives of young soldiers across the South and Ireland was destined to be staggering. Young Colonel Edward Porter Alexander, Longstreet's top artillery officer, wrote, "in taking the aggressive at all at Gettysburg [and] certainly in the place & disposition for the assault on the 3rd day, I think, it will undoubtably be held that [General Lee] unnecessarily took the most desperate chances & the bloodiest road" of all.[219]

4

The Army of Northern Virginia's Greatest Attack

With the arrival of warm sunrise on Friday, July 3, Lieutenant John Edward Dooley Jr., Major General George Edward Pickett's Division, was worried about the recent course of events that had sabotaged Lee's second invasion of the North. The loss of so many good officers and men at Chancellorsville on May 2, 1863, had been in vain—this was just another Pyrrhic victory for Lee and his hard-fighting army.

As mentioned, the missed opportunity of destroying Hooker's army at Chancellorsville had unleashed the Army of Northern Virginia for the push north across the Potomac and to a rendezvous with cruel destiny at Gettysburg. But Chancellorsville had taken a heavy toll on the Confederate leadership corps, including Stonewall Jackson. The death of Lee's top lieutenant was now coming back to haunt the Army of Northern Virginia—whose leadership was not in top form—at Gettysburg. Quite simply, high-ranking officers had let the common soldiers down, dooming many to needless deaths by their own mistakes.

Perhaps the son of an Irish immigrant said it best about Jackson's loss that had been strongly felt on July 2: "Who will fill great Stonewall Jackson's place, who indeed can ever replace our noble hero, so pure, so truly great?"[220] Instead of worrying about who would replace Jackson (who was irreplaceable, as realized at Gettysburg), Lee and his men should have been more worried about the Army of the Potomac's new commander who had just replaced "Fighting Joe" Hooker, Major General George Gordon Meade.

An Opposing Commander's Forgotten Irish Roots

While the Army of Northern Virginia was lacking in solid leadership performances, the Army of the Potomac had been benefiting immensely from Meade's leadership, especially on July 2. A veteran commander, Meade was as capable as his namesake, George Meade, who was the son of an Irish immigrant, Robert. The general's Irish roots was one reason for his stubbornness and excellent qualities of a fighter that proved invaluable at Gettysburg. Robert Meade was born in County Limerick in the picturesque Shannon River country. Hardly could the Irish soldiers of the Army of Northern Virginia have realized that the opposing army's commander had descended from an Irish Catholic immigrant who had migrated with high hopes to America in 1732. Robert Meade had established a sturdy foundation on which other Irish merchants had set up their business enterprises, based on shipping and links to the Atlantic, which transformed Philadelphia into the "Irish capital" of the thirteen colonies.

George Meade, the aspiring immigrant's son, was part of an active group of Patriot Irish merchants who played key roles in fueling the resistance effort, especially among the troops of Washington's Continental army. He was also a proud member of the city's leading Irish fraternal organization, the Friendly Sons of St. Patrick, organized on St. Patrick's Day in 1771. Like the vast majority of the Irish who migrated to America before the American Revolution, George Meade also served his country in the ranks of the Pennsylvania militia from 1775 to 1776. In this sense, Major General Meade was actually now only continuing his ancestor's role in defending Philadelphia and Pennsylvania.[221]

The fact that the Army of the Potomac's commander had descended from an ambitious Irish immigrant was perhaps as appropriate as it was symbolic on the bloody field of Gettysburg, where so many Irish on both sides fought and died for what they believed was right. Although an exaggeration—but still capturing much of the overall flavor of the Army of the Potomac, thanks in part to the Irish Brigade, hard-fighting regiments like the Sixty-Ninth Pennsylvania Volunteer Infantry, and many other Irish who were serving in Meade's Army—one modern historian wrote that the "Union army was among the greatest Irish armies that ever saw battle."[222]

Most important in regard to the final outcome of the battle of Gettysburg, President Lincoln had picked the right man at the right time and at the right place to command the Army of the Potomac in the most decisive

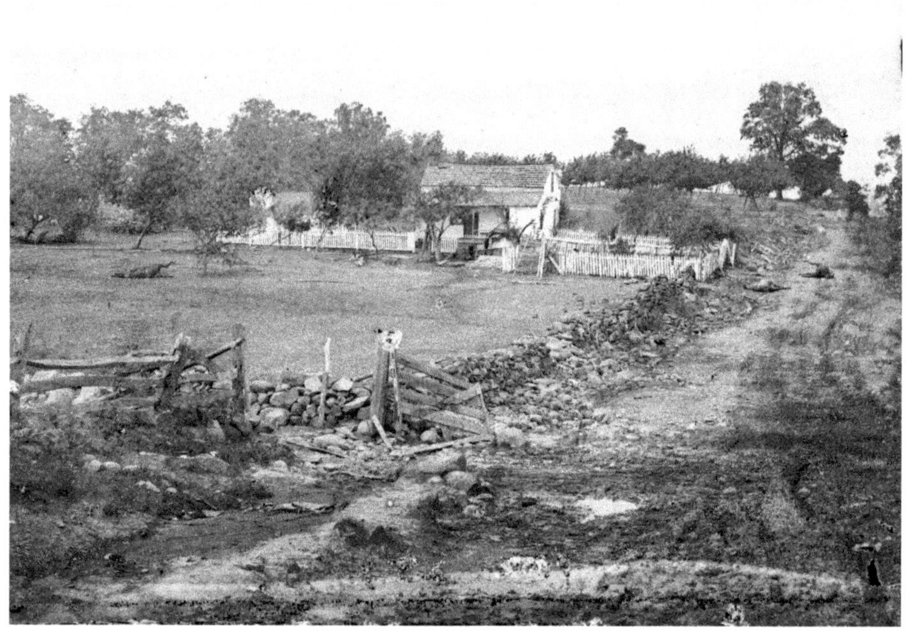

Major General George Gordon Meade's headquarters at the Widow Lydia A. Leister House on the Taneytown Road. Photo taken on July 6, 1863. *Courtesy of the Library of Congress.*

engagement of the Civil War. Making an appropriate analogy of his feisty general of Irish antecedents to a fighting cock, Lincoln knew that this hard-bitten Pennsylvanian, who would be most tenacious in defending home soil, was going to "fight well on his own dung heap."[223] The president's prophesy about General Meade and his typically Irish fighting spirit was proven true on July 2 and 3.

LINGERING IRISH LEGACIES

Ironically, on this warm Friday, July 3, 1863, America's fate was about to be largely decided by the combat performances of thousands of young men and boys on both sides who had not been born in the United States, nor even

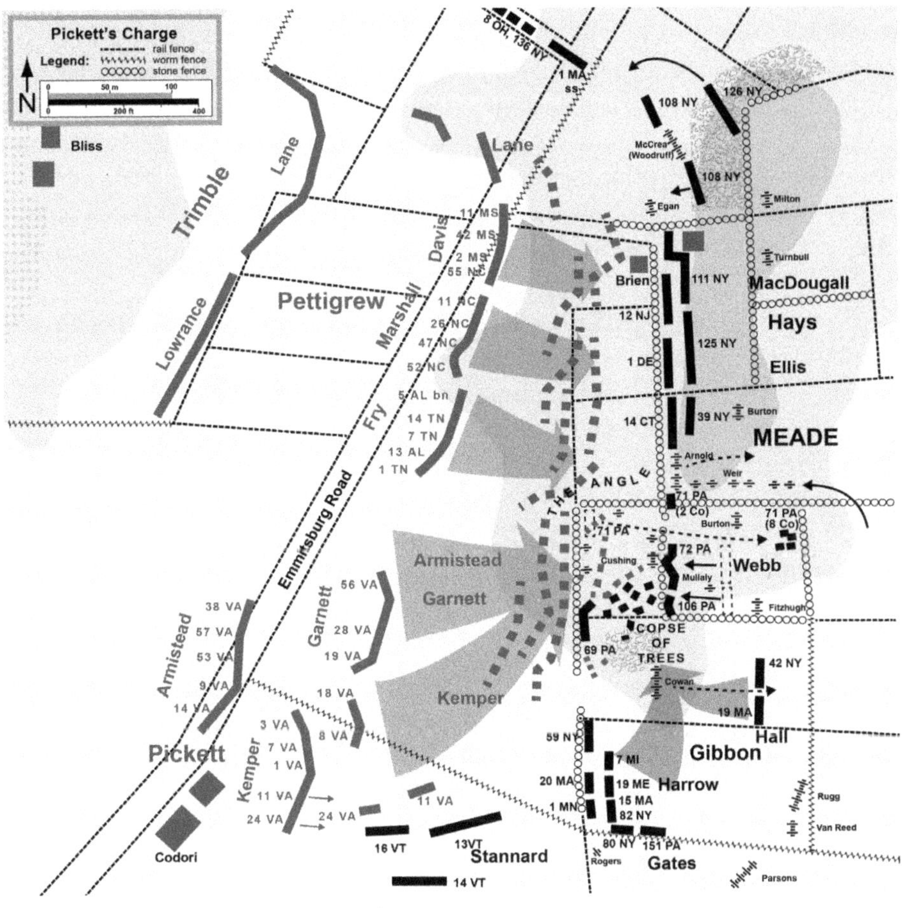

their fathers, grandfathers or great-grandfathers, for that matter. Ironically, the large number of Emerald Isle soldiers in both armies actually had far more in common, especially in terms of the Irish experience, than even they themselves realized on the third day at Gettysburg. Either they or their ancestors had grown up in the rural countryside of Ireland, but also in the lower-class ghettoes and Celtic-Gaelic ethnic communities on both sides of the Mason-Dixon line.

These distinctive ethnic communities in major northeastern cities had provided a relatively safe haven against the rising tide of discrimination (especially from the Know-Nothing Party, which led to anti-Irish riots in major northeastern cities) and the prejudice of non-Irish Americans. Natives of the United States had continued the anti-Irish cultural legacy of hatred from the people of Great Britain, especially military men and elitist politicians. But this ugly reality failed to diminish the heroics of the Irish Brigade soldiers who fought in part to overcome anti-Irish stereotypes. In fact, the men of the Irish Brigade naively believed that battlefield heroics would lead to better treatment for the Irish across the North. Of course, the South's less Irish-hating environment in both the cities and countryside was one fundamental reason why Lee's Irish fought so well at Gettysburg—they appreciated the more Irish-acceptable qualities they had found in the South rather than in the North.

The largest Irish enclaves in America were usually located near the docks, wharves and waters of the East River and in the infamous Five Points in lower Manhattan; along the banks of the Mississippi River in New Orleans; and on the banks of the Schuylkill and Delaware Rivers in Philadelphia. Ironically, these Irish from the North (the least represented of any immigrant group in the Army of the Potomac) and the South (the most represented of any ethnic and immigrant group in the Army of Northern Virginia) were about to meet during the climax of Lee's greatest offensive effort of the war.[224]

Instead of fighting and dying in large numbers at Gettysburg, these Irish soldiers, especially those who were die-hard Irish nationalists, should have been preparing to rise up on Ireland's soil to free the homeland. Instead, thousands of Irish of Lee's and Meade's armies were now facing each other to determine the fate of America rather than Ireland.

As mentioned, the sharpest divisions among the same Celtic-Gaelic people, including relatives, were best represented by the Irish Brigade's first commander, Thomas Francis Meagher, and the most inspirational leader of America's exiled Irish in the South, John Mitchel Sr. Like many fighting men in Lee's ranks, Meagher and Mitchel were united in the holy cause of Ireland's liberation. Indeed, Mitchel had forsaken a law career for the express purpose of joining "Meagher and other young Irishmen in a campaign to gain independence for Ireland."[225] But as a tragic fate would have it, Meagher's and Mitchel's most faithful followers were about to slaughter each other at an unprecedented rate on the decisive third day of the showdown in Adams County, Pennsylvania.[226]

Final Showdown for the Heart and Soul of America

Indeed, after failing to inflict a mortal blow on the Army of the Potomac on the two previous days, Lee now planned to deliver a far greater offensive strike. He had come so close to achieving decisive success (especially in Generals Hood's and Barksdale's sectors) on July 2 and believed that he had Meade's hard-hit army on the ropes. He was now convinced that the Union right-center was Meade's Achilles' heel. His thinking was fundamentally based on the certitude that Meade had reinforced his battered northern and southern flanks that had been nearly turned on July 2.

This had been especially the case far to the south in the Little Round Top sector, which had been mauled by Longstreet's First Corps, who had fought magnificently in attempting to overrun the high ground. Known for ascertaining his opponents' tactical thinking and their intentions with clarity that had always paid dividends in the past, Lee was now convinced that Meade had significantly weakened his right center to counter the July 2 threats to his flanks, leaving what he hoped was a golden opportunity to deliver a fatal blow to the weakened right-center along Cemetery Ridge.

For the upcoming massive attack, Lee now possessed an ace in the hole to exploit an irresistible opportunity of piercing a weak Union right-center: a single fresh division of seasoned Virginian troops that was the army's only fresh manpower. At this crucial time when every man was needed in the ranks, this division represented Lee's last remaining strategic reserve, General George Edward Pickett's Division of three veteran brigades. Indeed, Pickett's Division, the only such sized unit in the army consisting of soldiers from a single state, was now the only fresh command in the depleted army. Mercifully, Pickett's Division had been spared the bloodletting of July 1 and July 2, as if destiny itself had set the stage for its vital role on the afternoon of July 3.

Consequently, this all-Virginia division of fourteen infantry regiments was in overall good shape, especially when compared to Lee's other decimated divisions. Fortunately for Pickett and his men, they had missed the terrible slaughter at Chancellorsville, where Lee lost more than thirteen thousand men whom he could ill-afford to lose. Along with Longstreet's other troops, Pickett's Division had been dispatched south in early 1863 to southeast Virginia and laid siege to Suffolk, Virginia, because Lee had sought to protect the weakly defended area and gain supplies for his

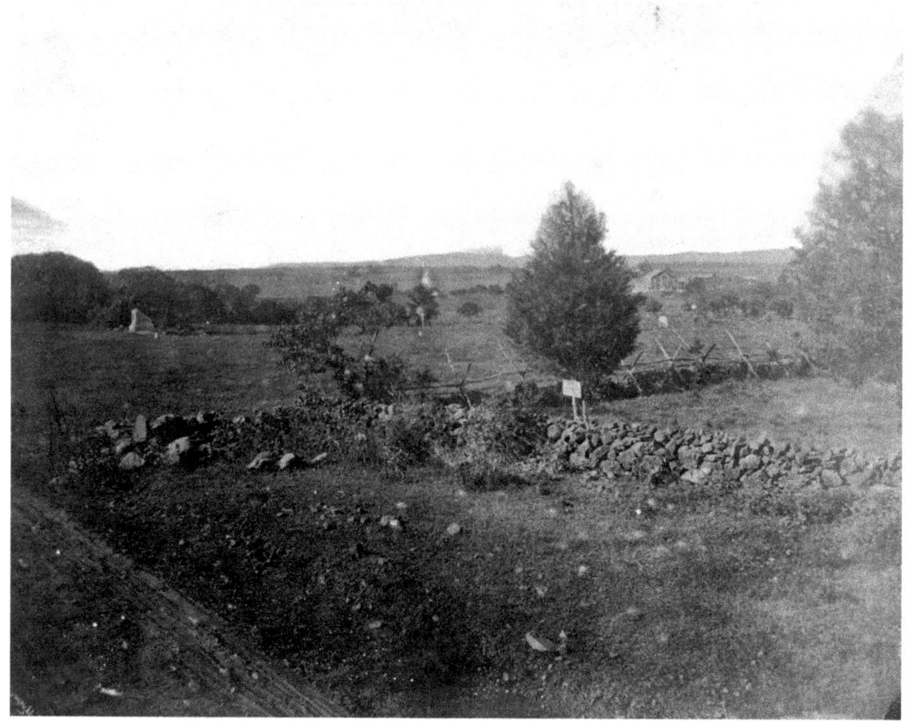

Preparations for General Lee's final bid to win it all, Pickett's Charge. The Army of the Potomac's weak right-center was targeted to receive the greatest impact of the Army of Northern Virginia's onslaught on the afternoon of July 3, 1863. *Courtesy of the Library of Congress.*

army's troops. Because of pressing circumstances, Pickett's Division was chosen to spearhead the great assault on which the Confederacy's fate now depended.[227]

Having brought up the army's rear along with the rest of Longstreet's Corps during the march east through Pennsylvania, the troops of Pickett's Division, recently encamped just outside Gettysburg along the clear waters of Marsh Creek in "a small copse of woods," including virgin sycamores that lined the bank, were on the move early on the humid morning of July 3.

In the words of Lieutenant John Edward Dooley Jr., from his journal:

> *Before the day has fully dawned we are on our way to occupy the position assigned to us for the conflict of the third day. As we turn from the main road* [Chambersburg Pike] *to the right* [or south], *Gen. Lee, or better known as Uncle Robert, silent and motionless, awaits our passing by, and*

> *anxiously does he gaze upon the only division* [Pickett's Division] *of his army whose numbers have not been thinned by the terrible fires of Gettysburg…it is impossible for us to be any otherwise than victorious and we press forward with beating hearts, hundreds of which will throb their last today."*[228]

And, of course, a good many of these were Irish hearts.

THE FORGOTTEN IRISH OF PICKETT'S DIVISION

Indeed, in many ways, it was most symbolic that General Lee had chosen Pickett's Virginia Division to spearhead the most important assault of the war. By 1860, Virginia had possessed more Irish immigrants (more than 16,500) than any other ethnic group and nearly twice as many as the number of Germans. Virginia's Irish population had increased by more than 44 percent since 1850. The Irish population of Richmond had risen from 685 in 1850 to 2,294 in 1860, representing a 234.9 percent increase, the highest increase of any Southern city other than Memphis, Tennessee, and far greater than the 20.8 percent increase for New Orleans.

Therefore, in 1860, the Irish, who occupied mostly unskilled positions, represented nearly 10 percent of the total white population of Richmond, compared with 4.5 percent ten years before. For such reasons, Pickett's Division contained a larger percentage of Irish, including the sons, grandsons and great-grandsons of Irish immigrants, than realized by generations of historians.[229] Therefore, in regard to Pickett's Division, Pickett's Charge certainly possessed a distinct Irish and Scotch-Irish flavor that has been overlooked by historians, including Gettysburg scholars, for more than a century and a half.[230]

Most symbolically, the youngest Irish Rebel in not only the ranks of Pickett's Division but also in Pickett's Charge was seventeen-year-old Private William Henry "Willie" Mitchel. He was the youngest son of Ireland's and the South's famed Irish nationalist and revolutionary, John Mitchel. Despite his youth and relative innocence among grizzled veterans, Mitchel had been detailed from Company D (Old Dominion Guard) to serve in the color guard of the First Virginia. To this young and idealistic Irish Rebel, such a prestigious position was considered the greatest privilege and honor.

Lieutenant John Edward Dooley Jr. described the young man called "Willie" in detail in his journal: "Poor little Willie left France with his father, Mr. John Mitchel, to join their fortunes with the Southern Confederacy. Last fall [1862] they reached Richmond and Willie immediately followed our army [of Northern Virginia] until he came up with us, when he enlisted in our company [C, the Montgomery Guard] as a private. He was then about 17 years of age and of very clear intellect and with talents more developed than is usual for one who had not enjoyed the advantage of early education. He had attended school in France however and was very assiduous in attending lectures in Paris, particularly those regarding insect life. He even pursued this study in camp, having a little manuscript book in which he entered all the discoveries he made with the aid of his microscope, describing minutely the figures and peculiarities of every unknown form of insect. We were nearly always together, messed together, hunted together and built our shelter together [and] Willie would tell us often of his adventures in Australia, of his long sojourn there while his father [exiled from Ireland for his revolutionary activities to free Ireland] was held a prisoner by the British government; of the strange animals, gorgeously feathered birds, and strange productions; of his father's escape; how he was unsuccessfully pursued; how [he journeyed to America] on the same boat with Mr. Mitchel" and other Irish.[231]

While the majority of the Irish who lived in Richmond had been unskilled laborers, such was not the case in regard to the Tidewater Irishmen of the Ninth Virginia Infantry, Armistead's Brigade, Pickett's Division. These Emerald Islanders had long worked at the Gosport Naval Shipyard (the former Norfolk Naval Shipyard), which had been destroyed after its May 1862 capture by Union forces in Portsmouth, Virginia.[232]

Revealing how the major Southern ports were filled with Irish sailors whose livelihood was the sea, these Tidewater Irish hailed from southeast Virginia, primarily the ports of Norfolk and Portsmouth. Here, they had labored as sailors, boatmen, mechanics (such as twenty-eight-year-old Private Richard H. McLean), shipwrights, ship caulkers, laborers (like Private Patrick O'Donnell) and ship's carpenters (like Privates Enos Murphy, fated to die in this war; John O'Donnell; and Rufus K. McCoy, wounded and captured on July 3). In addition, qualified members of the Ninth Virginia had been detailed from the regiment to work on the construction of Confederate naval vessels, including the famed CSS *Virginia* or the *Merrimack*, at the Gosport Naval Yard.

A number of Ireland-born soldiers of the heavily Irish Tenth Louisiana Infantry had also been transferred to serve on the *Virginia*. A first steam-powered ironclad of the Confederate navy, this casemate ironclad had been launched on March 8, 1862. Many Emerald Islanders of the Ninth Virginia had originally enlisted for duty at the Portsmouth Naval Hospital. Described as a "British subject" (Ireland was part of Great Britain), Private Robert W. Murry, Company B, had "family problems and business interests in the north of Ireland" and therefore resigned in late 1862.[233]

Among the Irish soldiers of the Ninth Virginia who were killed, wounded or captured in the assault on Meade's vulnerable right-center included Privates James M. McClenny, William McLaughlin, Henry and George W. Gyynn, Larkin M. Gill, William and Robert T. Daughtrey, and Sergeant William J. Barradall.[234]

General Pickett's Irish Face Their Greatest Challenge

After passing over fields littered with only "ghastly and mangled remnants" of soldiers cut down during the first day's fighting northwest of Gettysburg, the troops of Pickett's Division marched south on the morning of July 3 to its assigned position. Pickett's Old Dominion men then took position on the reverse, or west, slope of Seminary Ridge and halted to rest in the rising heat of another humid morning.

As Lieutenant John Edward Dooley Jr. explained the positioning of Brigadier General James Lawton's Kemper's Brigade, Pickett's Division: "we take temporary position in a hollow of a field [and] [b]efore us is a rising slope which hides the Yankee position [on Cemetery Ridge] from view.... Around us are some trees with very small green apples; and while we are resting here we amuse ourselves by pelting each other with green apples. So frivolous men can be even in the hour of death."[235]

Here, with his Fifty-Sixth Virginia aligned in a nearly ripe wheat field near the woods of Henry Sprangler, Lieutenant George Williamson Finley, of Irish heritage and proud of it, recalled how "some of the boys shinnied up the apple trees and shock those apples down. The boys began to stuff themselves with green apples. The gorged themselves on green apples [and they] didn't get sick [but] It would have served them right if they had [because that] might even have saved their lives."[236]

Quite naturally, the enthusiastic apple-eating by his men infuriated the commander of the Fifty-Sixth Virginia, Colonel William Dabney Stuart.

A promising commander, he was a graduate of Virginia Military Institute (Class of 1850) in Lexington. Stuart now could hardly believe his eyes at the sight of this indiscipline on the eve of the army's greatest assault. Therefore, when Stuart "realized what was going on, he lost his temper." He stopped the fun—the last in the lives of some of these young men and boys—by yelling, "You boys stop throwing those apples!"[237]

As a sad fate would have it, the handsome Colonel Stuart, of Celtic antecedents, was about to receive his death stroke in the assault against Meade's right-center. He breathed his last on this earth before the end of July.[238]

Lieutenant Finley observed that, about an hour before noon on July 3,

> *General Lee and his capable adjutant, Colonel Walter Herron Taylor, walked out of the [Spangler] woods near us. The General opened up a map and spread it out on a tree stump, and soon the staff officers began to gather around him. Those men were holding a council of war—in full view of our regiment* [the Fifty-Sixth Virginia]. *We could see them plainly* [and] [a]*fter about a quarter of an hour, the General folded up his map, and he and Colonel Taylor walked into the woods off to our left and disappeared. The staff officers disbursed to the four points of the compass, leaving us standing there with our mouths wide open. We didn't know it then, but General Lee had made a decision that was going to make Pickett's Division immortal.*[239]

Finley explained the tactical situation in simple terms of the common soldiers, who possessed a mindset that was comparable to that of the ever-aggressive General Lee, because so much was now at stake in the upcoming assault:

> *For the past two days, the Army of Northern Virginia and the Army of the Potomac had stood toe to toe like two old prize fighters and had slugged it out. The first day had gone to the South. The second day was about even, and this was the morning of the third day. So with food running low and ammunition running low, General Lee* [now] *decided to risk it all on one last throw of the dice. He had tried the Union right, and he hadn't broken it. He had tried the Union left, and he hadn't broken it, so he reasoned that the only place left to strike was the Union center. His plan was to hurl Pickett's entire division, with the 56th Virginia as part of the spearhead, right down the middle—straight into the center of the Union line—and if we could punch through, it just might mean victory.*[240]

However, and unfortunately for the Irish of Pickett's Division and for the bid to win it all, two of Pickett's brigades had been detached on assignments of relatively little importance. Now far away, these invaluable Virginia brigades were protecting Richmond, which was under no serious threat because the Army of the Potomac had moved north to pursue his army, as Lee had anticipated.

General Lee had hoped in vain that at least one brigade would eventually be allowed to rejoin Pickett's Division during the push north. A flurry of new Union activity on the Virginia peninsula had earlier caused an overly concerned Confederate leadership in Richmond to overreact. But, of course, and as Lee fully understood, a decisive victory on Pennsylvania soil was still the best way to secure Richmond from threats, especially if the Army of the Potomac was destroyed. Therefore, everything (not only Richmond's but also the Confederacy's salvation) was at stake with Lee's mighty offensive effort on the fateful afternoon of July 3.[241]

By relying on the tactical offensive and targeting the right-center of an overextended defensive line centered on Cemetery Ridge, Lee was going for broke. He was convinced that one final grand assault, spearheaded by Pickett's Division, would win it all for the Confederacy. Lee understood that delivering a decisive blow would save his slowly dying army and nation—now trapped in a brutal war of attrition—partly because of the steady flow of immigration, especially from Ireland, that replenished Union armies and compensated for losses.

Ironically, the contempt for the boys in blue, especially German immigrants, remained high among Lee's veterans, who had tasted victory for so long on Virginia soil. These soldiers were viewed as hirelings like the German Hessians employed by England during the American Revolution. Large numbers of Irish and Germans in the Union army only confirmed popular Southern stereotypes that the Yankee, especially the New Englander, was an inherent coward who needed more stalwart souls to win his battles. This myth, which still held sway among unsophisticated farm boys of the Army of Northern Virginia, was cruelly shattered at Gettysburg on the afternoon of July 3.[242]

Lieutenant John Dooley caught the representative mood of not only the Irish but also the non-Irish soldiers in the ranks in regard to what they felt was now at stake: "We were the last representatives of free government, and that when we fell the right of self government or the rights of States and peoples to govern themselves would fall with us."[243]

Clearly, the men of this largely Scotch-Irish or Anglo-Celtic army felt the heavy burden of the responsibility for the overall welfare of their people, whom they felt they must save, and even for future generations of Southerners. In this sense, Lee's Irish fought for a brighter future in an independent Southern nation—not only for the Southern people but also the Irish people. Therefore, greater opportunities for the Irish people were anticipated with the winning of independence.

A UNIQUE CULTURAL FUSION

The sense of compassion for the underdog status of the Irish, especially immigrants, was well known even in other countries. In general, the Irish, including former U.S. soldiers of Mexico's St. Patrick's Battalion during the Mexican-American War, felt a strong affinity toward the long-suffering Mexican people of the same faith, Catholicism. Contrary to the black-hating stereotype supposedly wholeheartedly embraced by them, many Irish identified with the plight of lowly blacks because the Irish people had been Europe's underdog for centuries as a result of English domination. After touring the town of Cork, in County Cork, Frederick Douglass, a former Maryland slave and the son of a white master and slave mother, was astounded by the fact that the Irish people "did not judge people on the color of their skin [like white Americans] but on their merits as human beings."[244]

In cities across the South, especially in major ports, lower-class free blacks and whites often lived, danced, worked and drank in "grog shops," and got together in both casual and longtime relationships, crossing society's strict racial barriers meant to safeguard the racial integrity and alleged purity of white Protestants. After all, both people (blacks and Irish) shared a comparable history of social and economic oppression, finding release in shared passions of the common working man. Blacks, slave and free, danced Irish jigs, and the enterprising Irish incorporated aspects of African music and culture into their own in what was a melting pot fusion combining cultural, musical, and racial ingredients into one.

After the outlawing of the traditional Irish harp (a revered nationalist symbol and a cherished icon that had distinguished quite a few Irish family coats of arms as early as the thirteenth century) and harpers by the English, fiddling evolved to be the most popular music among the Irish. Thanks largely to massive Irish migration to America since before the American

Revolution, fiddling in turn became a passion among blacks (free and slaves) across America and as far west as the Texas frontier, where whites often sang old slave songs to fiddling even before the Texas Revolution of 1835–36. This interracial activity on multiple levels between the Irish and free blacks and slaves had naturally caused great concern among Southern civil and societal leaders, who "became nervous about the potential of an Irish challenge to the prevailing racial hegemony."[245]

This forgotten blending of black and white cultural traditions was evident even in the ranks of Pickett's Division. Lieutenant John Dooley, First Virginia of Kemper's Brigade, described how, just before the slaughter at Gettysburg, the best-singing Virginians, under William "Bill" H. Dean, Company G, First Virginia—who was fated to die in a filthy Northern camp as a prisoner of war—provided soothing entertainment that was thoroughly enjoyed by the men in the ranks. Indeed, they made "the woods in our immediate vicinity reecho with all the old negro songs and glees that have been composed many years back."[246]

A member of General William Barksdale's Mississippi Brigade, Longstreet's First Corps, teenager James "Little Jimmie" Dinkins described how he and his Magnolia State comrades "sang all kinds of plantation songs," including "Sallie, Get Your Hoe Cake Done."[247] In addition, Virginians of the Army of Northern Virginia often sang the popular song "Bonnie Jean," which reflected the cherished folkways and traditions of the Celtic-Gaelic homeland, keeping Irish cultural influences alive and well in the Army of Northern Virginia.[248]

The Forgotten Irish of Pettigrew's Division

While Pickett's Division had been chosen by General Lee to spearhead the assault on the right, or south, he envisioned a sweeping assault over the open fields across a wide front of two divisions. Therefore, Brigadier General James Johnston Pettigrew's Division—formerly under the command of erratic General Henry "Harry" Heth (West Point class of 1847), a cousin of Pickett known affectionately as "Cousin Hal," who had been wounded in the head on July 1—was placed on Pickett's left, or north, to protect that flank. Pettigrew's Division of four brigades was part of Lieutenant General Ambrose Powell Hill's Third Corps. Pettigrew's left on the north was protected by two brigades of Hill's corps—the division of the lamented Major General William Dorsey Pender.

As mentioned, the promising North Carolina–born commander (still another rising star who met a tragic end) of the so-called Light Division had fallen mortally wounded in the bitter fighting northwest of Gettysburg on July 2. To protect Pickett's right on the south, General Richard Anderson's Division, Hill's Third Corps, was chosen to play a key supporting role but failed to advance in line with Pickett's three brigades at the same time as the front-line attackers to provide adequate protection of the division's southern, or right, flank.[249]

At this time, the Irish of the North Carolina Brigade were still saddened by the loss of the popular Colonel Henry King Burgwyn Jr. He was one of the most promising regimental officers from North Carolina, having led the Twenty-Sixth North Carolina in the attack with his usual hard-hitting leadership style. A proud Virginia Military Institute graduate known in the army as the daredevil "boy colonel" at age twenty-one, Colonel Burgwyn was fatally cut down on July 1 while battling the crack westerners of the Iron Brigade, whose sobriquet was bestowed because of their toughness in battle. The Irish from his Tar Heel State regiment were always inspired whenever he had ordered the regimental bands to play traditional Celtic tunes like "The Girl I Left Behind Me" and "The Campbells Are Coming."[250]

LIKE SO MANY UNITS of this fine division, the Twenty-Sixth North Carolina had been decimated during the nightmarish combat on July 1, when the fast-firing Tar Heels had cut down a large number of Yankees "as if shooting squirrels," in General Pettigrew's words of admiration.[251] Here, a good many Irish soldiers fell on the savage fighting that had swirled with intensity just northwest of Gettysburg, including men of the Pee Dee Wildcats (Company K, Twenty-Sixth North Carolina, led by Captain John C. McLauchlin) from Anson County, North Carolina. West Pointer Captain William W. McCreery, of Scotch-Irish descent, a member of General Pettigrew's staff and assistant inspector general of the North Carolina Brigade, was killed leading the attack on that awful first day that had culled so many soldiers from Lee's ranks, minimizing overall chances for success on the afternoon of July 3.[252]

Of course, "The Campbells Are Coming" appealed most to the Scottish soldiers in the Army of Northern Virginia's ranks, and the Scotch-Irish to a lesser degree. Lieutenant Archibald W. McGregor was one such Scottish soldier sacrificed during Pickett's Charge. Appropriately, and just as he would have it, McGregor led a company known as the "Scotch Boys," Company F, Eighteenth North Carolina.[253]

After having ascertained that the weakest point along the Cemetery Ridge line was located at the copse of chestnut oak trees that dominated the right-center, Lee envisioned a carefully coordinated assault to split Meade's army in two. Not unlike on the previous day, Lee's ambitious plan once again went awry, however. Longstreet, desiring to conduct a flank movement around the Round Tops like the day before, was not ready to assault on the early morning of July 3 as planned. And then General Ewell, commanding the Second Corps, struck too early in the predawn hours at the defenders of Cemetery Hill and Culp's Hill, reaping no tactical gains.

Despite these setbacks combined with other ill omens, Lee was not deterred. Most of all, he remained adamantly determined to win the decisive victory that had long eluded him. He therefore continued to prepare for the launch of the massive assault throughout the morning. Fortunately for the men of Pickett's Charge, Ewell's assaults on the north had prevented Meade from dispatching reinforcements south to bolster his weak right-center that remained vulnerable, as Lee had correctly anticipated with tactical clarity. Therefore, this battered section of Cemetery Ridge's lengthy defensive line was vulnerable.[254]

In his journal, and similar to what was witnessed by Lieutenant John Williamson Finley in the ranks of Garnett's Brigade to the left, or north, of Kemper's Brigade, Lieutenant John Edward Dooley Jr. described knowing that the assault was about to begin. He wrote that the troops of Kemper's Brigade watched while "Genls. Lee, Longstreet, and Pickett are advising together and the work of the day is arranged. Soon we are ordered to ascend the rising [western] slope [of Seminary Ridge] and pull down a fence in our front, and this begins to look like work....Again, orders come for us to lie down in line of battle; *that all the cannon* on our side will open at a given signal, will continue for an hour and upon their ceasing we are to charge straight ahead over the open field and *sweep from our path* any thing in the shape of a Yankee that attempts to oppose our progress. This order is transmitted from Regt. To Regt., from Brigade to Brigade, and we rest a long time awaiting the signal" to attack.[255]

MAJOR GENERAL GEORGE EDWARD PICKETT AND MEMORIES OF GLORY IN MEXICO

Assigned to spearheading the massive assault of roughly one third of Lee's Army despite graduating last in his West Point class in 1846 and other troubling signs now ignored, General Pickett hailed from Virginia's Tidewater planter class. Lee and Pickett, who shared Old Dominion cavalier bonds, believed that this was the offensive strike that would save Virginia. Fate and history have merged to earn immortality for Pickett on the afternoon of July 3, as the most important attack in American history became his namesake (although he commanded fewer than half of the attackers). Born in Richmond and of French Huguenot heritage, Pickett was a Virginia gentleman and dandy of the Tidewater planter class and acted accordingly. He had long enjoyed the upper-class status of a member of a privileged neo-feudal and slave-owning society that still looked unfavorably upon the lowly immigrant Irish, who were seen as uneducated newcomers and social inferiors—basically, part of the unwashed masses that had invaded America from foreign shores.[256]

Ironically, the Irish immigrant soldiers of Pickett's Division were not aware that Pickett, as a younger man, had played a key role in sealing the tragic fate of a good many Irishmen much like themselves, including many recent immigrants, during the Mexican-American War. On September 13, 1847, on the outskirts of Mexico City, General Winfield Scott's forces were knocking on the door of the capital after more than a year and a half of America's first foreign war having been fought mostly below the Rio Grande River. The U.S. Army, consisting of both United States regulars and volunteers, had marched inland from Vera Cruz, Mexico, all the way into the lush Central Valley of Mexico.

Protecting the southern approach to Mexico City and standing like a guardian to protect the capital barely two miles away to the northeast was the Castle of Chapultepec, the home of Mexico's Military Academy, which had been transformed into a defensive position. Here, situated atop a commanding two-hundred-foot-high hill amid a sea of flowing cornfields on lower and mostly level ground, was Chapultepec. This sacred hilltop, once the home of Aztec rulers, had to be captured by Scott's troops before Mexico City fell.

Recently taken captive in the bloody defense of the Convent of Churubusco were surviving Irishmen of the St. Patrick's Battalion. Named in honor of Ireland's patron saint, this crack unit consisted of Mexico's elite fighting men, mostly Irish Catholic immigrants who had deserted the U.S. Army largely because of abusive treatment from Irish-hating Protestant officers. They were also motivated in their desertion by the desire to worship Catholicism as they had back in Ireland (not possible in the mostly Protestant U.S. Army, which had no Catholic chaplains). Now, these men mostly from the Green Isle stood in wagons with nooses around their necks on a small hill near the village of Mixcoac. While on their makeshift scaffolds, they faced the imposing heights of Chapultepec. These faithful sons of St. Patrick had fought with distinction against the *norteamericano* invaders, including at the Battle of Buena Vista, under Ireland's emerald green battle flag for the people of Mexico. But like the Republic of Mexico, the ill-fated men never had a chance against a more powerful opponent from the north. These Sons of Erin, who had once worn the uniform of blue, were about to suffer a cruel demise. They had been ordered to be hanged as soon as the Mexican flag, waving proudly from the castle's tower near the eastern edge of the complex that included Mexico's Military College, was lowered by victorious Americans.

As fate would have it, a young lieutenant of the army's newest regiment, the Eighth U.S. Infantry, named George Edward Pickett led the way in the headlong assault toward the castle complex located on its hilltop perch just southwest of Mexico City. He had already been commended for valor in the attack on Churubusco, where most members of the San Patricio Battalion had been captured on August 20, 1847. In one gallant rush through the open fields below the heights, Lieutenant Pickett grabbed the regimental colors from a fallen James Longstreet. After scaling the projectile-swept heights, Pickett lowered the Mexican banner from the flagpole of the tower. He then raised the U.S. colors to the wild cheers of the victors. Garnering laurels, Pickett's battlefield exploits made him famous not only throughout the army but also across the United States.[257]

The red-white-green flag of Chapultepec was lowered on September 13, giving the long-awaited signal to begin an atrocity that shocked the Mexican people and Europeans. The hapless Irishmen—including Francis O'Connor, who had lost both legs at Churubusco—in their stylish Mexican army uniforms (more Napoleonic-influenced than American uniforms) were hung like common criminals. One spunky Irishman, before meeting a grisly death, cursed the U.S. officer in charge of the mass execution and mocked "your dirty old flag." Other doomed Irishmen cheered the courage of the Mexican defenders, including the teenage boy cadets (half a dozen were killed) from the Military Academy, who valiantly defended Chapultepec after older and more seasoned soldiers had fled in panic.

Meanwhile, the execution of thirty unlucky men of St. Patrick's Battalion was unknown to Pickett and other U.S. regulars who stormed the heights of Chapultepec. The Mexican people, including priests who witnessed the mass hanging, and the international community were appalled by the cruelty administered to Mexico's heroes. They protested and lamented the tragic deaths of "our luckless Irish soldiers" whose lives were suddenly ended—like their dream of ever again seeing Ireland.[258]

Clearly, like so many chapters of the tortured course of Irish history, this tragic fate of the Emerald Islanders of the St. Patrick's Battalion mocked the sad adage of "luck of the Irish." Another example of Irish bad luck can be seen in the case of one unfortunate Irishman of the First Virginia, Pickett's Division: Patrick McGee. He deserted his regiment because he wanted to go home, but he was eventually captured and returned to the camp from which he had fled. Made a highly visible example of, the unlucky "Pat" McGee, who might have still spoken with an Irish brogue, was executed by a Confederate firing squad in January 1863.[259]

Some Irish of the Civil War generation still felt shame and embarrassment over the fact that so many Irish had deserted the U.S. Army and fought in the St. Patrick's Battalion, a distinctive Irish unit, not seen in Scott's Army in 1847. This perceived blemish on the Irish character was a factor—although not significant in overall terms and relatively low on a long list—motivating the Irish in gray and butternut (but of course more for Irish Brigade soldiers because they were Irish Catholics like most St. Patrick's Battalion soldiers) to serve with distinction in battling for the Confederacy.[260]

OTHER LEGACIES LINGERED TO cause resentment among the Irish at Gettysburg on July 3. Lieutenant John Edward Dooley Jr. would have been incensed had he known that fellow Emerald Islanders of General Meagher's Irish Brigade had encamped on the grounds of the Jesuit's Georgetown College, where he had attended before the war, not long after reaching Washington, D.C., from New York City.[261]

Ironically, like Pickett's Irish soldiers who now wore crucifixes in the hope that God would protect them in the upcoming attack, the division commander now wore a small crucifix around his neck that had been given to him by a Mexican priest, evidently a member of the Franciscan order. This man of God had long bestowed spiritual faith to Mexico's soldiers, perhaps members of the ill-fated St. Patrick's Battalion, when the Mexican Republic's life had been at stake. General Pickett was given this crucifix by the good priest not long after the capture of Chapultepec, where he had won everlasting fame. Deciding to go into the attack mounted on his warhorse, Pickett would need all the protection he could obtain from every possible source on this afternoon.[262]

While the Irish, especially the Catholics, in the division's ranks would have identified with Pickett now wearing a crucifix for spiritual protection and God's blessings, the Emerald Islanders in gray and butternut would not have relished the thought of the well-mannered Virginian's friendly association with British officers in scarlet uniforms when he had been a young officer stationed in the Washington Territory near Vancouver Island along the Canadian border. Even worse from the viewpoint of the lowly Irish, Pickett was a member of the aristocratic elite, much like these haughty and arrogant English officers, having grown up in the upper class of the Virginia Tidewater. Like the British in general, he and other West Pointers looked at lowly Irish as part of an "inferior class."[263]

Most of all, Pickett was anxious to be unleashed in the attack once the final word was given by Longstreet, who had been delegated this key mission. In one of Gettysburg's ironies, the defensive-minded "Old Pete," as ordered by Lee, was now in charge of orchestrating the largest assault ever unleashed by the Army of Northern Virginia, although he was against the concept of a frontal attack. As mentioned, when a younger man, Longstreet had fallen in the assault up Chapultepec's slope on September 13, 1847, but he handed the regimental colors to young Lieutenant Pickett; the situation somehow almost seemed to seal their fates for the leading roles they were destined to play on July 3. During the march east toward Gettysburg, Pickett had felt the sting of the humiliation of having been ordered to bring up the army's rear.

Therefore, he now sought redemption for himself and his Old Dominion men, and this equated to leading the assault calculated to split the Army of the Potomac in two. Pickett wanted to show what his fresh Virginia division could accomplish before the eyes of Lee, the entire army and the world on this afternoon of decision. As if intent on recapturing his long-lost youth, the long-haired general was determined to relive past glories that included that old "climactic thrill of Chapultepec," when he had been a much different man.[264]

On the left flank of Garnett's Brigade (Pickett's old brigade, known as the "Gamecock Brigade" since the Battle of Seven Pines during the 1862 Peninsula campaign), the Fifty-Sixth Virginia served as a solid anchor on the northern end of Pickett's lengthy assault formation. Irish clans of family members in this excellent regiment included the McAlisters, McCauleys and McGehees (eight McGehee boys in total since the war's beginning, including one wounded and two family members captured at Gettysburg). Among the soldiers of the McCauley kinship group, one member was destined to be wounded and another would be captured on July 3.[265]

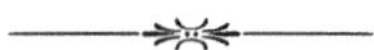

TWENTY-FOUR-YEAR-OLD LIEUTENANT GEORGE WILLIAMSON Finley, who began the war as captain of the Clarksville Blues, now commanded Company K, Fifty-Sixth Virginia. Of Irish heritage, which he still revered, the lieutenant had placed his small pocket Bible over his heart for physical and spiritual protection (a double insurance), trusting in God and hoping for the best. Finley believed that his Holy Bible would shield him from harm in the upcoming attack against the high ground.

As Finley explained,

> *I always carried this little Testament in my inner pocket over my heart. I carried it for three reasons. First, because my wife* [Margaret] *gave it to me. Second, because nothing will give you greater spiritual comfort than a New Testament. And Third, because absolutely nothing will stop a minie ball better than a New Testament! With luck, that rifle ball will enter at the first chapter of Matthew and stop somewhere short of the last chapter of Revelation.*[266]

Consisting of Tidewater soldiers from southeast Virginia, the Fifty-Third Virginia was positioned in the center of Armistead's Brigade of veterans. Like the rest of Pickett's regiments, Irish and Scotch-Irish were heavily represented in the seasoned ranks of the Fifty-Sixth Virginia. Listed as a British subject rather than born in Ireland because of the harsh realities of an earlier conquest by way of Anglo-Saxon imperialism, Private William H. McCabe was one of the Irish teenagers who served in this regiment. Meanwhile, some Fifty-Third Virginia Irishmen who served in the ranks included Private Edward P.W. McComas, an ex-farmer of Company F. He was about to fall wounded in the assault, as was Private John W. McComac of the same company (Edmonds Guards) of Halifax County. Ireland-born

Private Bernard Marron, who had dark hair and eyes and from Halifax County, Virginia, was another Son of Erin, who stood in the lengthy assault formation of the Fifty-Third.

In Company K (the Charles City Guards), Fifty-Third Virginia, Sergeant John McLees had been born in Ireland on June 5, 1833. When only an infant, he had migrated with his parents, Dennis and Sarah Jane Patton McLees, to Brooklyn, New York City, in 1837. In search of a better life, this Irish family then moved south to Charles City, Virginia, in 1852. Here, the blue-eyed and dark-haired John was employed as a stonemason, but the war erupted to change his life forever. John McLees repeatedly proved his abilities on the field of strife, rising to the rank of corporal. Standing taller than his comrades at five feet and nearly ten inches, the Emerald Islander was about to make a good target when advancing through the open fields before Cemetery Ridge.

McLees had already been wounded in the face at Seven Pines, and not far from his home. The wound was slight, and the close call that left facial scars failed to dampen John's enthusiasm to beat the Yankees, especially on Gettysburg's third day. But on this day of destiny, McLees, who had been promoted to sergeant on May 19, was about to receive a far more grievous wound in the assault on Cemetery Ridge.[267]

PETTIGREW'S STOIC SURVIVORS

Although Pickett's Division was ordered to spearhead the assault because it was Lee's only fresh unit, or strategic reserve, the troops of Pettigrew's Division (formerly under General "Harry" Heth until he was wounded on July 1) now stood in lengthy formations on the Virginians' left, to the north. In the frontal assault lines alongside the three brigades of Pickett's Division positioned just to the south, Pettigrew's troops occupied a "post of honor" by their advanced position. Unlike Pickett's Virginians, and as mentioned, Pettigrew's command had been cut to pieces on the first day; the butchery resulted in a staggering loss of as much as 40 percent of the young men and boys who had marched with confidence into Pennsylvania with high hopes.[268]

Nevertheless, these veteran fighting men were durable and resilient, in part because of the command's largely Celtic-Gaelic composition. For such reasons, when Pettigrew's North Carolinians had crossed the Potomac River with a chorus of cheers, the musicians of their brass bands planned favorite tunes that included rollicking Irish songs.[269]

Most important, a good many dependable Irish soldiers filled the formations of Pettigrew's Division at the lower and higher levels. The port of Wilmington, North Carolina, contained the largest number of North Carolina Irish at the war's beginning. As in Pickett's command, Pettigrew's ethnic soldiers drew inspiration and moral strength from analogies to the many heroic struggles for liberty in the Celtic past, especially in regard to fighting against the odds. Of Irish descent, Colonel Robert M. Mayo now led the Virginia brigade known throughout the army as Brockenbrough's Brigade. On Garnett's right, Colonel Birkett D. Fry, of Scotch-Irish descent, commanded his veteran brigade of Tennessee and Alabama troops.

An old Nicaragua filibuster who had served under the deceivingly placid-looking William Walker (the fiercely ambitious, precocious son of a Scotland-born father), who had led the mostly American volunteers of the Army of the Republic of Nicaragua that had included Celtic and Irish volunteers from the United States, Fry now commanded the brigade. This was an opportunity for the Virginia-born Fry, who was also a seasoned Mexican-American War veteran. As mentioned, General James Jay Archer had been captured in the July 1 combat by a strapping Irishman, Private Patrick Maloney, of the Iron Brigade.

Meanwhile, handsome Colonel James Keith Marshall, age twenty-four, led the North Carolina brigade (Pettigrew's old command before his promotion to divisional commander after General "Harry" Heth was wounded on July 1), which was positioned on Fry's left. Of Celtic antecedents going back to Wales (paternal side) and Scotland (maternal side), young "Jimmy" Marshall, a promising Virginia Military Institute graduate, was one of the army's rising stars. He was destined to fatally fall in the upcoming assault.[270]

Hailing from the Virginia aristocracy like Pickett, Marshall was the grandson of Chief Justice John Marshall, who was Thomas Jefferson's cousin. In the beginning of the American Revolution, when the patriotic spirit ran high on the western frontier of Virginia, John Marshall had served as an officer of the Fauquier (County) Rifles. This volunteer company consisted heavily of Scotch-Irish frontiersmen hailing from the western frontier at the foot of the Blue Ridge Mountains in the Culpeper, Virginia area. The Fauquier Rifles became part of the battalion known as the Culpeper Minutemen. These experienced riflemen in hunting shirts carried the famed rattlesnake flag reading "Don't Tread on Me," boasting of a feisty fighting spirit.

Ironically, these western frontiersmen, who were armed with long rifles and looked more like Indian warriors than traditional soldiers, were commanded by William Pickett, an ancestor of General Pickett. If not for this distinguished legacy in the Pickett clan during America's struggle for liberty from 1775 to 1783, young George might never have chosen a military career that led him to West Point, Chapultepec and now the field of Gettysburg. Indeed, from "his earliest years he had been inculcated into the military tradition of 'the Fighting Picketts of Fauquier County.'"[271]

To protect the left of Pettigrew's Division (or the left of Marshall's North Carolina Brigade), Brigadier General Joseph Robert Davis's Mississippi and North Carolina Brigade, Hill's Third Corps, was positioned farthest north. A moon-faced young Irish soldier named Thomas F. McKie, Eleventh Mississippi Infantry, was about to be killed in the upcoming assault, as were a good many other Sons of Erin on the left flank, which was especially vulnerable to enfilade fire from the guns on Cemetery Hill to the northeast.[272]

THE GREAT ARTILLERY BOMBARDMENT

A key component of smashing through Meade's right-center at the copse of trees was the unleashing of the greatest artillery bombardment of the war. Positioned in the center of Kemper's Brigade with his First Virginia in the veteran brigade that occupied the right of Pickett's Division, Lieutenant John Edward Dooley Jr. described the volcanic firestorm that erupted about an hour after noon from the lengthy rows of Confederate artillery pieces, which then garnered the inevitable return fire of the Union artillery from the high ground:

> *the earth, mountains and sky seem to open and darken the air with smoke and death dealing missiles. Never will I forget the scenes and sounds. The earth seems unsteady beneath this furious cannonading.... In one of our Regs. Among the killed and wounded, even before going into the charge, amounted to 88 men; and men lay bleeding and gasping in the agonies of death all around, and we unable to help them in the last* [and] *some companion would raise his head disfigured and unrecognizable, streaming with blood, or would stretch his full length,*

> *his limbs quivering in the pangs of death. Orders were to lie as closely as possible to the ground, and I like a good soldier never got closer to the earth than on the present occasion.*[273]

In the ranks of the Fifty-Sixth Virginia, Garnett's Brigade, Lieutenant John Williamson Finley wrote, "with a great crash and crescendo…every gun on the Confederate line on Seminary Ridge open fire!...Our gunners stood to their pieces and fired peal after peal in salvos. The guns bucked and roared like caged lions, and we could feel the very ground tremble beneath our chests [while] the air was filled with murderous iron. The incoming storm of shot and shell killed or wounded many a man lying face down in the tall grass, and the moans and screams of the wounded and dying mingled with the sound of the tempest" that roared to a level not seen in any previous battle.[274]

Perhaps some Irish defenders in blue poised on Cemetery Ridge still recalled John Mitchel's fiery words that had helped to earn him banishment from Ireland by British authorities: "The people sovereignty—the land and sea and air of Ireland for the people of Ireland—this is the gospel that the heavens and earth are preaching, and all hearts are secretly burning to embrace.…It is the mighty, passionate struggle of a nation hastening to be born into new national life."[275]

And now infused with the heady idealism of Southern nationalism and thoughts about the Irish past, Lee's Irish were now determined to reap a decisive victory with identical idealistic goals in mind: winning the independence of the infant Southern nation.

Meanwhile, Captain Robert A. Bright, one of Pickett's staff members, relayed final instructions to brigade commanders. It was a risky mission, undertaken while riding across open ground under long-range fire of rifled cannon well-positioned atop Cemetery Ridge. After giving the last directives to General Kemper, whose seasoned brigade was positioned on the far right of Pickett's Division on the south, Bright then galloped up north before the lengthy lines of gray and butternut, back to General Pickett. Here, the observant Pickett noticed that the rowel of one of the young captain's brass spurs had been bent by an iron shell fragment. Captain Bright looked down and realized that he just had a narrow escape. Pickett laughed to himself while still in danger in the open field while thinking about "the Irishman's story [another tale that mocked the Irish] that one spur was enough, because if one side of your horse went, the other side would be sure to go also."[276]

Colonel Edward Porter Alexander, meanwhile, busily scanned the ridgetop along Meade's right-center with his binoculars from his perch on the commanding open ground of Seminary Ridge. He had the vital assignment, bestowed by Lieutenant General Longstreet (Lee's most senior corps commander, in charge of orchestrating the assault), to ascertain "the most opportune moment for our attack." Colonel Alexander was concerned about the rapid depletion of a large number of his artillery rounds, which pounded Cemetery Ridge far longer than planned, because Federal artillery in the right-center was not withdrawing as anticipated. Consequently, the native Georgian dispatched a hastily written message to Pickett around 2:30 p.m.: "If you are to advance at all, you must come at once or we will not be able to support you as we ought."[277]

In a hurry, Pickett then rode over to Longstreet to inform him of Alexander's note and to request permission to begin the assault. Young Alexander had quickly followed the first missive with another note when he saw more than a dozen Union guns suddenly withdraw from Meade's right-center, departing the battered crest of Cemetery Ridge. This was a sight that seemed to have fulfilled the artilleryman's chief objective of eliminating Federal guns in the targeted sector and thus considerably enhancing the odds for a successful assault: "The eighteen guns have been drawn off, For Gods sake come on quick or we cannot support you in the assault."[278]

"Old Pete" Longstreet, age forty-two and now gloomy about upcoming developments, was unable to speak in regard to giving the fateful order. He therefore merely nodded his grudging approval that it was now time for the massed concentration of troops to go forward across the shallow valley of open ground (fields and pastures) separating Seminary and Cemetery Ridges.

Not sharing Longstreet's ever-deepening sense of defeatism, Pickett responded with a smart salute and the fateful words, "I am going to move forward, Sir." The finely uniformed Virginian then rode to his anxiously awaiting men. Pickett issued the necessary orders to his staff officers, who galloped forward to inform Generals Kemper, Garnett and Armistead that the time had come to launch the army's greatest assault in its storied history. Shortly, these three experienced brigade commanders barked out orders for their troops, who had already gathered excess gear, such as haversacks and knapsacks, in neat piles to prepare for the attack.[279]

In the center of Kemper's Brigade with the First Virginia stood a good many Irish soldiers, including Lieutenant John Edward Dooley Jr. He

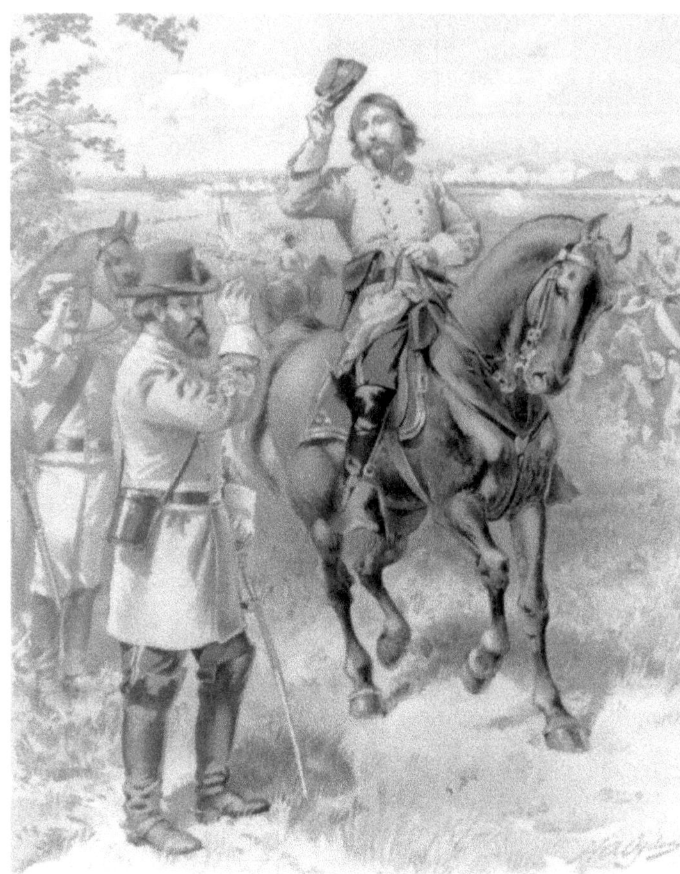

Major General George Pickett received the reluctant orders from Longstreet to launch the great attack. *Courtesy of the Library of Congress.*

described, in a hardened veteran's words, the dramatic moment: "Our artillery has now ceased to roar and the enemy have checked their fury, too. The time appointed for our charge is come [but] there is no romance in making one of these charges [and] when you rise to your feet as we did…the enthusiasm of ardent breasts in many cases *ain't there*, and instead of burning to avenge the insults of our country, families and altars and firesides, the thought is most frequently, Oh, if I could just come out of this charge safely."[280]

Knowing that relatively few men would possibly survive a headlong assault over such a lengthy stretch of open ground, Irish Catholics in gray and butternut crossed themselves in silence, with eyes closed and thinking of loved ones far away, almost as if not wanting to see the grim reality of what lay before them. The Sons of Erin, including those men who still spoke ancient Gaelic, said silent prayers to the revered saints, especially Ireland's patron saint, St. Patrick.

Perhaps, just before the great attack, some Irish soldiers recalled the heroics of America's first martyr, Ireland-born Major General Richard Montgomery, who fell in leading his doomed assault on the mighty fortress city of Quebec in a desperate bid to transform Canada into an American possession, the fourteenth colony. They knew that nothing had been more desperate than that ill-fated assault launched with too few Continental soldiers against a defensive bastion during a raging snowstorm. One of the most desperate attacks faltered when General Montgomery met his tragic end, killed by a hail of canister fired at close range from a cannon. He fell into the snow of a Quebec street on December 31, 1775. This courageous Irishman was the first general killed in the history of the American army. One of America's most promising general officers, Montgomery had been born in County Dublin, Leinster Province, not far from the city of Dublin.[281]

Ironically, to reveal a shared heritage between Irish Confederates and Irish Federals, General Montgomery's heroic legacy equally motivated the Irishmen in blue, especially in the Irish Brigade, which had been bloodied in the vicious struggle for possession of the Wheatfield, located just northwest of Little Round Top, on July 2. Irish Brigade soldiers in cities like Boston, New York City and Philadelphia had rallied to the flag with the cry, "Come, my countrymen, in the name of Richard Montgomery" and in the name of other heroic Irishmen, like Andrew Jackson.[282]

Indeed, from the war's beginning, Irish Brigade men had been posed a simple question and a still inspiring historical example not far from their hearts and minds: "What is asked of an Irishman in this crisis? He is asked to preserve that government which [General Richard] Montgomery died to create."[283] Of course, Lieutenant John Edward Dooley Jr., who now stood in the ranks of the Montgomery Guard (named after General Montgomery, who led an assault that was as desperate as Pickett's Charge), First Virginia, thought differently, as did hundreds of Irish soldiers who were now part of the army's greatest offensive effort.[284]

DESPITE AN INCREASING AMOUNT of foreboding and anxiety, more than twelve thousand young men and boys from across the South were ready to do their duty on this hot early afternoon. What lay before them on this Friday afternoon was a wide stretch of rolling ground that extended for more than twelve hundred yards to Meade's over-extended defensive line that spanned

Cemetery Ridge's length. Realizing that he was about to play a key role in the largest assault he had ever been a member of, Pickett galloped to the front of his lengthy line, which stretched north–south across the high ground of the open crest of Seminary Ridge. Before his ranks of silent and contemplative men, who knew that the long-awaited moment had come at last, Pickett then yelled, "Remember today that you are from Old Virginia!"[285]

Despite the danger of charging Cemetery Ridge, the final order to go forward actually came as a relief to many soldiers in the ranks. In Lieutenant John Williamson Finley's words:

> *The men began to stand up all down the line, and oh, what a relief that was! We had lain under the hot sun under fire so long* [more than two hours] *that we scarcely appreciated the danger. Anything was better than lying under that hot sun and cannon fire any longer.... The drummers* [including Irish musicians] *began to beat the long roll, and the color bearer in each regiment uncased his colors and shook them out. The battle flags blossomed like red and blue flowers all down the Confederate line. Forty two regiments of infantry—forty two battle flags* [including the blue banner of] *the Old Dominion, the Commonwealth of Virginia.... We had lain down in our usual order of battle, so when we stood up we were ready to move forward.*[286]

A large percentage of these men were of Celtic heritage, the sons, grandsons and great-grandsons of Irish immigrants, especially the Ulster Irish, who had been living in the South for two generations before the American Revolution. Some Emerald Islanders were distinguished by especially dark hair, eyes and complexions—the so-called black Irish. These were common characteristics among the people who lived around the ports of Galway and Limerick on the Shannon River, the longest watercourse in Ireland. Black Irish now stood in the ranks, perhaps aware of the old tale that they had descended from Spanish sailors of the Spanish Armada, whose ships had wrecked on the rugged Irish coast.

Most of all, the Irish soldiers of the Army of Northern Virginia knew that what was at stake on this sunny afternoon in Adams County was the very life of their infant nation conceived in revolution. Quite simply, it was now or never for the Army of Northern Virginia and the Southern republic, and these young men and boys instinctively realized as much. Like the army itself, the disproportionately high Irish presence (mostly Scotch-Irish) among the battle-hardened men of Pickett's Charge was most symbolic on this day of decision. This was not an unprecedented representation at a key moment in American history. After all, during the darkest periods of America's struggle for independence, a disproportionate percentage (from 40 percent to 50 percent) of Irish fighting men had served in George Washington's Continental Army, including at the Battle of Trenton, which reversed the war's course by way of a miraculous victory, in the snows of Valley Forge during America's darkest winter of discontent, and during the final showdown at Yorktown.[287]

Unfortunately for Irish souls of Lee's Army just before the assault, no man of God in gray bestowed a general absolution for the final forgiveness of sins in preparation for so many soldiers about to meet their Maker. As mentioned, such a much-needed spiritual gesture on the eve of battle had been granted to the thankful 530 Irish Brigade soldiers on July 2. At that time, they knelt in silent reverence amid a haunting silence while peals of musketry roared in the near distance just before they entered the hellish combat of the Wheatfield. A humble son of an Irish immigrant, Father William Corby was one of the Irish Brigade's most respected men. He stood atop a rocky outcropping to give a general absolution and to inspire the Irishmen to perform their best in the upcoming challenge. From this perch above the bowed troops, and wearing a black clerical suit of clothes as if presenting a sermon at church at a Catholic Cathedral back home in a quieter time of more innocence, Corby granted absolution to the Irish Brigade's veterans now led by Ireland-born Colonel Patrick Kelly.

For the first time in the history of the U.S. Army, a general absolution was granted to soldiers about to go into battle and die for their country: a significant spiritual event that would have shocked the Irishmen of the St. Patrick's Battalion of Mexican-American War fame. On the afternoon of July 3, as mentioned, a comparable general absolution was not granted to the Irish. Consequently, Lee's many Emerald Islanders in the ranks were now on their own in regard to making spiritual preparations, unlike their fellow countrymen of the Irish Brigade on the previous day.[288] These Irish Brigade soldiers had long fought by the Gaelic motto *Riamb nar druid o sbairn lann* ("never retreat from the clash of spears"), and this martial legacy from an ancient warrior ethos had helped to fuel their fighting prowess on July 2. In the same way, the Irish of Pickett's Charge were inspired and motivated to not give up and to fight to their last breath, if necessary, to gain a decisive victory on the afternoon of the third day.[289]

Launching the Civil War's Most Famous Attack

General Pettigrew, commanding the veteran division situated on the left of Pickett's Virginians, and General Pickett, leading his division on the right, spoke well-chosen words of encouragement to their troops now facing their greatest challenge. At long last, Lee's most desperate assault of the war began to slowly roll off Seminary Ridge with a momentum of its own. It then moved over the open fields of summer in lengthy lines that stretched as far as the eye could see.

On the right of Pickett's Division with the Virginians of Kemper's Brigade, Lieutenant John Edward Dooley Jr., First Virginia, described General Kemper's and his officer's attempts to maintain alignment of the ranks and a proper distance from the right of Garnett's Brigade to the north:

> *Onward—steady—dress to the right—give way to the left—steady, not too fast—don't press upon the [brigade's] center—how gentle the slope! steady—keep well in line—there is the line of* [Union] *guns we must take—right in front—but how far they appear! Nearly one third of a mile, off on Cemetery Ridge, and the lines stretches round in almost a semicircle. Upon the center of this we must march. Behind the guns are strong lines of infantry. You may see them plainly and now they see us perhaps more plainly.*[290]

Indeed, in the targeted vulnerable sector at Meade's right-center, which had taken a severe beating in the cannonade, held by the Second Corps, Vermont-born Lieutenant Franklin "Frank" Aretas Haskell, who was fated to die in America's bloodiest war, watched the unbelievable sight in the open fields from Cemetery Ridge: "None on that crest now need to be told that *the enemy is advancing.* Every eye could see his legions, an overwhelming resistless tide of an ocean of armed men sweeping upon us!...The red flags wave [and] they move, as with one soul, in perfect order, without impediment of ditch, or wall or stream, over ridge and slope, through orchard and meadow, and cornfield, magnificent, grim, irresistible."[291]

To the north of Lieutenant Dooley and Kemper's Brigade, Lieutenant John William Finley and his Fifty-Sixth Virginia comrades obeyed what they had been told by their tough "First Sergeants [who] gave the final orders: 'Advance slowly with arms at will. No cheering, no firing, no breaking from common to quick step, dress on the center.'"[292]

The strict discipline and precision of thousands of advancing Rebels was a sight to behold to the Yankees watching from the commanding ground. But what the Union gunners now had before them as far as the eye could see was an artilleryman's dream come true. Along the open crest of Cemetery Ridge, rows of cannon blasted away at the assault formations now exposed in the open.

Caught in the long-range leaden storm, Lieutenant John Edward Dooley described the punishment suffered on the right of Pickett's Division from the rapid fire of Federal artillery, which continuously "belch forth their flame and smoke and storms of shot and shell upon our advancing line; while directly in front, breathing flame in our very faces, the long range of gun which must be taken thunder on our quivering melting ranks. Now truly does the work of death begin [in earnest and] [t]he line becomes unsteady because at every step must be closed and thus from left to right much ground is often lost."[293]

Likewise, Lieutenant Haskell, a former attorney with a promising future if he survived this war (he would not), watched the escalating devastation delivered upon the surging Rebels, who somehow had to be stopped on an afternoon when everything was at stake: "the ability of these two trefoil [Second Corps] divisions to hold the crest and repel the assault depended not only on their own safety or destruction, but also the honor of the Army of the Potomac and defeat or victory at Gettysburg....All our available guns are [ablaze] and from the fire of shells, as the range grows shorter and shorter, they change to shrapnel, and from shrapnel to canister; but in spite of shells, and shrapnel and canister, without wavering or halt, the hardy lines of the enemy continue to move on."[294]

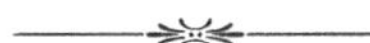

A GOOD MANY IRISH of Company C (Montgomery Guard), First Virginia, steadily moved onward through the storm of projectiles. Irish immigrants and the sons of Celtic-Gaelic immigrants of the Montgomery Guard included not only Lieutenant John Dooley but also a good many other Emerald Islanders who were as determined as this proud citizen of Richmond: Captain James Hallinan, a twenty-one-year-old laborer who had been promoted to a captain's rank in late August 1862; thirty-eight-year-old Sergeant Edward Byrnes, a Richmond mechanic; Sergeant Charles Kean, age thirty-four; a reliable noncommissioned officer who led by example,

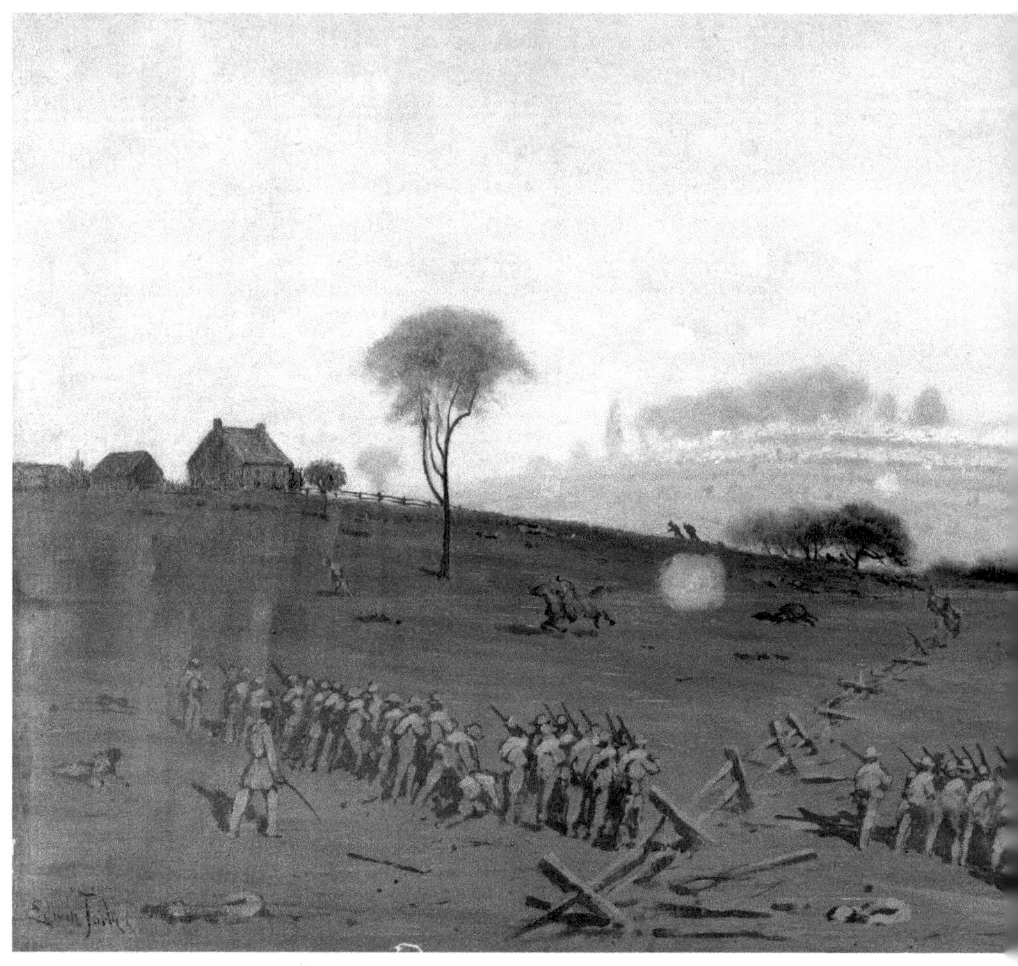

The attackers of Pickett's Charge advance over the wide-open fields, surging over rail fences that had been torn down by skirmishers in preparation for the assault. This is an Edwin Forbes painting from his sketch taken from personal observations of the great attack. *Courtesy of the Library of Congress.*

twenty-eight-year-old Sergeant John Moriarty, a Richmond laborer; and Privates Hillery W. Collins, Benjamin J. McCary, James McCrossen (a twenty-four-year-old laborer), E.R. Maiden (who had enlisted in February 1863), Samuel H. Gillespie and Richard Giles. All of these men of Irish descent were cut down during the assault.[295]

All the while, the extensive span of Confederate linear formations rolled onward with a neat precision. The sight presented an impressive spectacle reminiscent of Napoleon Bonaparte's great assaults that had brought

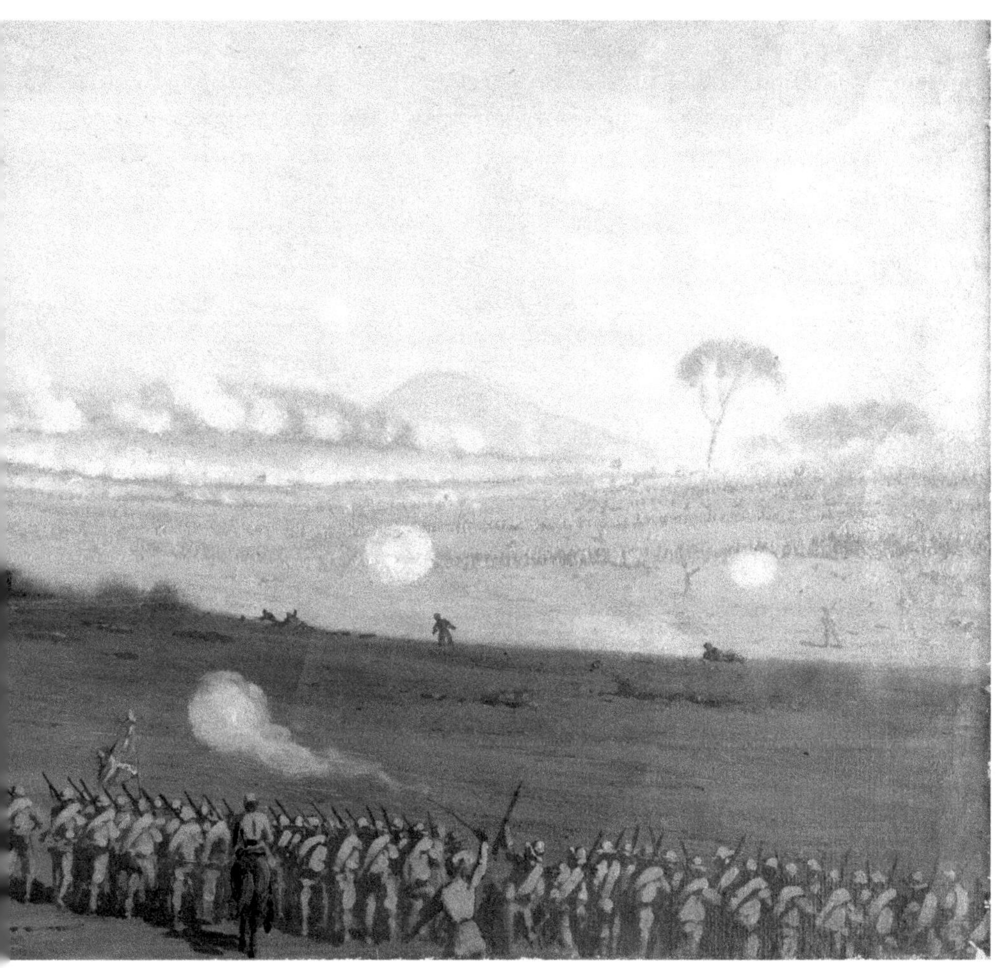

decisive victories on so many European battlefields, except against Great Britain, which had defied him to the bitter end. After fleeing the failed revolution of 1798 and the Emerald Isle, thousands of Irishmen had filled the ranks of Napoleon's army, including the famed Irish Legion. Napoleon's Irish Legion had continued the martial tradition of the "Wild Geese" of exiled Irish soldiers who served with distinction across Europe in armies of Spain and France.[296]

Stretching across the open fields of summer, these Napoleonic-era assault formations of the Army of Northern Virginia presented ideal targets to veteran artillery commanders such as Captain James McKay Rorty. He was a die-hard Irish nationalist and dedicated Fenian (a revolutionary member of the Fenian Brotherhood), whose great dream was focused on liberating the oppressed native homeland. But instead of killing British regulars who had long crushed any hint of an uprising among the common people, Rorty and his artillerymen were now killing their fellow Irish charging across the fields with rapid fire from his well-served cannon of Battery B, First New York Light Artillery.[297]

In the First Virginia's surging ranks in the center of Kemper's Brigade, Lieutenant John Edward Dooley Jr., known as "Gentleman Jack" by his Richmond friends (what now seemed a lifetime ago), was sickened by the sight of the rain of projectiles that cut down additional Irishmen. Officers raised cries of "Close up! Close up the ranks when a friend falls, while his life blood bespatters your cheek or throws a film over your eyes! Dress to the left or right, while the bravest of the brave are sinking to rise no more! Still onward! Capt. [James] Hallinan has fallen and I take his place [but] [s]o many men have fallen."[298]

Like his fellow comrades, Dooley was horrified to see the fall of their revered captain, age twenty-one. Fatally cut down in the killing fields, Captain James Hallinan was a highly respected Son of Erin who had long led the Emerald Islanders of Company C, the Montgomery Guard. Dooley now took the place of his fallen captain, encouraging everyone onward in the nightmarish advance to gain the fiery heights wreathed in smoke before it seemed that everyone would be cut down in the open fields.[299]

In the Fifty-Sixth Virginia's ranks, positioned on the left of Garnett's Brigade, Lieutenant George Williamson Finley felt a strange sense of "inner peace" even while additional comrades fell and projectiles buzzed around him like angry bees. This fine officer of Irish descent recalled what he had recently read from the well-worn pages of his pocket Holy Bible that had long provided so much spiritual comfort to him: "I know whom I have believed and am persuaded that He is able to keep that which I have committed unto Him against that day."[300] And, to Finley, that very day of trials and tribulations was now this awful Friday, after reading the inspirational passages when he had suddenly "opened this little book at random." Finley felt and "somehow knew that everything would be all right."[301]

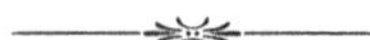

MEANWHILE, REGIMENTAL MUSICIAN RICHARD Roland Carney, age twenty-three and with deep Celtic-Gaelic roots in Emerald Isle soil, continued to move forward at the head of the surging formations of

Armstead's Brigade, which advanced just to the rear of Garnett's Brigade. The Irishman beat his steady, rhythmic cadence so that the Ninth Virginia's veterans, with muskets on their right shoulders, now marched in near perfect step over the flowing fields. An ex-farmer of Company I, the Irish drummer had been wounded in the fighting the previous summer in Virginia, but the memory of that painful injury failed to diminish Carney's assigned duties as a musician playing a part in inspiring the troops onward. Amid the exploding shells hurled from the fast-firing guns of Cemetery Ridge, Carney kept pounding on his drum until he was finally cut down.[302]

Before Armistead's Brigade's formations, the troops of Garnett's Brigade, to Kemper's left, continued to surge ahead with firm discipline and flags waving through the bursting shells and drifting smoke. On Garnett's left, the veterans of the Fifty-Sixth Virginia moved steadily onward while ignoring the shell-fire and fallen comrades who littered the ground in ever-increasing numbers, especially after additional Union artillerymen gained the exact range. Lieutenant John Williamson Finley described the breathtaking sight of a new danger that loomed before the butternut and gray formations spanning across the open fields: "About three quarters of the way out you could see the Emmittsburg [sic] Road in the distance crossing the field. There was a fence that ran alongside the road, and behind that fence you could see the Union skirmish line waiting for us. The bluecoats [including veteran Irish soldiers] were so thickly planted that they looked like a regular line of battle."[303]

Advancing with the Eighth Virginia, Garnett's Brigade, Sergeant Randolph Shotwell described, with a touch of Irish-related humor, the hot firefight with the large number of bluecoat skirmishers who were attempting to slow the sweeping advance through the shallow valley: "we are hotly engaged with the Federal sharpshooters [skirmishers]; firing on Paddy's rule in a 'skirmage'—'Whinever ye see a head, hit for it.'"[304]

Upon nearing the Emmitsburg Road and the slight ridge, where the bluecoat skirmishers were aligned to take advantage of the higher ground, upon which ran the road, Lieutenant John Williamson Finely marveled at the striking difference between the ragamuffin attackers and the well-uniformed Yankee skirmishers. "I was struck by the appearance of that [most advanced] Union infantry [because] [e]very man dressed like each other [and] [e]ach man clutching a shiny, new Springfield [.58 caliber] rifle-musket [and] [y]ou could see the sunlight gleaming on the barrels. The bluecoats represented all the wealth and power and might of the Federal government [while among the attackers] [n]o two dressed alike. Some of them bare footed [and] [m]any of them wearing butternut trousers."[305]

All the while, the large numbers of Pickett's Irish soldiers continued relentlessly toward Cemetery Ridge and seemingly destiny itself, including the Charlottesville Irish of Company F (Montgomery Guards), Nineteenth Virginia, Brigadier General Richard B. Garnett's Brigade. Captain Bennett Taylor, a former teacher of age twenty-four, commanded this excellent Emerald Isle company. Captain Taylor was about to fall wounded; capture awaited him. Symbolically, in what the South now considered the Second American Revolution, Taylor was a descendant of Thomas Jefferson of Monticello, the picturesque hilltop nestled in the Virginia Piedmont where Taylor was destined to find a final resting place.

Quite a few Company F Irish were skilled in a single occupation other than farmer, the most common occupation of the enlisted ranks. The company of the Nineteenth Virginia contained a disproportionate number of carpenters, men who had once worked with their skilled hands for a livelihood, creating wooden products of beauty. Those hands were now bent on destruction. These former carpenters, who marched toward Cemetery Ridge, of Irish descent, included Sergeant Abram S. McLain (age twenty-four) and Privates Philip Kennedy (thirty-one) and Charles McDonald (thirty). Some of the Nineteenth's former carpenters would never work with wood again after this afternoon in hell.

Meanwhile, additional numbers of Irish soldiers were cut down, including Lieutenant James Davis McIntire, a twenty-year-old former clerk, and Private Edward J. Herndon, a twenty-two-year-old carpenter. Herndon fell then later lost a leg by amputation. He died on July 10 after an agonizing ordeal. Company H (Jeff Davis Guard) was another heavily Irish company of the Eleventh Virginia, under Major Otey Kirkwood, who was about to fall wounded in the attack. These seasoned Irishmen hailed mostly from Lynchburg and the surrounding area of western Virginia, where they had long worked as railroad laborers and rail hands, making a living from the ample number of jobs supplied by the railroad. Private Cyrus Fitzgerald, a twenty-two-year-old farmer; Sergeant Henry Doyle, a printer; and Corporal John P. Daniel, a laborer of twenty-four, were Irishmen who served Company H's ranks and fought for what they believed was right. Daniel was fated to be badly wounded, losing two legs to amputation, and he died a painful death far from home before the end of July.[306]

In the surging ranks of Pettigrew's Division, which advanced on the left of Pickett's Division and now featured the youngest brigade commander

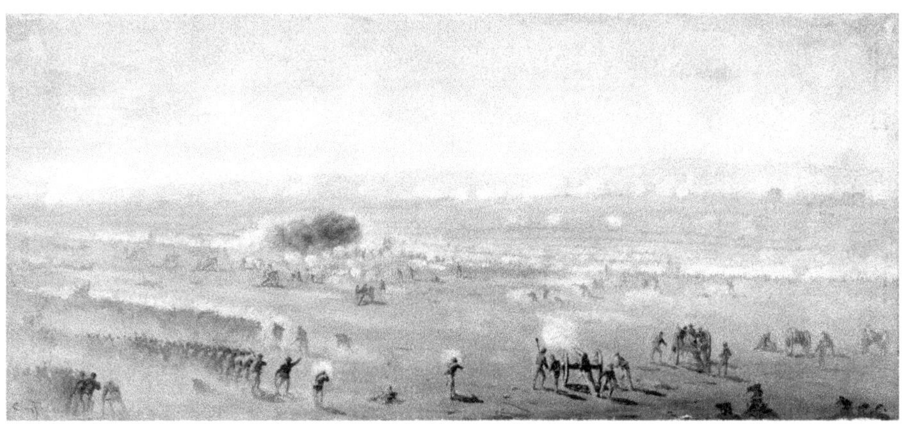

View of the zenith of Pickett's Charge from the Federal side, while the combat rages in and around the clump of trees located near the crest of Cemetery Ridge. *Courtesy of the Library of Congress.*

leading the way in the front ranks of Pickett's Charge north of Pickett's Division, mounted Colonel "Jimmy" Marshall continued to encourage his four North Carolina regiments forward. As fate would have it, he was only one day removed from the three-year anniversary of the most important day of his young life, when he had graduated with distinction from the Virginia Military Institute. This former commander of the Fifty-Second North Carolina, advancing on the brigade's far right, encouraged his Tar Heels forward while mounted and wearing a resplendent gray uniform, as General Pettigrew had earlier implored to inspire his troops onward into the din with the cry, "for the honor of the good Old North State."[307]

The advancing veterans of Company F, Eighteenth North Carolina, were known as the "Scotch Boys" because of their distinctive Celtic heritage. These Celts had been organized by Captain Charles Malloy of Irish descent, but they were now led by Lieutenant Archibald "Archie" McGregor. He descended from the McGregor clan of Scotland. McGregor encouraged his men forward in a desperate bid to gain Cemetery Ridge or die in the attempt. Fated to be shortly killed while at the head of his Scotch Boys, he yelled while waving his saber before his men: "Hurrah for Dixie! Follow me, boys. Let us show them what we can do."[308] One soldier never forgot the inspiring sight of this dynamic Celtic officer in the heat of combat. In his opinion, "none responded with more alacrity than did Lt. McGregor," who had risen magnificently to the challenge of taking the strategic high ground at any cost.[309]

Irish of the Forgotten Tennessee Brigade

Perhaps the most forgotten troops of Pickett's Charge hailed from the Volunteer State. They were forgotten especially because of the longtime obsessive focus of generations of historians and writers, especially from Virginia, on General Pickett and his Virginians, almost as if no other attackers existed. Advancing on the far right of Pettigrew's Division and to the left of Garnett's Virginians to the south, the so-called Tennessee Brigade was a unique combat unit on a number of levels. Containing six companies of Wilson County boys, the Seventh Tennessee advanced across the open fields under the blazing early July sun and hot fire from not only Cemetery Ridge in front but also flank fire from East Cemetery Hill to the north.

A good many Irish and Scotch-Irish served in the Lebanon Greys (from Lebanon, Tennessee, located just east of Nashville) and Wilson Blues (from Wilson County, Tennessee): the nucleus of the Seventh Tennessee. Significantly, a large number of these men of Company H and K were of Scotch-Irish descent. In more peaceful days, some of these soldiers, who traced their ancestry to Ulster Province, had attended the Presbyterian school at Cumberland University, established in 1842. Cumberland University boys also served in other regiments of the Tennessee Brigade, including the Fourteenth Tennessee, which was fated to lose half of its strength during the nightmarish combat at Gettysburg.[310]

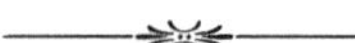

Advancing across the meadows and fields donned in bright summer hues, which lay between the two parallel ridges (Seminary and Cemetery Ridges), the lengthy Confederate assault lines made ideal targets for the fast-firing Union cannon not only along Cemetery Ridge's crest but also on Little Round Top to the south. From the rocky summit of this commanding perch situated just to the north of Big Round Top, long-range rifle artillery pieces—10-Pounder Parrotts—unleashed a terrible flank fire that swept the surging ranks exposed in the open.

In the Fifty-Sixth Virginia, George Williamson Finley described the living nightmare:

> *we passed the center of the* [wheat] *field, the Union artillery on Little Round Top off to our right began to open fire on us. Shells poured down upon us, and as they descended they shrieked and screeched and hissed like frightened birds. The first shell landed in Company A* [Mecklenburg Guards]. *It knocked six men down and scattered them about like so many rag dolls* [while] [t]*he second shell landed in Company D* [Buckingham Yancey Guards]. *It knocked five men down. The third shell struck on the extreme right of Company H* [White Hall Guards under Captain James C. Wyant, in his first battle as company commander]—*the largest company in the regiment—37 men. All 37 men were swept away by a single shell.*[311]

Upon advancing closer to the Emmitsburg Road line with high fences on both sides, an even hotter rifle fire from the Union skirmishers was poured forth to inflict even greater damage. Lieutenant Finley wrote, "enemy fire grew hotter and faster [and] bullets buzzed about our ears like angry hornets. The air was so full of flying lead that you could raise your hand above your head and catch a bullet. Men were falling from the ranks as a cart spills meal."[312]

Finley marveled at the courage of the primary leaders of the charge, especially the mounted General Richard B. Garnett—not General Pickett, who lingered behind his surging ranks. Out in front just north of Kemper's Brigade, the handsome general, born at the family's "Rose Hill" estate in Essex County, Virginia, in 1817 and a West Pointer (class of 1841), implored his troops to maintain their discipline under the steady pounding, "Steady men. Steady. Save your strength for the end."[313]

All the while, the killing not only continued unabated across the open fields, it also increased to higher levels. As Lieutenant Finley lamented, "By this time men were falling like stalks of grain before the grim reaper, but there was never a pause in that slow and steady movement" toward the flaming crest of Cemetery Ridge.[314]

"As we approached the fence at the Emmittsburg [sic] Road, the Union skirmishers pulled back, ran up the hill, jumped down behind the stone wall, and rejoined their comrades" to add strength to the formidable defensive position located just below the crest of Cemetery Ridge, wrote the lieutenant of Irish descent.[315]

At this time, the large number of Irish and Scotch-Irish soldiers had no idea that they were now pushing across the picturesque farmlands owned by a French immigrant named Nicolas Codori. Codori now lived on York

Street in Gettysburg, renting out the stately house located on the east side of the Emmitsburg Road. The renters who now occupied the house were an Irish family, John and Talithia Reily. On this afternoon, the fine house of this family was engulfed by the tide of disciplined Virginians of Pickett's Division, which flooded around both sides of the structure as the attackers closed in on Meade's right-center, which had been severely punished by the Confederate cannonade.[316]

MEANWHILE, THE IRISH OF the Sixty-Ninth Pennsylvania of Brigadier General Alexander Webb's Second Brigade, Brigadier General John Gibbon's Division, Second Corps, which was under the extremely capable Major General Winfield Scott Hancock, remained firmly in position behind the stone wall on the sloping ground (the ridge's western slope) just before Cemetery Ridge's crest. Defending home soil, the troops of the Philadelphia Brigade were saddled with the heavy responsibility of defending the Angle, located just north of the copse of trees. But the veteran Irishmen of the Sixty-Ninth Pennsylvania were in the forefront.

These experienced Emerald Islanders were aligned just to the south of young Lieutenant Alfonso Hersford Cushing's two most advanced guns of Battery A, Fourth United States Artillery, positioned inside the Angle. These two cannon, three-inch Ordnance Rifles were, like the battery's other guns, well manned by the gunners of the Wisconsin-born, twenty-two-year-old West Pointer (class of 1861, like George Armstrong Custer, also of part Irish descent). Just in time to greet the attackers, they had been pushed down the slope nearly to the stone wall for a better field of fire. Meanwhile, the battery's other four cannon were poised to the right rear, higher up the slope and near the open crest that was now the most strategic ground on the Gettysburg battlefield.

At this time, the troops of the Seventy-First Pennsylvania were aligned near the crest to the Sixty-Ninth Pennsylvania's right-rear, while the Seventy-Second was positioned as a strategic reserve behind the clump of trees now in full summer foliage. Without wavering or panicking, these Pennsylvanians, sweating and with dry mouths, gamely held their ground while the seemingly endless number of Confederates advanced ever closer.

Shouting encouragement to his Irish soldiers in blue and reminding them to perform at their best this afternoon, Colonel Dennis O'Kane had been born in Tireighter Townland Park Village Claudy, County Derry, north Ireland, in 1818. He had long worshiped at St. Mary's Catholic Church before immigrating to America and starting anew in a strange land. O'Kane now commanded the Sixty-Ninth Pennsylvania, known as "Paddy Owen's Regulars" and the "Irish Volunteers." Hailing from tough Irish neighborhoods and ethnic enclaves in Philadelphia, these highly motivated Sons of Erin (especially when defending Pennsylvania soil of the adopted homeland) were positioned to protect a key strategic point that General Lee had targeted as the best place to achieve a dramatic breakthrough of lines of blue.

Holding firm while thousands of screaming Rebels poured toward them, these Philadelphia troops were now the primary force of infantry that protected the half dozen rifled pieces of Lieutenant Cushing's field pieces of Battery A, Fourth U.S. Artillery, located inside the Angle. Only age twenty-two, the Wisconsin-born Lieutenant Cushing was performing beyond the call of duty and experiencing his finest day, one that eventually earned him a Medal of Honor. Here at the Angle, which contained Cushing's fast-firing guns that were in exactly the right place at the right time, the stone wall of whitish limestone turned east over the open ground toward the open crest before again continuing north up Cemetery Ridge and parallel to the strategic crest.

Major James Duffy, a fierce Irish nationalist, was a principal Irish leader of the Sixty-Ninth Pennsylvania and its 292 fighting men, who were determined to hold firm to the strategic high ground at all costs. Symbolically, this fine regiment's nucleus had been founded on prewar Irish militia units such as the Hiberian Greens. These ethnic units were first formed in the 1850s to protect the Irish people from Irish-hating Americans, especially the so-called Nativists. Relying on brute force and the ugliest form of racism rather than mere hate-filled rhetoric, the Nativists (mostly Anglo-Saxons) wanted no Irish presence on American soil to stain the United States' name, which the Sons of Erin now fought at Gettysburg to save. A good many of these men in blue were still passionate Irish nationalists who even now lusted for Ireland's liberation.

Now positioned nearest to the Angle, Company I, Sixty-Ninth Pennsylvania, anchored the regiment's right flank on the far north of the thin defensive line. Captain Michael Duffy now led the boys of Company I with his usual skill. He was ably assisted by a number of no-nonsense Irish sergeants who led by example and exerted profound influence among the enlisted ranks. Providing solid leadership were Sergeant William Richardson, age twenty-three, born in County Derry; Patrick McMahon, the oldest sergeant at twenty-eight; Christian Rooney, age twenty-five; Joseph Garrett; and James Tooney. During this crisis situation, when so much was at stake, they inspired their fellow Irishmen, like printers Private Frank McClarren and Ireland-born Thomas Flynn, to hold their ground against the onslaught while thousands of Rebels drew closer with blue and red battle flags flapping in the sunlight. As fate would have it, the Sixty-Ninth Pennsylvania, especially Company I on the far right, was about to become the eye of the storm.

After having been swept by the intense artillery barrage from Seminary Ridge, the Irish from the Keystone State were eager to reap a measure of revenge; they had suffered losses and survived a harrowing ordeal. In Company A, under the command of Irish Captain John McHugh, Private John Harvey Jr., was struck in the head by an iron shell fragment. Fortunately for him, Private John Harvey Sr., was nearby to rush to his assistance and help to bandage his son's bloody head.[317]

Leading the Fifty-Sixth Virginia of Armistead's Brigade, meanwhile, Colonel William Dabney Stuart continued to inspire his well-disciplined regiment farther across the pastures and fields, plunging ever deeper into the leaden storm. He had a bright future, having graduated third in his 1850 class at Virginia Military Institute. Stuart's intellectual gifts allowed him to become an assistant professor of mathematics and instructor of tactics at VMI. He then served as the headmaster of classical studies in Washington, D.C., and later took a comparable position at a school in Richmond. Despite outstanding success in his professional and personal life, Colonel Stuart never forgot that his grandfather, Archibald Stuart, had departed Ireland to escape the Old World's corruption and abuses. The father of two sons and a daughter, Colonel Stuart, thirty-three, who might have seen himself as a modern Virginia Achilles given his love of the ancient classics, especially the heroic story of the stoic Greek warriors of the *Iliad*, was about to receive a mortal wound at the head of his troops.[318]

Other Celtic-Gaelic soldiers of the Fifty-Sixth Virginia about to fall in Gettysburg's holocaust included the following good fighting men: Private Robert W. McCauley, who was destined to be captured and die in a dirty Maryland prison; Private George V. McGehee; Sergeant Leonidas J. Gee, who was mortally wounded; and his brother Private Benjamin C. Gee, who was killed in the leaden tempest that survivors never forgot.[319]

GREATER DESTRUCTION AT THE FENCES OF THE EMMITSBURG ROAD

The only physical obstacles on the open ground for the men of both frontline divisions of Pickett's Charge were the two high rail fences that lined both sides of the north–south Emmitsburg Road, which led northeast to Gettysburg's southern end. Therefore, a nasty surprise greeted the brown and gray tidal wave of panting Rebels when they finally gained the dusty road that ran along the shallow ridge that also pointed toward the town. Lieutenant George Williamson Finley described the shock that was so fatal to so many young men and boys at this crucial point, while under a severe fire from Cemetery Ridge's defenders: "When we got to the fence at the [road], we discovered to our horror that what we thought was going to be another worm fence [as in Virginia and across the South] was instead [more sturdy] post and rail. That Pennsylvania Dutch [German] farmer had dug post holes alongside the road, sunk upright posts in the holes, cut slots into the tops of the posts, and fitted them with slatted boards." This method created a more formidable obstacle for the already weary infantrymen.[320]

Consequently, "we had to climb the fence to get to the enemy! Men were falling all around us, and cannons and muskets were raining death upon us."[321] However, once over the high board-and-rail fences, the ranks were hurriedly reformed by the survivors, who remained under an intense fire. Clearly, a remarkable level of discipline was displayed by these veteran soldiers at this especially fatal point, while additional comrades fell beside them.

Then, after the reformed troops unleashed a cheer, the charge continued in the determined bid to reach Cemetery Ridge before too many soldiers were shot down. Although relatively gentle just beyond the fence lining the road, the open slope beyond, or east of, the Emmitsburg Road became steeper and more difficult to charge up for weary soldiers, who were now sucking for air in the afternoon heat during the deadly race to reach Cemetery Ridge's strategic crest before losses eliminated any chance for a decisive breakthrough on Meade's right-center. Atop the slope stood the clump of trees situated just below the Angle, crowning the crest of the open ridge and looking like a green beacon to the attackers surging up Cemetery Ridge's western slope.

Leading the Fifty-Sixth Virginia, Lieutenant George Williamson Finley, the never-say-die Irish American officer who was highly respected throughout the command, described the strategic objective for which so many lives had already been lost:

> *And on the other side* [east] *of the Emmittsburg* [sic] *Road the ground rose up gently to other high ground called Cemetery Ridge. There was a long stone wall or fence that ran along the top of the ridge* [and] *in the center of the line the wall made a sharp, right angle turn* [the Angle]. *There was a grove of umbrella shaped trees inside the angle* [and earlier] *Colonel Stuart pointed* [with his VMI saber] *towards the trees at the center of the wall and said in a loud voice, 'Men, you see that wall there? It's full of Yankees. I want you to help take it.'"*[322]

(William Dabney Stuart, of the Virginia Military Institute, class of 1850, and a former Richmond teacher and school official, was about to fall mortally wounded.)

But of course, the most daunting challenge for the attackers, who had already suffered high losses in charging across such a wide stretch of open ground, was reaching the strategic crest. Some Irish Yankees now defending Cemetery Ridge had been recruited to serve their country after having read recruitment posters that compared the Confederacy to Ireland's ancient enemy, England: "The Cotton Lords and Traitor Allies of England Must be Put Down!"[323] Such emotional anti-England appeals caused Irish brothers to serve on opposite sides and die in different colored uniforms. Ironically, as if arranged by a vengeful English God, the Irish brothers' war was now being played out in full in the struggle for possession of this strategic point on Meade's right-center.[324]

In the Irish ranks of the Montgomery Guard, First Virginia, who advanced in the center of Kemper's Brigade, Lieutenant Dooley described the desperate situation upon nearing the flame-lined crest that had to be captured at all costs:

> *On! men, on! Thirty more yards and the runs are ours; but who can stand such a storm of hissing lead and iron? What a relief if earth, which almost seems to hurl these implements of death in our faces, would open now and afford a secure retreat from threatening death. Every officer is in front* [and General] *Garnett on the right, Kemper in the center and Armistead on the left; Cols., Lieut. Cols., Majors, Captains, all press on and cheer the shattered lines.*[325]

Perhaps, at this critical moment, some Irish members of the Montgomery Guard, First Virginia, still recalled the stirring battle cry of "Remember Limerick!," which had fueled the successful bayonet charge of the Irish

Brigade, French Army, that won the day at the Battle of Fontenoy (Belgium). It was this dramatic victory that became a legend to generations of Irish, especially impassioned nationalists and including the large number of Irish soldiers now charging toward Meade's weakened right-center.[326]

Most devastating of all, the blasts of canisters erupting from the cannon's mouths knocked down clumps of attackers as they neared Cemetery Ridge's crest, cutting men down like a giant scythe. Lieutenant Finley, Company K (Harrison's Guards), Fifty-Sixth Virginia, described the horror: "Canister turned a cannon into a giant shot gun on wheels [and was] so devastating against infantry [that they] called it 'canned hellfire'."[327]

In front of the First Virginia, in his first battle since enlisting in November 1862 and carrying the colors to inspire his comrades even farther up the bullet-swept slope amid the drifting smoke, teenager "Willie" Mitchel was hit. But he refused to go rearward to the field hospital, as expected of him. He wanted to stay beside his friends and the hard-hit regiment while they were going for broke. Willie ignored the painful wound and mustered his remaining strength, continuing up the ridge's western slope. Seemingly on the strength of willpower alone, the young man from Richmond surged even farther into the tempest that so rapidly consumed lives of the best and brightest of Pickett's Division. A fellow member of the regimental color guard, which had been decimated by this time, realized the ugly truth as a second bullet found its target, when he saw that "Willie clasped his hand over his abdomen, showing he had been wounded fatally."[328] The promising youngest son of the South's leading Irish nationalist and revolutionary had been "shot through the lower part of the abdomen… and fell near the breastworks," or stone wall, that stood just below the crest and protected a blazing line of bluecoats, who continued to blast away with desperation.[329]

Meanwhile, to the left of Garnett's Brigade, Pettigrew's troops—including cooks and walking wounded who had been added to the ranks at the last minute for this one supreme offensive effort—of the assault's left wing continued through exploding shells and gunfire to keep pace with Pickett's Virginians on their right. So far, only Brockenbrough's brigade of Virginians, which had suffered severely on July 1, advanced on the far left flank of the attack to the north that had early faltered. On what was certainly not the Old Dominion's finest day in this northernmost sector, Brockenbrough's Virginia soldiers failed to match the determination of their comrades on the opposite flank, Pickett's troops, who were serving as the assault's spearhead to the south.

But this was not completely the Virginians' fault, because this small brigade had early on fallen under a severe flank fire of cannon from the north from first Cemetery Hill's well-positioned artillery and then an enfilade explosion of musketry had then erupted from the advanced ranks of the Eighth Ohio Volunteer Infantry. However, Davis's steady Mississippi and North Carolina Brigade had quickly replaced Brockenbrough's shell-shocked men in protecting Pettigrew's extremely vulnerable left flank, which then continued onward to make up for the hard-hit Virginia brigade's systemic collapse. Therefore, the attackers north of Pickett's Division now advanced in conjunction with those attackers on the south.

Courageous leaders, like General Pettigrew, steadily led the onrushing troops of their division, and Colonel Marshall, who was still leading his North Carolina Brigade, continued to inspire troops toward the strategic crest. Because these two dynamic officers were mounted and leading the way across open ground, it was only a matter of time before the inevitable projectile struck home to eliminate one or both of them. Indeed, Marshall was shortly wounded and knocked off his horse by a shell burst, but he quickly remounted to continue leading his men toward the blazing crest. The young colonel's inspiring example played a role in keeping the assault's left wing moving relentlessly through the hail of lead, with battle flags waving through the drifting smoke. Like Pickett's men, Pettigrew's troops were under orders not to fire until they gained an advanced point very close to the strategic crest of the open ridge, and these strict directives were obeyed: a demonstration of a remarkable measure of discipline while under a murderous fire.

Most important, Pettigrew's men had likewise succeeded in getting over the two fatal post-and-rail fences that proved so formidable and time-consuming for breathless men. After crossing the fences, they, like the Virginians to the south, hurriedly realigned and then surged up the ridge's western slope in alignment with Pickett's advancing troops, despite a good many officers and men cut down at the dual wooden obstacles on both sides of the dusty road. Tempting fate in leading the way for such a long distance and so close to the Federal defensive line that now seemed all ablaze, Colonel Marshall was killed when he was hit by two bullets in the forehead. Young Marshall fell from his horse, ending a most promising career when he dropped lifeless on Pennsylvania soil. After losing their respected commander, the North Carolina troops of Marshall's brigade surged up the slope with renewed vigor as if motivated to avenge their colonel's fall. Despite panting for wind and drenched in sweat, they raced toward the stone wall of white rocks north of the Angle without order but, more important, with great determination. Meanwhile, the erudite General Pettigrew, now on foot after his horse had been shot from under him, encouraged everyone onward and farther into hell itself, because so much was at stake this afternoon.[330]

Before the expansive formations of the steadily advancing North Carolinians and positioned behind the stone wall along the ridge about six hundred feet north of the clump of trees, an especially defiant Irish commander implored his men to hold firm against the onslaught. Brigadier General Thomas Alfred Smyth, born on the Emerald Isle, and his veterans of the 1st Delaware (his old regiment), 12th New Jersey, 14th Connecticut, and the 108th New York were ready to greet the onrushing Rebels with especially close-range fire. Commanding the Second Brigade, Second Corps, General Smyth was a fine commander and every inch a fighter, as recently demonstrated in the brutal combat that had swirled through the dark forests of Chancellorsville. He was exactly the kind of dynamic Irish leader who was needed to face the massive onslaught of seemingly innumerable attackers who seemingly could not be stopped.

The capable Smyth had immigrated to New York City in 1854 to begin his life anew, never again seeing his picturesque Celtic-Gaelic homeland across the sea. The hard-fighting general was destined to fall wounded on this afternoon of decision while defending his perch against a fierce onslaught of fanatical Rebels. Often overlooked in the story of Pickett's Charge, this dark-haired Irish general was a key reason why his troops—Second Brigade of Brigadier General Alexander Hays's Third Division of Major General Winfield Scott Hancock's Second Corps—held firm and fought so well on this afternoon. However, a cruel fate dogged this brave Irishman in the years ahead, when his luck finally ran out. Thomas Alfred Smyth was fated to be the last Union general killed in the war. He fell to rise no more on the Palm Sunday that General Lee surrendered the Army of Northern Virginia at Appomattox Court House on April 9, 1865.[331]

All the while from the commanding heights of Cemetery Ridge, General Smyth watched the steady advance of Pettigrew's troops, who continued to surge onward as if nothing in the world could stop them. However, because Pettigrew's Division had lost about 40 percent of its strength in the first day's combat northwest and west of Gettysburg, Lee was now forced to depend more on Pickett's fresh troops, because they had been spared the nightmarish bloodletting of the first and second days. In this sense, Pickett's three Virginia brigades were fulfilling the traditional role of a strategic reserve in now spearing the assault in Lee's final bid to win it all.

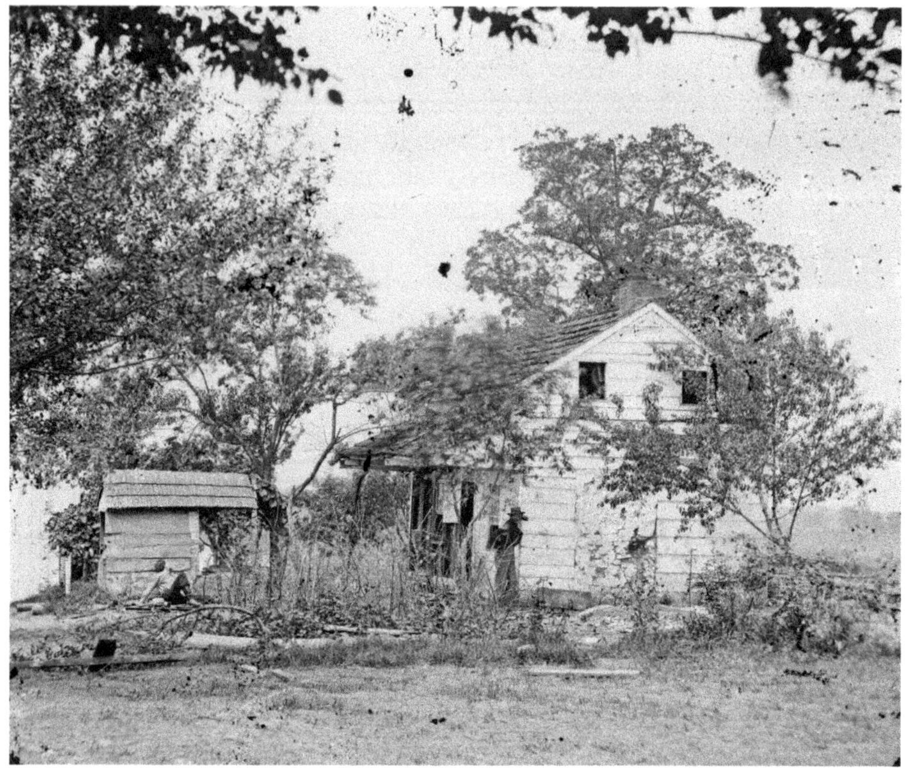

The small wooden house of the free black family of Abram Bryan located at the defensive sector of Meade's Cemetery Ridge line north of the clump of trees and the Angle. *Courtesy of the Library of Congress.*

As fate would have it, the mini–civil war among the Irish was played out in full on this dramatic stage of Pickett's Charge. Of Irish descent, George Williamson Finley described how the high ground that loomed before his Fifty-Sixth Virginia comrades, who continued to advance on the left of Garnett's Brigade, was defended by "the men of the Philadelphia Brigade" under the command of Brigadier General Alexander Stewart Webb. Most important, the combat prowess of the Philadelphia Brigade (Second Brigade, Brigadier General John Gibbon's Second Division of Hancock's Second Corps) was considerable increased by the veteran Irish fighting men of the Sixty-Ninth Pennsylvania Volunteer Infantry. They were determined to do or die this afternoon. [332]

But what most astounded the attacking Irish of Pickett's Division was the sight of the green flag of Ireland waving through the drifting palls of smoke on the strategic crest of Cemetery Ridge! In some astonishment, Lieutenant

Finley wrote, "69th Pennsylvania had a Stars and Stripes flag, but it was proudest of its own special regimental flag of green silk. There were three things on the green field: [an Irish] round tower, [an Irish] sunburst, and [an Irish] wolf to show that the regiment was solidly Irish."[333]

Indeed, in part because of the inspirational Irish legacies of this green flag and the memories of heroic Irish warriors of old, the Philadelphia Brigade's soldiers gamely stood firm behind the wall of stone with grim determination. Positioned just below the copse of trees, adjacent to Lieutenant Alonzo Hersford Cushing's guns of Battery A, Fourth United States Artillery (part of the Second Corps' Artillery Brigade) situated on the north side of the clump of trees and bolstering the left of the Philadelphia Brigade, the five guns of Scotland-born Captain Andrew Cowan inflicted severe punishment on the attackers, especially on Pickett's right.

Meanwhile, one of Cowan's field pieces of the Sixth Corps Artillery Brigade bellowed fire from a position behind the wall of white stones just north of the clump of trees. Hardworking New York Irishmen, like "that 'wild Irishman' Mike Smith" and Private Jacob McIlroy, who shortly fell when shot in the head, cut down additional Virginia attackers with each blast from the fast-firing guns of the First New York Independent Battery. Capable Irish lieutenants, like Milton A. Kinney and Peter Kelly, also provided Cowan with invaluable support in this crisis situation. These guns, fired by cannoneers mostly from Cayuga County in Upstate New York, helped to bestow greater confidence to the Irish soldiers of the Philadelphia Brigade to stand fast in the face of the onslaught. Young Cowan, born in Ayshire, Scotland, displayed dynamic leadership and a bold example to encourage his artillerymen. He kept his New York boys busily loading and firing at a rapid rate, blasting away at the attacking Rebels—too many to miss at such close range.[334]

Behind the stone wall that lay just below the smoke-wreathed crest, the troops of the Philadelphia Brigade's reserve, the Sixty-Ninth Pennsylvania, under Colonel Dennis O'Kane (born in County Derry, Ulster Province) waited for the arrival of the screaming attackers who continued charging up the grassy slope with wild abandon. If the howling Rebels broke through the first thin blue line positioned along the stone wall that paralleled Cemetery Ridge's crest, then it would be up to the mostly Sons of Erin of the Sixty-Ninth Pennsylvania to plug the gaping hole before it was widened and led to disastrous results.

In Colonel O'Kane's Sixty-Ninth Pennsylvania, Ireland-born Corporal John Cassidy was one of the many Sons of Erin who stood firm while awaiting the seemingly overpowering Confederate onslaught, when nerves were especially taut and tension high at Meade's targeted right-center. The Irish corporal—as tough as any sergeant—felt some comfort in the fact that he still possessed his small prayer book given to him by the regiment's Catholic chaplain on June 27, 1862, at Poolsville, Maryland. It was now positioned in his breast pocket in protective fashion. Providing solace in such a deadly and crucial time, the prayer book was entitled *The Manual of the Christian Soldier*. Ironically, Cassidy was indeed a Celtic-Gaelic holy warrior who was just like the large number of Irish now surging ever closer to Meade's severely battered right-center with a determination to split the Army of the Potomac in half.[335]

Surprise Union Flank Attack

Meanwhile, the troops of a green Vermont Brigade, under General George Jerrison Stannard, performed like veterans on this day of destiny, delivering a hot flank fire to enfilade the right flank of Kemper's Brigade from the south. Aligned along a lengthy rail fence and with their muskets resting on wooden rails for "perfect aim," the "Green Mountain Boys" of the Thirteenth Vermont, along with troops of its sister regiments the Fourteenth and Sixteenth Vermont, blasted away at close range. They inflicted severe damage on the Virginia boys with a brutal flank fire. On Kemper's far right, the Twenty-Fourth Virginia took the most severe punishment, and Old Dominion soldiers dropped like fallen leaves on a windy autumn morning in the Virginia Tidewater. Leading the way and performing exceptionally well, the Thirteenth Vermont had been the initial command that had faced north and perpendicular to Kemper's right to deliver deadly enfilade fire until Stannard ordered the Sixteenth Vermont to add its musketry to the punishing firepower.

Spunky Irish soldiers of the Thirteenth Vermont (one of the three Vermont regiments of the Third Brigade of Major General Abner Doubleday's Third Division, First Corps) were among those men who fired into Kemper's vulnerable right flank that hung in midair on the open fields southwest of the clump of trees. Positioned on the regiment's flank because of its dependability and appropriately named the Emmett Guards, this Irish company (A) from Burlington, in northwest Vermont on the eastern shore of Lake Champlain, was the regiment's best company. This distinct ethnic company consisted of Irish Catholics (the majority) and Protestants, including those who had emigrated from Ireland because of the horrors of the Great Potato Famine.

Some Company A Irishmen, under staunch Irish nationalist Captain John Lonergan, who possessed a "wild Irish spirit" and won the Medal of Honor for his gallant performance at Gettysburg, came from humble roots like so many Sons of Erin on both sides. He had worked in the West Rutland marble quarries near Burlington, performing manual labor to make a meager living for daily survival. Emerald Isle teenagers served in Company A's ranks and fought with distinction on this bloody afternoon. Major General Winfield Scott Hancock, who continued to command the Second Corps with consummate skill, ordered the two Vermont regiments to counterattack to hit the attackers' vulnerable right flank—an offensive thrust (basically a surprise attack) calculated to apply pressure to squeeze the attackers into a more compact mass to create even better targets for the Union artillery and muskets lining Cemetery Ridge. This devastating punishment from the south forced Pickett's men to gradually shift north to escape the blistering enfilade fire from the fast-firing Vermonters.[336]

Displaying remarkable discipline in having resisted the temptation to return fire on their tormentors for such an extended period of time, Pickett's men finally returned fire when close to the crest, within only one hundred yards of the stone wall. Lieutenant Dooley described the first return fire unleashed by Pickett's survivors: "Just here—from right to left the remnants of our braves pour in their long reserved fire; until now no shot had been fired, no shout of triumph had been raised; but as the cloud of smoke rises over the heads of the advancing divisions the well known southern battle cry which marks the victory gained or nearly gained bursts wildly over the blood stained field and *all that line of guns is ours*."[337]

In the brigade (under General Garnett) advancing to the left of John Dooley's regiment in the center of Kemper's Brigade, Lieutenant George Williamson described the moment when, at long last, "we reached a point about 100 yards from the stone wall, a junior officer [Colonel Stuart already had fallen] couldn't stand it any longer, and he gave the order we had all been waiting for: 'Take good aim, aim low, fire!' We fired one time, and then he said, 'Now let's holler!'...The rebel yell rent the air for the first time that day. We screamed like fiends and demons from hell."[338]

Because the Confederate cannonade had inflicted considerable damage on Union artillery defending the Angle and the copse of trees sector, Lieutenant Alonzo Hersford Cushing's battery (Battery A, Fourth United

States Artillery), located amid the open ground inside the Angle, was in bad shape. This excellent battery of six three-inch Ordnance Rifles had been cut to pieces, but Lieutenant Cushing had ordered his gunners to fight to the last man because the high ground had to be held at all costs. A good many cannoneers had been killed or wounded by this time; other gunners had fled for shelter. Encouraging his artillerymen, the gallant Lieutenant Cushing staggered when hit. Refusing to retire to the rear after suffering a serious wound, the West Pointer remained defiantly on the front line. Here, he had implored his sweat-stained gunners to fire faster until Cushing was finally killed by a bullet that struck him in the mouth.

However, two defiant cannoneers of Cushing's Battery remained beside one of the guns waiting for the attackers to get as close as possible before opening fire. Lieutenant Finley wrote:

> *when we reached a point about 50 yards from the wall, there were only two* [of Cushing's] *gunners left* [and they] *both dropped down on their stomachs* [while] [e]*ach man had his hand on a lanyard, and each lanyard was attached to a three inch rifled-gun triple shotted with canister. When we were about 50 yards out.... They jerked their lanyards simultaneously, and the two cannon rock back from the wall with a splitting report. They fired their last shots full into our faces and so close to me that I distinctly felt the flame against my left cheek.*[339]

The fiery explosions of canister at such close range had a devastating effect among the compact mass of attackers who had already believed that the gun was theirs. Indeed, these two "shots cut a bloody swath in our ranks [and] Captain [James C.] Wyant, our acting commander, was shot in the face [and] fell in front of the wall."[340]

Lieutenant Dooley no longer led his troops of Company C, Montgomery Guard, after the fall of Irishman Captain Hallinan, who had led the way with a remarkable degree of courage and determination. In Dooley's words: "Shot through both thighs, I fall about 30 yards from the guns" and went down among the clumps of dead and wounded.[341]

On the crest with the increasingly nervous defenders, Lieutenant Haskell was now "wondering how long the Rebel ranks, deep though they were, could stand our sheltered volleys [when suddenly] [t]he larger portion of [Brigadier General Alexander Stewart] Webb's brigade [the Philadelphia Brigade, Second Corps, and positioned just south of the Angle] there by the group of trees and the angles of the wall was breaking from the cover of their works, and...were falling back, a fear-stricken flock of confusion! The fate of Gettysburg hung upon a spider's single thread!"[342]

With Cushing's last gunners manning their field pieces, positioned above (north of) the copse of trees, shot down or fled rearward, the howling Virginians gained and then charged over the stone wall en masse. Here, any remaining Federals were quickly bayoneted, clubbed down or taken prisoner. Before the charging troops of Garnett's Brigade, Lieutenant Finley described the incredible sight that revealed the extent of the amazing success at the collapsing right-center of the Army of the Potomac: "For the next few minutes, there were no bluecoats in front of our regiment [and then we] saw General Garnett ride up to the wall, [but] at that moment, the 72nd Pennsylvania came over the hill [crest of Cemetery Ridge] on the other side of the wall [and] [t]hey leveled as one, pulled triggers and fired a terrible volley straight into us [and] General Garnett was on horseback [and] took a minie ball right between the eyes and toppled off his horse stone dead."[343]

Indeed, fortunately for the Union, the Seventy-Second Pennsylvania Volunteer Infantry was in the right place at the right time to unleash a counterattack. Now a fierce struggle raged between the exhausted survivors of Garnett's Brigade and the Seventy-Second Pennsylvania. Lieutenant George Finley wrote: "We exchanged one or two volleys with the 72nd Pennsylvania, and they pulled back and went over the hill [Cemetery Ridge's crest just east of the copse of trees] from whence they had come.... Just as the 72nd withdrew [up the slope for the safety of the crest just to the east], General Armistead arrived at the head of the remnants of his brigade."[344]

The arrival of General Armistead and his elated soldiers, including many Irish soldiers, of the Thirty-Eighth, Fifty-Seventh, Fifty-Third, Ninth and Fourteenth Virginia, from left to right (or north to south), could not have been more timely. Displaying dynamic leadership necessary to exploit gains, Armistead sparked the resurgence of the Virginia offensive effort beyond the stone wall and toward the strategic crest, which had to be captured if a decisive victory was to be had. Like when, fresh from the halls of West Point, fueled by the reckless courage of youth that inspired his comrades in the Mexican-American War, Armistead led his men, here, over the stone wall, around which were strewn so many bodies of blue and gray, with sword in hand, while shouting encouragement for his men to hurry on to gain the crest.

As Lieutenant Finley described the renewed charge of the rejuvenated Virginians beyond the stone wall and higher up the slope toward the crest: "The men began to follow the General over the wall—that is, those of us

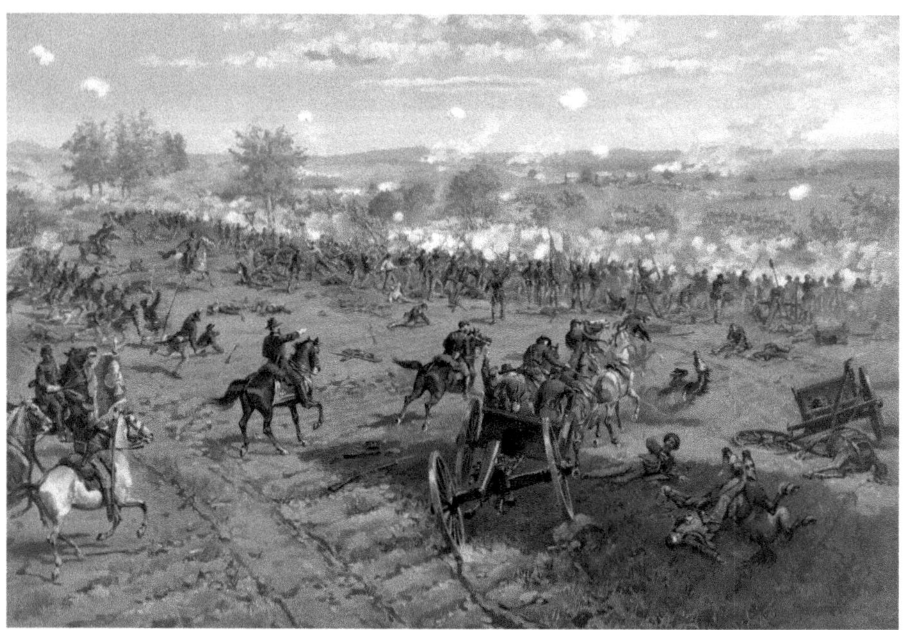

Painting of Major General Winfield Scott Hancock, commander of the Second Corps, Army of the Potomac, and his timely efforts to thwart Pickett's Charge. Painting entitled *Hancock at Gettysburg* by Thurede Thulstrup. *Courtesy of the Library of Congress.*

who were still able to walk…there couldn't have been more than several hundred of us left, but every man who was able followed the General over the wall. I hesitated, and then I remembered the [inspiring and comforting] words that I had read from the little pocket Testament.…So I jumped the wall, and landed in the worst fight I have ever been in my life!"[345]

Now the bloody struggle for possession of the strategic crest swirled to new heights during some of the most savage combat of the war. Lieutenant Finley was not the only Irishman who now had a pocket Testament or prayer book in his breast pocket for comfort and spiritual protection. At the peak of the vicious combat of desperate men, Colonel O'Kane led the Sixty-Ninth Pennsylvania, Philadelphia Brigade, into the fray to regain the wall of stone. In the ranks of the Sixty-Ninth, dark-haired Corporal John Cassidy was knocked over when a Confederate bullet struck him in the chest. Fortunately, the right half of the corporal's small prayer book, *The Manual of the Christian Soldier*, took the main impact of the bullet's force, saving the Irishman's life—but only for a brief period. This faithful Son of Erin was destined to die in his hometown in less than two weeks from the lingering effects of the nasty wound.[346]

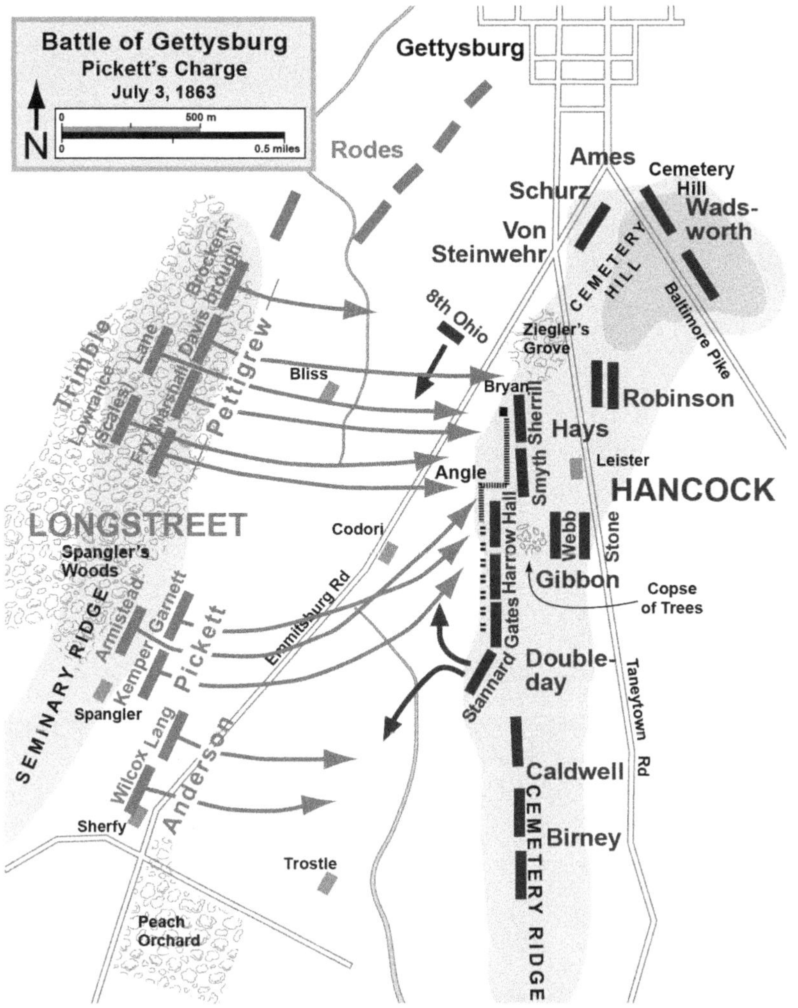

Most important at this crucial moment, the sight of the counterattacking Irish of the Sixty-Ninth Pennsylvania inspired a good many other Emerald Islanders in blue. Mike Smith, an Irishman who had manned one of the six guns of Captain Cowan's First New York Independent Battery positioned on the slope just below the clump of trees, became unnerved by the sight of thousands of charging Rebels continuing to make significant gains and surging ever closer to the crest. He hastily mounted a horse to ride rearward to save himself. But he suddenly turned and looked north toward the dramatic breakthrough of the screaming Rebels. The eyes of the powder-stained Irishman widened when he now

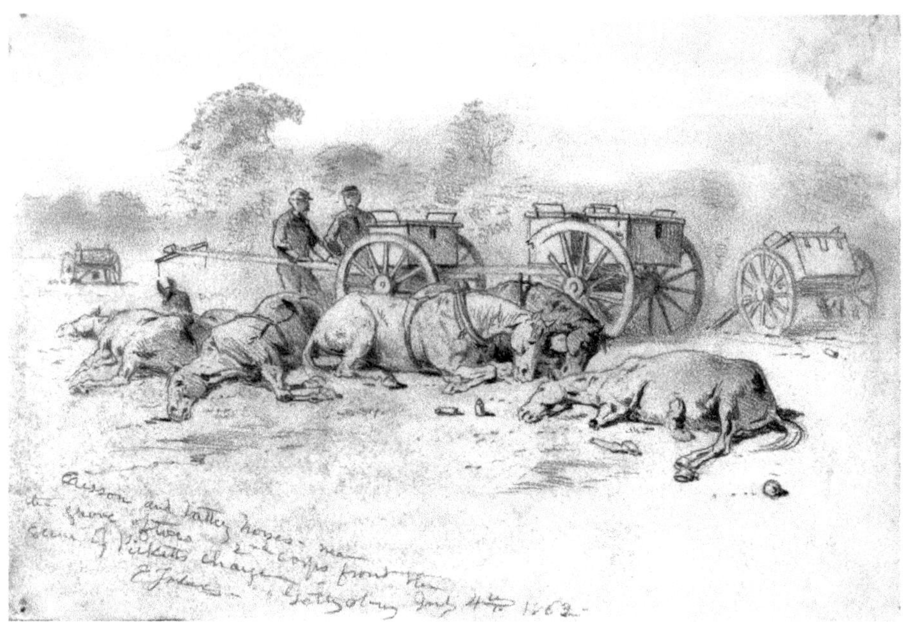

Wrecked battery near the clump of trees. *Courtesy of the Library of Congress.*

saw the emerald-green banner of the Sixty-Ninth Pennsylvania Irish waving through the drifting battle smoke and flying defiantly before the throng of attackers.

The breathtaking sight of the green battle flag fueled the fighting spirit of every Irishman who saw the silken emerald banner that represented so much to them. Scotland-born Captain Cowan, proving himself to be a true Celtic warrior and resourceful leader in this crisis situation, never forgot the "wild Irishman," who was invigorated by the sight of the green flag: "Instantly raising himself up in the stirrups and waving his whip, with wild excitement, [Mike Smith] shouted, 'Hurrah for the ould flag.'"[347] Significantly at this key moment of the Confederate breakthrough, that "ould flag" was that of Ireland, and the sight of this green banner brought back a flood of memories to a good many Irishmen in blue.

After having just jumped over the stone wall with a handful of his Company K (Harrison's Guards), Fifty-Sixth Virginia, one survivor described the close-range firefight that raged just below the crest: "Both sides came ever closer to one another. We were so close that we were literally shooting into each other's faces. The muzzle flashes of the muskets were scorching the shirts off of our chest [and] [i]n some places there wasn't room to load and fire, so the men threw down their muskets and fought fist to fist, rock to rock, tooth to tooth [and] [e]very man fought on his own hook."[348]

At such a close and deadly range, an ever-increasing number of Irish soldiers in gray and butternut were astounded to see the unbelievable sight that emphasized the horrors of this increasingly bitter civil war among the Irish: the gold harp of Ireland, a revered nationalist symbol of the Emerald Isle, was prominently displayed on the battle flags of the Philadelphia Brigade Irish, who met the final rush of Pickett's Virginians, including Irish soldiers, with fixed bayonets and a feisty fighting spirit.[349]

The Bitter End

As tragic fate would have it, the best efforts of the men of Pickett's Charge were doomed. Shocked by the sheer magnitude of the losses and the carnage, Lieutenant John Edward Dooley Jr., who was now lying wounded about thirty yards from the crest, described the bitter end of the most ambitious of Confederate dreams: "There—listen—we hear a new shout, and cheer after cheer rends the air. Are those fresh troops advancing to our support? No! no! That huzza never broke from southern lips....Oh, if there is anything capable of crushing and wringing the soldier's heart it was this day's tragic act and all in vain! But a little well timed support and Gettysburg was ours. The Yankee army had been routed and Pickett's division earned a name and fame not inferior to that of the Old Guard of Bonaparte."[350]

With a handful of remaining survivors of the Fifty-Sixth Virginia standing firm on the high ground with fixed bayonets and only a few rounds remaining in leather cartridge-boxes, Lieutenant George Williamson Finley described the bitter end to the most famous charge in American history in the most crucial sector: "We were surrounded on three sides, and I could see that our situation was hopeless. So to avoid the further highest ranking officer left standing at my end of the line [therefore] I gave the order to the men around me....'Cease fire! Lay down your arms and surrender!'"[351]

During the largest battle on the North American continent, the three days of slaughter in Adams County, Pennsylvania, were unprecedented. In his desperate bid to reap a decisive success before this brutal war of attrition doomed his army and the Confederacy to the ash bin of history, Lee had gone for broke in hurling one assault after another at the high-ground defensive positions. Thus, he threw the lives of thousands of young men and boys away in a desperate attempt to gain a victory that never came for the South and reverse the course of America's most tragic war.

Lieutenant John Edward Dooley Jr., First Virginia, Kemper's Brigade, perhaps said it best: "Oh God! Virginia's bravest, noblest sons have perished here today and perished in vain!"[352] Indeed, the First Virginia lost a staggering 120 out of 150 men who had advanced over the open fields in Lee's bid to deliver a knockout blow to the Army of the Potomac.[353]

Saddened by the fate of his fellow Virginians, Ted Barclay, Liberty Hall Volunteers (Company I, Fourth Virginia Infantry), Stonewall Brigade, Ewell's Second Corps, wrote in a letter of the ultimate horror of Gettysburg and loss of some of the finest Old Dominion generals: "We suffered heavily. The first two days fighting was entirely in our favor. How unfortunate it was we attempted to drive them from an impregnable position [on Cemetery Ridge]. We had two Gens. killed, Brigs. Gens. Garnett and Kemper, and ten wounded."[354]

In a bitter irony, Lieutenant Dooley, who had been wounded in both thighs before reaching the blazing stone wall that was situated just below the crest, was placed in an ambulance "along side a wounded Yankee [who was] a coarse bloated looking Irishman [and] I long to get rid of my loathsome companion and hail with delight the approach to the field hospital."[355]

But young Dooley, who still revered the ill-fated revolutionaries of the Young Ireland Movement of 1848, shortly received a greater shock at the field hospital, learning in greater detail about what was most forgotten about the dramatic showdown during the three days at Gettysburg, including during Pickett's Charge: essentially, a mini–civil war had been waged with a savage intensity between Irish soldiers on opposing sides. In Dooley's words:

> *A Yanko-Irish* [or Anglo-Irish] *soldier told me he was from Lowell, Mass., and that he had been a soldier under John Mitchel in '48. Having heard that John M*[itchel]*'s three sons were in the Confederate army he wished to hear something about them. He seemed much pleased when he learned that I could give him so much information about the Mitchels. And then* [the Third Virginia's twenty-three year-old Private Edgar] *Cronin* [wounded and captured and fated to die the following July as a prisoner of war] *and I began questioning him and asking him how it was possible for him who had in '48 fought or intended to fight for the same cause for which we were contending, how could he consistently*

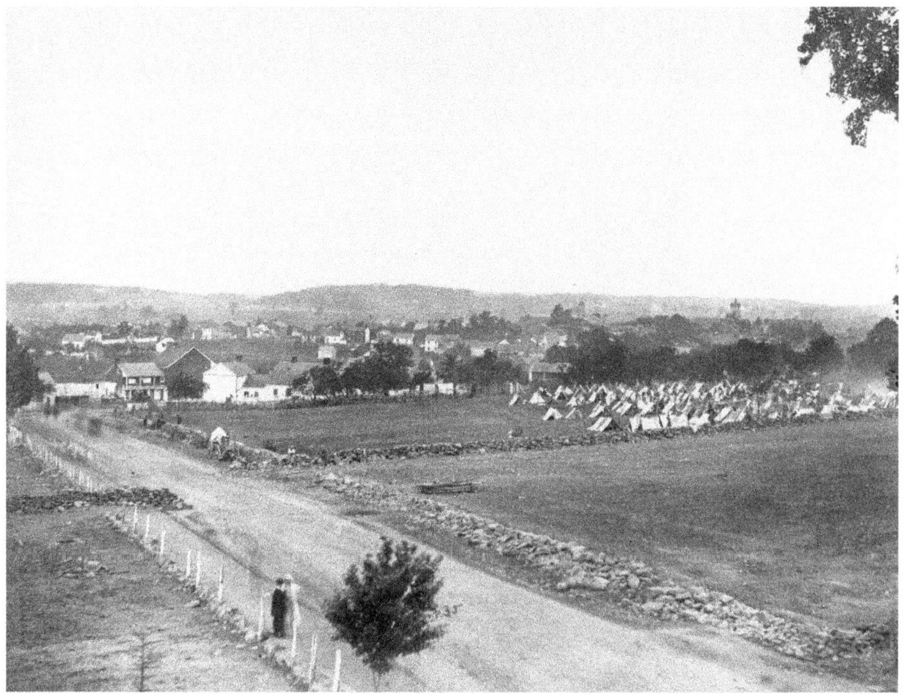

Union troops encamped outside Gettysburg and on the high ground of Cemetery Hill. The town of Gettysburg is seen in the background of this July 7, 1863 photograph. *Courtesy of the Library of Congress.*

> *turn his back on his principles and for the pitiful hire of a few dollars do all in his power to crush a brave people asserting their right of self government; and now that he was engaged in the cause of tyranny, fighting against honesty, Justice and right, and moreover against those very gallant young men he was seeking to hear of, what, we asked, would Mr. Mitchel think of him?*[356]

Like an ancient warrior of old, Lieutenant "Archie" McGregor was one of the Celtic officers who fell to rise no more during Pickett's Charge. He had gone down while leading his troops of the Eighteenth North Carolina, Jim Lane's Brigade, Pender's Division, Hill's Third Corps. One soldier never forgot how McGregor had led the way up the grassy slope when "a minnie ball pierced his left breast near the heart, and he fell and shortly expired. He fell in a stranger's land."[357]

Finally, and belatedly, the last reinforcements—troops of Major General Richard Herron Anderson's Division of Hill's Third Corps—pushed forward in a bid to protect Pickett's open right flank that had hung dangerously in midair in the open fields, but it was too little, too late. Equally as ill-fated in regard to poor timing, these reinforcements, Brigadier General Cadmus M. Wilcox's Alabama Brigade and Colonel David Lang's Florida Brigade, were far too few to make any difference.

The Irish of the Eighth Alabama, which was part of Wilcox's Brigade of five Alabama regiments, the Emerald Guards (Company I, the regiment's color company), led the way, representing their Mobile and the Green Isle so far away. Leading Company I, Captain C.P.B. Branagan was a gray-eyed bachelor and a former merchant and clerk from the port of Mobile. With a dark complexion and vivid memories of the Emerald Isle, Branagan had demonstrated his worth as a fine officer in past battles, including at Salem Church, located just west of the town on the Rappahannock River, Fredericksburg.

This dynamic Irish leader from Mobile fell with three wounds, going down like other Irish soldiers of the Emerald Guards. Branagan later died of his wounds, having given all for God, his adopted country, and Ireland. Lieutenant John McGrath, who had been commended for bravery during the 1862 Peninsula campaign, took command of what little was left of the decimated Irish company after the fall of Branagan and so many others.

As could be expected in an assault lacking proper coordination and launched far too late to assist Pickett's Virginians, Wilcox's and Lang's attacks were easily repulsed during the last phase of Pickett's Charge. The final offensive effort resulted in no gain, signifying a dismal end to the greatest offensive effort ever launched by the Army of Northern Virginia. In his diary, Virginia-born Robert Garlick Hill Kean, who headed the Confederate Bureau of War and whose ancestors had migrated from Ulster Province, north Ireland, about the time of the American Revolution, penned an undeniable truth: "The battle of Gettysburg was a virtual, if not actual defeat [because] the center of the enemy resisted successfully all of Longstreet's efforts."[358]

Indeed, the final repulse of Anderson's attackers from Florida and Alabama was the last chapter of the tragedy of Pickett's Charge, representing another waste of Southern courage and lives, especially for the Irish. General Lee's desperate bid to win it all had only resulted in lengthening the long list of killed and wounded soldiers who never again saw their homes and families across the South.

Epilogue

The Irish Confederates fought in disproportionate numbers from 1861 to 1865 for the dream of the independence of a new Southern republic with the enduring legacies of the Irish experience and their beloved native homeland in mind. This was especially the case in regard to the Army of Northern Virginia, which consisted of a largely Celtic and mostly Scotch-Irish soldiery, and in part explained why that resilient army was the best fighting force in the history of the Confederacy.

Just before dying of his wounds, John Mitchel Jr. perhaps said it best in illuminating what was buried deep inside the hearts and minds of many Irish Confederates who fought and died while still thinking of Ireland and envisioning the much-dreamed-about possibilities for a new Irish republic free of British domination: "I die willingly for the South, but oh! that it had been for Ireland."[359]

Indeed, this was one of the great ironies and tragedies of Pickett's Charge, when Lee went for broke in his desperate bid to win it all: the Irishmen in blue and gray who killed each other with a ferocity seldom seen. Even more, by slaughtering each other with an unbridled enthusiasm, the Emerald Islanders at Gettysburg were also killing the greatest dream of Irish nationalists and the nationalist Irish Republican, or Fenian, Brotherhood. This revolutionary organization was the successor to the revolutionary United Irishmen and Young Ireland Movements, appropriately founded on St. Patrick's Day, 1858. The Young Ireland Movement of 1848 had been primarily a "Fenian uprising" of die-hard Irish nationalists and patriots who refused to accept Ireland's dismal fate.

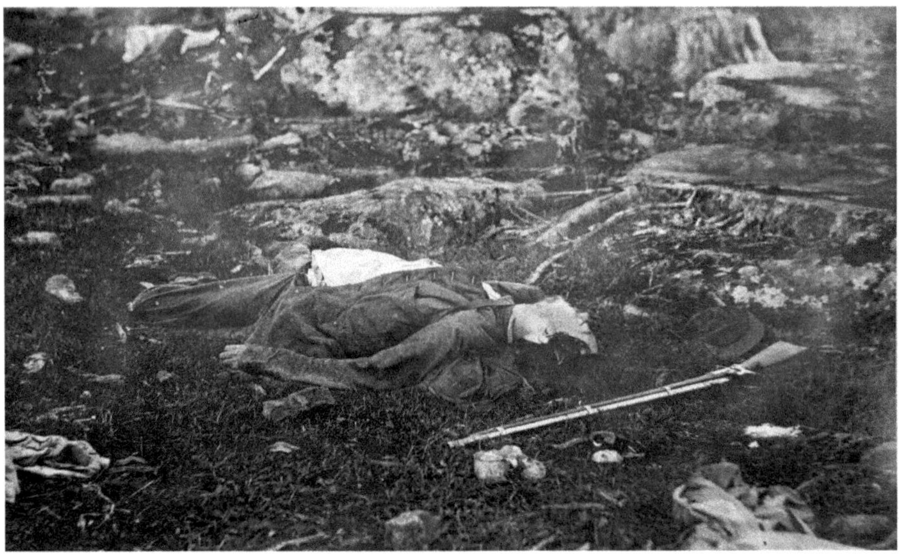

Alexander Gardner photograph of a Confederate dead soldier on the southern slope of Devil's Den. *Courtesy of the Library of Congress.*

Most of all, the Fenians (officially formed in 1858 and the antecedent of the Irish Republican Army), with active revolutionary cells in Charleston, Memphis, New Orleans and Savannah, hoped that the Civil War would serve as a training ground for Irishmen on both sides in preparation for defeating British redcoats so that "Ireland shall be restored to her rightful place among free nations." Therefore, the Fenians were heavily recruited during the war years on both sides, including to fill the Irish Brigade's ranks. In the words of Thomas Francis Meager, a die-hard Fenian of the Young Ireland Movement and the Irish Brigade's first commander who shared Mitchel's great dream of liberating Ireland, the Civil War provided the best experience in obtaining training and combat experience, because these tried veterans then "will not be likely to shrink on the day (when will it dawn, that white day) that they will have the comparatively light task of whipping their weight of red-coats."[360]

A journalist of the *Nation*, in Dublin, Ireland, lamented the tragic waste of Irish lives, both blue and gray, in the awful bloodletting that was unprecedented in the nation's history: "Enough! enough! Your blood was given….But mightier is the claim of heaven, And urgent that of motherland."[361] Reflecting his grim determination to free Ireland at any cost, General Meagher concluded, "It is better to reduce the island [the

Green Isle] to a cinder than let it rot into an obscure quagmire, peopled with reptiles."[362]

Likewise, known for the "violence of his hatred" of England that had been instilled in his sons who wore the gray because the Northern government was viewed as analogous to the oppressive British rulers in London, Mitchel bitterly detested the powerful British political and economic system that sought to "exterminate" the Irish people.[363]

Clearly, the high sacrifice of Irish on both sides was a central tragedy of the Battle of Gettysburg and Pickett's Charge long overlooked by historians, including Irish historians. In this sense, the Battle of Gettysburg and Pickett's Charge had even transcended the omnipresent burning dream of the Emerald Isle's nationalists, who still envisioned a bright, new day for Ireland and its long-suffering people in the future. Even while surging with high-pitched Rebel yells toward Cemetery Ridge, a good many Irish Confederates still thought about the idealistic vision of a future Ireland free of British.

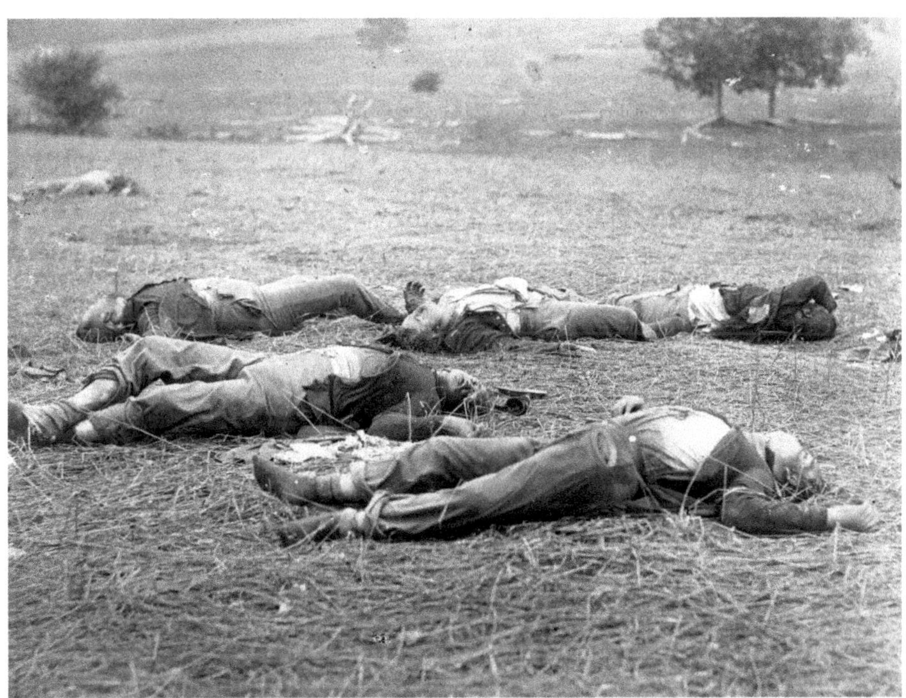

Group of soldiers who made the ultimate sacrifice at Gettysburg. *Courtesy of the Library of Congress.*

As mentioned, teenager Willie Mitchel was one such determined attacker who might have played a role in Ireland's liberation in the future had he not been struck down during the attack. He was carrying the colors of the First Virginia when he fell, to rise no more. During the withdrawal from Cemetery Ridge, the young man was not seen by his concerned comrades, and no one knew of his exact fate. Was Mitchel taken prisoner like other Rebel wounded who had been left alive on the battlefield? No one in his regiment knew the answer.

Young Mitchel's uncertain fate was first brought to light to the Southern public in a July 13, 1863 article about the decimation of the First Virginia that appeared in the *Richmond Daily Dispatch*: "The 1st Virginia carried in [Pickett's Charge] 175 men....They brought out between thirty or forty, many even of them being wounded....Wm Mitchell [sic], son of John Mitchell, in command of the color guard of the regiment, is wounded and missing."[364]

Hoping and praying that the missing boy might have been captured and was recovering from his wound under the good care of a Union physician as a prisoner of war, the anxiety-ridden members of the Mitchel family conducted a desperate search for the teenager. The existing widespread connections of John Mitchel, who was still respected by the Irish on both sides of the Mason-Dixon line, resulted in an extensive quest to ascertain the whereabouts of Willie, which appeared in the pages of the *Irish-American*, of New York City, in late August 1863: "'A correspondent writes to us from Maryland requesting us to relieve the anxiety of an old friend [John Mitchel] by communicating publicly the fate of Private William Mitchel, who fell on the field of Gettysburgh [*sic*], killed or wounded.' If any of our readers can inform us whether such a person was among the Confederate prisoners taken at Gettysburg or otherwise, we shall feel obliged by a communication of the facts as speedily as possible."[365]

The awful truth as to the Richmond teenager's ultimate tragic fate finally became known. The mystery was revealed in the pages of the *Richmond Sentinel* on September 17, 1863:

> *We are sorry to learn that Wm. Mitchel, youngest son of John Mitchel, editor of the* [Richmond] *Enquirer, who was reported missing after the battle of Gettysburg, is now believed to have been killed in the hard-fought struggle. Young Mitchel was only eighteen years old, and is represented to have been a young gentleman of fine attainments, and an excellent soldier, and behaved with especial gallantry at Gettysburg. He has two brothers in the Confederate Service.*[366]

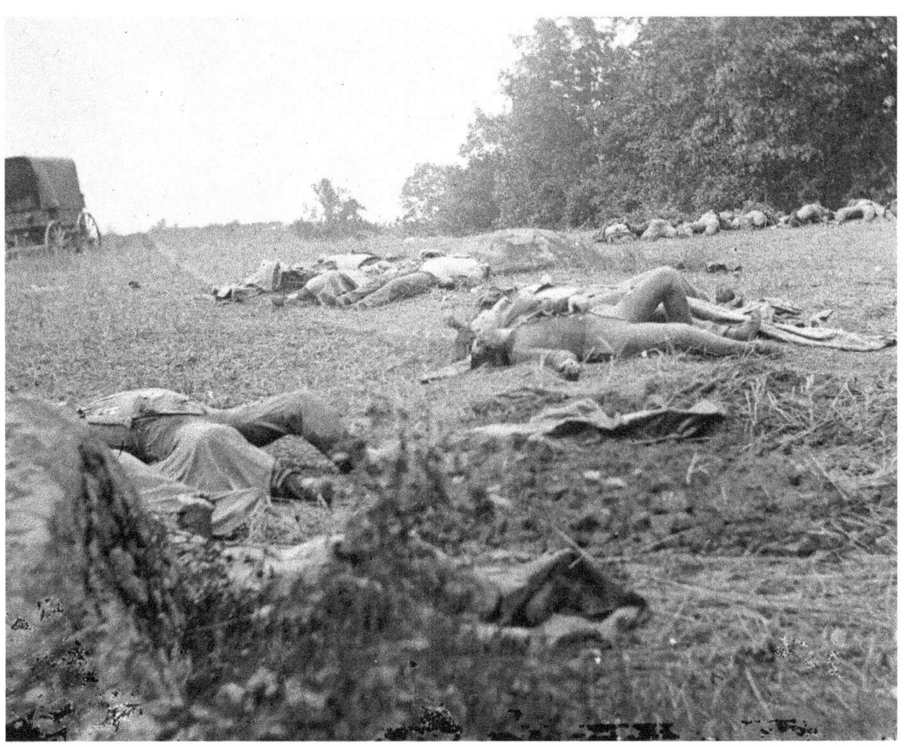

Young men and boys who paid a high price. This group of Confederate dead were collected and laid out for burial at the edge of the Rose Woods. *Courtesy of the Library of Congress.*

In a rare tribute to a Confederate soldier, especially a lowly private, the pro-Union *Irish-American*, which was widely read by the Irish community, paid its final respects to Willie Mitchel:

> *We have received with sincere sorrow the intelligence that William Mitchel, the youngest of John Mitchel's sons, fell mortally wounded on the battle-field of Gettysburgh* [sic], *shot through the lower part of the abdomen. He was in the color-guard of the 1st Virginia regiment, and fell near the breastworks.…He was a young lad of the highest promise, and never failed to endear himself to those with whom he was brought in contact, by the sterling goodness of his disposition and the many excellent traits of character he displayed. Few who remember the bright, open-hearted boy, who, three short years ago, was the life of a yet unbroken family circle in the vicinity of this city, but will join in the regret which we now record his untimely fall.…Mr. Mitchel's family have been sorely afflicted.*[367]

The sad news of the fall of Willie Mitchel was spread throughout Ireland by the *Dublin Nation* on September 26, 1863:

> *Amongst the sons of Ireland whose blood was poured on the slaughter-field of Gettysburg, was one whose fall will be learned with sorrow in many an Irish home. William Mitchel has given his young life in the cause to which his father early devoted his whole heart and his great intellect and surely if there is to be at this moment a grief keener than all other in the parental heart of the brave exile, it is that the life of his* [first]*born, so gallantly yielded on the battle-field, was not given, as* [nationalist and revolutionary hero Patrick] *Sarsfield said, "for Ireland."*[368]

Ironically, in this same month, September 1863, a captured Lieutenant John Edward Dooley Jr., First Virginia, learned as a prisoner of war the awful truth from a firsthand source. He recorded in his journal on September 21: "Lieut. Kunningham [William Henry "Pete" Keiningham, Company D (Old Dominion Guards), First Virginia, who was wounded and captured in Pickett's Charge] puts an end to all hopes regarding the surviving of Willie Mitchel. The Ensign Wm. [M.] Lawson [a twenty-three-year-old clerk from Richmond and a fellow member of the color guard who was wounded in the right arm, which was amputated by a surgeon in a field hospital] saw him fall…and Willie clasped his hand over his abdomen, showing he had been wounded fatally."[369]

In a sad letter, Willie's Ireland-born mother, Sarah Jane, wrote to her surviving son James—who also had served in Company C (Montgomery Guard), First Virginia, and who had fallen seriously wounded at the battle of Williamsburg on the Virginia peninsula on May 5, 1862—of what she knew about the demise of her youngest and favorite son. Four of Pickett's survivors of the great attack

> *were going on the field looking for wounded soldiers. And that they found Willie rolled in a blanket pinned with three pins. The center one being a large one with a black head and two others common pins—that his face had been washed and there was a slip of paper pinned to the blanket with his name "W*[illiam] [Henry] *Mitchel" son of the Irish patriot—with the help of a colored man they dug a grave on the banks of a small cabin so close that no plow would ever disturb it—and laid him there and took the paper and fastened it to a piece of cracked board and hammered*

> *it there at the head of the grave. It was near a little brick house* [of the Nicholas Codori farm] *that the body was found* [where he had fallen].[370]

Dark-haired Willie Mitchel, distinguished by a boyish handsomeness and innocence, was "buried at the Codori house," which, symbolically, was now rented by an Irish family.[371]

The grieving mother (who hailed from Limerick, Ireland) of the slightly built Private Mitchel, who looked even younger than his seventeen years, described in her postwar letter of her last, most heartfelt wish in regard to her lamented youngest son: "I would like to find that grave. It was years before I gave up the hope that he would some day appear. I got it into my head that he had been taken prisoner and carried off a long distance but that he would make his way back one day—this I knew was very silly of me but the hope was there nevertheless." And it remained for years.[372] Proving to be as stoic as the young man's Ireland-born mother, the elder Mitchel, the patriarch, wrote in grief: "Our poor Willy, in that terrible slaughter of Pickett's Division, was shot through the body and at once killed....He could not have fallen in nobler company, nor as I think, in a better cause."[373]

Nor had his comrades forgotten the likeable and boyish Willie, whom they looked upon as a son (especially the older men in the ranks) and a brother (the soldiers around his own age). Lieutenant John Edward Dooley Jr. penned in his journal about how he was haunted by the memories of the pleasant young man who was no more: "Dreamed for the fourth time last night that Willie Mitchel is still alive."[374]

The loss of so many good fighting men like Mitchel in part caused General Lee to write to President Davis in a rather remarkable letter that revealed the following: "I have been prompted by these reflections [about the battle of Gettysburg and the terrible losses in vain] to propose...the propriety of selecting another commander" for the Army of Northern Virginia.[375] What should not be forgotten in either America or Ireland are the almost unbelievable courage and heroics of Willie Mitchel and thousands of other Irish soldiers and the sons, grandsons and great-grandsons of Emerald Islanders during those three bloody days at Gettysburg.

Ironically, no monument or marker to the Irish Confederates of this largely Celtic army (primarily Scotch-Irish) has to this day been erected on the field of Gettysburg—the most monument-covered and marker-dominated battlefield in the world. However, a truly magnificent monument can be seen at the edge of the Rose Woods to honor the heroism and sacrifice of Irish soldiers. But this exquisite monument was not erected to honor any Irish Confederates who fought at Gettysburg. Instead, this beautiful monument, built from the donations of New York City Irish and distinguished by a large Celtic cross, has long paid a fine tribute to the Irish Brigade, which fought at the Wheatfield just south of where Pickett's Charge was launched.

In a greater irony that certainly would have horrified the Irish survivors of Pickett's Charge—very much a traditional Celtic charge, almost as if launched against ancient enemies of the Emerald Isle homeland, from the Vikings to the English—was the fact that the Irish Brigade monument that stands today on America's most visited battlefield was carved by a self-taught sculptor and Irish Confederate veteran who fought at Gettysburg as a teenager, Virginia-born William Rudolf O'Donovan. He served throughout the war in a Virginia command before paying the ultimate tribute to his brave countrymen of the Irish Brigade.[376]

But the South's far larger number of Irish and other Celtic warriors, including fighting men of Scottish and Welsh heritage, were never honored not only by a monument, but also not even by headstones to mark the final resting places of these fallen fighting men on Pennsylvania soil. In the words of one North Carolina soldier who lamented the loss of Celtic warrior Lieutenant "Archie" McGregor, who suffered the same tragic fate as so many Irish and Celtic soldiers during Pickett's Charge:

> *He fell in a stranger's land. His remains were consigned to their last resting-place by stranger hands. No polished slab, no towering shaft, nor even a simple board, mark the last resting-place of our noble Archie, but his memory will ever live green in the minds of those who knew him.... Freely has the Old North State poured out her richest blood as a libation upon the altar of her country in this terrible struggle for freedom and independence, and I will here venture to say, that no purer or nobler sacrifice has been offered than the blood of Lt. McGregor.... He is gone!*[377]

In the end, the Irish in blue and gray who met in mortal combat at Gettysburg and during the climax of Pickett's Charge in the Angle and around the copse of trees played a large role in ultimately deciding the Civil War's outcome and America's destiny. Of course, this was a most ironic development, because the majority of these Sons of Erin who fought and died at the bloody apex of Pickett's Charge had been born more than four thousand miles away from Adams County, Pennsylvania.

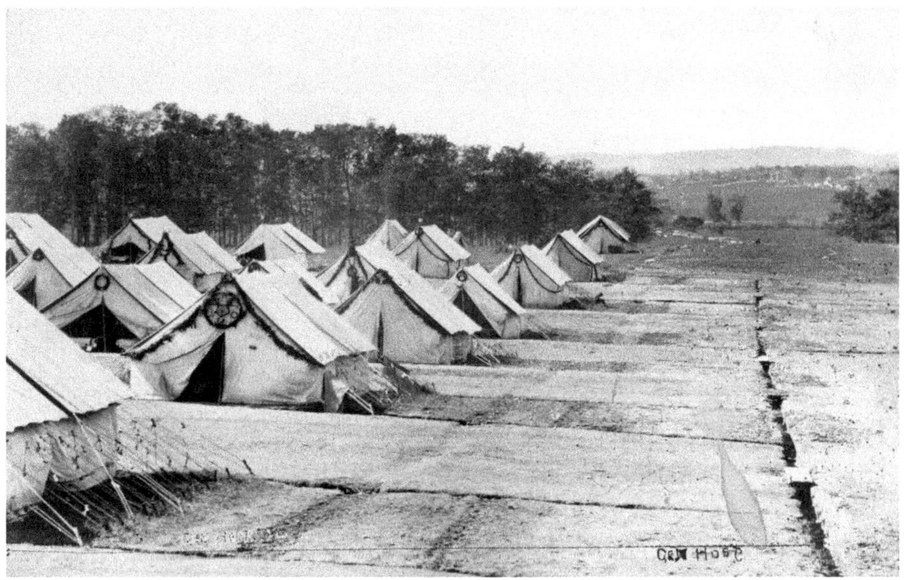

Thousands of wounded survivors of the three days of combat at Gettysburg recovered in farmhouses, barns, private homes and hospital tents. This is an August 1863 photo of the General United States Hospital at Camp Letterman at Gettysburg. *Courtesy of the Library of Congress.*

Nevertheless, these Irish soldiers in gray and butternut battled courageously for what they believed was right and against a cruel fate that could not be overcome. Consequently, in the end, these self-sacrificing Emerald Islanders on both sides played a large role in determining the ultimate fate of America that has been long unappreciated by historians of not only the Civil War but also of the Irish experience.

Therefore, even after the 150th anniversary of the Battle of Gettysburg, the general obscurity and absence of Irish contributions from the pages of Gettysburg historiography and the story of Pickett's Charge, although this most famous attack in American history consisted of largely Celtic (Scotch-Irish) attackers, has been a striking paradox. Clearly, this unfortunate situation has revealed one of the great ironies of not only Gettysburg and Civil War history but also of American history. The purpose of this book has been to rectify this long silencing of the importance of the Irish contribution while filling a gaping void in Civil War, Irish and Gettysburg historiography.

In a classic case of history coming full circle, a knowledgeable English politician emphasized to his aristocratic and upper-class peers in the British Parliament of the forgotten vital role played by large numbers of mostly lowly Irish rebels from 1775 to 1783 because they had significantly contributed to England's greatest reversal in its history: "We have lost America through the Irish."[378]

In much the same way, the largest battle ever fought on the North American continent was lost by the Confederacy in no small part by the heroic defense of the hard-fighting Irish in blue, especially those of the Philadelphia Brigade, who played a leading role in repulsing Pickett's Charge. Indeed, thousands of Irish and descendants of Irish immigrants nearly won it all for the Confederacy on July 3 and actually came closer than is generally recognized today.

Ireland-born Sergeant James Hand, Company D, Sixty-Ninth Pennsylvania Infantry, was one of the courageous Philadelphia Brigade men who played a part in halting Pickett's Charge at the "High Water Mark of the Confederacy" and paid the ultimate price. Sergeant Hand was an inspirational leader of the common soldiers in the ranks, and he helped to rally his men during the supreme moment of crisis. This highly capable sergeant was also a man who loved his Irish family, who prayed for his safe return to their home at 1319 North Sixteenth Street in Philadelphia and to his former life as a doting father and printer. James's wife, Jane, who was also born in Ireland and in her late twenties like her husband, prayed in vain for the return of Hand, who never again saw his two young daughters, Mary Jane and Lucy. Even more, Hand never learned of the birth of his first son, James Charles, who was born near the end of July 1863, less than a month after the sergeant was killed.[379]

Captain Charles McAnally, an Irish immigrant like Sergeant Hand and destined to win the Medal of Honor for his May 1864 heroics in the bitter fighting at Spotsylvania Court House, Virginia, had commanded Company D, Sixty-Ninth Pennsylvania, which had been positioned on the regiment's right-center during the great attack. Only two days after the repulse of Pickett's Charge, he sat down to write his most difficult letter, because Sergeant Hand had been a close friend. In fact, the middle name of Hand's infant son (Charles) was almost certainly a tribute to Captain Charles McAnally, who had been born in Ireland in May 1836.

Therefore, on July 5, a war-weary Captain McAnally wrote to Jane Hand about the sad fate of her husband, whom he affectionately called "Jas":

> *It is a painful task for me to Communicate the sad fate of your husband (my own Comrade) he was killed on the 3rd inst he received a ball through the breast & one through the heart & never spoke after* [he was hit when]

> *we were at it hand to hand* [with Pickett's men when] *they charged us twice & we repulsed them [and] they then tried the Regt on our Right & drove them which caused us to Swing back our right then charged them* [General Armistead's breakthrough into the Angle] *on their left flank & in the charge James fell may the Lord have mercy on his Soul [and] he never flinched from his post & was loved by all who knew him....* [T]*he loss in the battle on the 3rd was heavy but all did not discourage the boys [who were mostly Irish because] we were determined that as long as a man lived he would stand to be killed too rather than to have it said that we left on the battle field the Laurels that we so dearly won in Strange States* [like Virginia].... [T]*here was never a battle fought with more determination....Mrs. Hand please excuse this letter as I am confused & I hope you will take your trouble with patience* [because] *you know God is mercifull* [sic] *& good to his own* [and] *no one living this day was more attached than Jas & my self* [to each other] *when I was engaged in front* [before Cemetery Ridge in command of the skirmish line of the Sixty-Ninth Pennsylvania] *he wanted to get out to my assistance* [and] *I lost a loyal comrade in him no more at present from your Sorrowing friend.*

Quite likely, this battle-hardened Irish captain of immense faith and bravery shed tears while writing this heartfelt letter to a young widow. Like Captain McAnally, Jane Hand also hailed from Ireland. She had immigrated in the hope of finding happiness in America, but she found tragedy instead.

Like the dreams of generations of Irish nationalists and patriots and the hopes of young Ireland-born wives of Irish soldiers in blue like Jane Hand, the dream of the Irish Confederates had been dashed forever at Gettysburg. The golden opportunities that had been presented there would come no more for the Army of Northern Virginia. When Lee's greatest attack was repulsed on Meade's right-center, the hopes for Confederate independence faded away like a cool Celtic mist blown by a stiff breeze over the waters of the Irish Sea.

Because so few Irish Rebels survived the slaughter at Gettysburg, especially Pickett's Charge, and the following bloody two years of war, relatively little has remained of the legacy of these determined but doomed Celtic-Gaelic warriors who served in disproportionate numbers and suffered disproportionate losses from 1861 to 1865. Even more, the story of these Sons of Erin has been overshadowed by the South's postwar Anglo-Saxon myth and Lost Cause romance, obscuring their significant wartime contributions.

Therefore, these Emerald Islanders in gray and butternut have been largely forgotten to this day despite the leading roles they played at Gettysburg and in Pickett's Charge.

In the end, only the bodies of a good many Irish warriors left smoldering in shallow graves and burial trenches at Gettysburg provided a grim testament to their sacrifice and die-hard commitment to a people's struggle that was as doomed as the once-vibrant dream of independence to generations of revolutionaries on the Green Isle. Relatively few Irish Confederates lived to tell their tales of what they had seen and achieved during the three-day showdown at Gettysburg. These disproportionately high losses ensured that the Irish Rebels were the Confederacy's—and the Civil War's—most forgotten warriors, fueling the misconception (one of the great myths of the war) that the Irish played no significant role in fighting and dying for the South, especially at the Battle of Gettysburg.

For too long, the mere thought that large numbers of Irish on both sides played leading roles during the three days at Gettysburg and in Pickett's Charge—not only in the tactical offensive but also in the tactical defensive—seemed inconceivable if not entirely incomprehensible. This was the case not only for the American public but also for generations of traditional non-Irish historians. Unfortunately, these historians have taken relatively little interest in the supreme importance of the Irish role during the climactic showdown at Gettysburg, ensuring a hidden history that has existed for more than a century and a half.

Notes

Chapter 1

1. Grady McWhiney, *Cracker Culture, Celtic Ways in the Old South* (Tuscaloosa: University of Alabama Press, 1988), xiii–xiv, xxi–xxiii, xxxviii–xliii, 1–50; Thomas G. Rogers, *Irish-American Units in the Civil War* (Oxford: Osprey, 2008), 3; David T. Gleeson, *The Irish in the South, 1815–1877* (Chapel Hill: University of North Carolina Press, 2001), 1–54; James Webb, *Born Fighting: How the Scots-Irish Shaped America* (New York: Broadway Books, 2004), 1–233; Ella Lonn, *Foreigners in the Confederacy* (Chapel Hill: University of North Carolina Press, 2002), xi–xii, 1; Mike Cronin and Daryl Adair, *The Wearing of the Green, A History of St. Patrick's Day* (New York: Routledge, 2002), xxi–64; Thomas G. Rodgers, *Irish-American Units in the Civil War* (New York: Osprey, 2008), 3
2. Webb, *Born Fighting*, 5.
3. Richard B. Harwell, editor, *The Confederate Reader, How the South Saw the War* (New York: Dorset, 1992), 58; Terry Golway, *For the Cause of Liberty, A Thousand Years of Ireland's Heroes* (New York: Simon and Schuster, 2000), 10–38.
4. Webb, *Born Fighting*, 221.
5. Rodgers, *Irish-American Units in the Civil War*, 3–4.
6. *Memphis Daily Appeal*, Memphis, Tennessee, April 30, 1862.
7. Webb, *Born Fighting*, 232.
8. Gleeson, *Irish in the South*, 140; Rogers, *Irish-American Units in the Civil War*, 18.
9. Jay P. Doylan, *The Irish Americans, A History* (New York: Bloomsbury, 2008), 9.

10. Ibid.
11. Gleeson, *Irish in the South*, 143.
12. Thomas Fleming, *Washington's Secret War: The Hidden History of Valley Forge* (New York: Smithsonian Books, 2005), 141–42, 259–60, 285; Charles Murphy, The *Irish in the American Revolution* (Groveland: Charles Murphy, 1975), 1–103; Gleeson, *Irish in the South*, 13; Cronin and Adair, *Wearing of the Green*, 8–11.
13. *Poulson's American Daily Advertiser*, Philadelphia, Pennsylvania, February 28, 1815; *New York Gazette and Weekly Mercury*, New York, New York, April 24, 1780; Murphy, *Irish in the American Revolution*, 45.
14. Robert L. Tonsetic, *1781: The Decisive Year of the Revolutionary War* (Havertown, PA: Casemate Publishers, 2011), 11.
15. G.A. Hayes-McCoy, *Irish Battles, A Military History of Ireland* (New York: Barnes and Noble Books, 1997), 1.
16. Owen B. Hunt, *The Irish and the American Revolution: Three Essays* (Philadelphia: private printing, 1976), 31.
17. Gleeson, *Irish in the South*, 69.
18. Murphy, *Irish in the American Revolution*, 64.
19. Gleeson, *Irish in the South*, 141.
20. Ibid., 143; Bell Irvin Wiley, *The Life of Johnny Reb, The Common Soldier of the Confederacy* (Baton Rouge: Louisiana State University Press, 1978), 109–110, 323; *Historic Mobile, An Illustrated Guide* (Mobile, AL: Junior League of Mobile, 1974), xi–xiii; Lonn, *Foreigners in the Confederacy*, 6–11; Phillip Thomas Tucker, *"God Help The Irish!, The History of the Irish Brigade* (Abilene, TX: McWhiney Foundation, 2007), 21; Rodgers, *Irish-American Units in the Civil War*, 5, 8, 19–20; Gerald A. Patterson, *From Blue to Gray, The Life of Confederate General Cadmus H. Wilcox* (Mechanicsburg, PA: Stackpole, 2001), 24, 33, 56–58; Sean Michael O'Brien, *Irish Americans in the Confederate Army* (Jefferson, NC: McFarland, 2007), 107.
21. Lonn, *Foreigners in the Confederacy*, 92; Rodgers, *Irish-American Units in the Civil War*, 19.
22. Phillip Thomas Tucker, *Irish Confederates: The Civil War's Forgotten Soldiers* (Abilene, TX: McWhiney Foundation, 2006), 34.
23. Kelly J. O'Grady, *Clear the Confederate Way!, The Irish in the Army of Northern Virginia* (Mason City: Savas Publishing Company, 2000), ix, 255, 258–59
24. G.A. Hayes-McCoy, *Irish Battles, A Military History of Ireland* (New York: Barnes & Noble, 1969), 1.
25. Webb, *Born Fighting*, 232.

26. Gleeson, *Irish in the South*, 156.
27. Lonn, *Foreigners in the Confederacy*, 55.
28. Wiley, *Life of Johnny Reb*, 324; Walter Bryan, *The Improbable Irish* (New York: Ace Books, 1969), 22; Tucker, *"God Help the Irish!*, 55–176; Peter Haining, *Great Irish Humor* (New York: Barnes and Noble, 1996), 14–16; Gleeson, *Irish in the South*, 148, 151; Rodgers, *Irish-American Units in the Civil War*, 3–4, 18; O'Brien, *Irish Americans in the Confederate Army*, 7.
29. Webb, *Born Fighting*, 232.
30. Ibid.
31. Ibid; Myles Dungan, *How the Irish Won the West* (New York: Skyhorse, 2011), ix–8; Phillip Thomas Tucker, *How the Irish Won the American Revolution: A New Look at the Forgotten Heroes of America's War of Independence* (New York: Skyhorse, 2015).

Chapter 2

32. Jay P. Dolan, *The Irish Americans, A History* (New York: Bloomsbury, 2008), 84.
33. Dolan, *Irish Americans*, 68; Timothy Egan, *The Immortal Irishman: The Irish Revolutionary Who Became an American Hero* (New York: Houghton Mifflin Harcourt, 2016), 40–42.
34. Dolan, *Irish Americans*, 75; McWhiney, *Cracker Culture*, xiii–50.
35. John E. Dooley, SJ, Papers, Special Collections, Georgetown University, Virginia; Joseph T. Durkin, SJ, editor, John Dooley, *Confederate Soldier, His War Journal* (Tuscaloosa: University of Alabama Press, 1945), ix, xi; Brian Lalor, editor, *The Encyclopedia of Ireland* (New Haven, CT: Yale University Press, 2003), 630, 982.
36. Durkin, *John Dooley*, ix; Dolan, *Irish Americans*, 74–77; Lalor, *Encyclopedia of Ireland*, 630–633, 982.
37. Dooley, SJ, Papers, GU; Durkin, ed., John Dooley, p. ix; Lonn, *Foreigners in the Confederacy*, 31–32; Rodgers, *Irish-American Units in the Civil War*, 40–42; Sean Michael O'Brien, *Irish Americans in the Confederate Army* (Jefferson, NC: McFarland, 2007), 8.
38. Dolan, *Irish Americans*, 82, 85.
39. Dooley, SJ, Papers, GU; Durken, ed., *John Dooley*, x–xi; Gleeson, *Irish in the South*, 1–140; ibid., 136, 141; Egan, *Immortal Irishman*, 43–44.
40. Lalor, *Encyclopedia of Ireland*, 729–730; Dooley, SJ, Papers, GU; Durkin, *John Dooley*, x–xi; Dolan, *Irish Americans*, 82, 99; Gleeson, *Irish in the South*, 69–71; CVSR, NA; Egan, *Immortal Irishman*, 43–44.

41. Dooley, SJ, Papers, GU: Gleeson, *Irish in the South*, 1–140; Durkin, ed., *John Dooley*, xi, xiv; David Mould and Missy Loewe, *Remembering Georgetown, A History of the Lost Port City* (Charleston, SC: The History Press, 2009), 16.
42. Gleeson, *Irish in the South*, 160.
43. Ibid., 140.
44. Ibid.
45. Dooley, SJ, Papers, GU; Durken, ed., *John Dooley*, x–xi, xiv, 1–2; Durkin, ed., *John Dooley*, 177; Tucker, *Irish Confederates*, 88–89; CVSR, NA; O'Brien, *Irish Americans in the Confederate Army*, 7–8.
46. Gleeson, *The Irish in the South*, 140, 156; Dooley, SJ, Papers, GU; Durkin, ed., *John Dooley*, x–xi, xiv–xv, 1–2, 6 note 10; CMSR, NA; David D. Ryan, ed., *A Yankee Spy in Richmond: The Civil War Diary of "Crazy Bet" Van Lew* (Mechanicsburg, PA: Stackpole Books, 1996), 37.
47. Gleeson, *Irish in the South*, 143, 154; Rodgers, *Irish-American Units in the Civil War*, 18; O'Brien, *Irish Americans in the Confederate Army*, 9.
48. Damian Shiels, *The Irish in the American Civil War* (Charleston, SC: The History Press, 2013), 30–34.
49. CVSR, NA; Durkin, *John Dooley*, xiv–xv.
50. Gleeson, *Irish in the South*, 156.
51. Rodgers, *Irish-American Units in the Civil War*, 5, 12–13, 17.
52. CVSR, NA; Durkin, ed., *John Dooley*, xi; O'Grady, *Clear the Irish Way*, 7.
53. Ryan, ed., *Yankee Spy in Richmond*, 33.
54. Ibid., 5, 25.
55. Rodgers, *Irish-American Units in the Civil War*, 41.
56. CVSR, NA.
57. CVSR, NA; Durkin, ed., *John Dooley*, xv.
58. Durkin, ed., *John Dooley*, ix, xi–xii; Dooley, SJ, Papers, GU; Ryan, ed., *Yankee Spy in Richmond*, 35.
59. Robert V. Remini, *Andrew Jackson and His Indian Wars* (New York: Penguin Books, 2001), 7–9, 12–19.
60. Ibid., p. 13.
61. Rodgers, *Irish-American Units in the Civil War*, 38–39.
62. John W. Stevens, *Reminiscences of the Civil War, A Soldier in Hood's Texas Brigade, Army of Northern Virginia* (Hillsboro, TX: Hillsboro Mirror Print, 1902), 79.
63. Ibid., 80; CTSR, NA.
64. J.B. Polley, *Hood's Texas Brigade, Its Marches, Its Battles, Its Achievement* (New York: Neale, 1910), 281.
65. Lonn, *Foreigners in the Confederacy*, 105.

66. Rodgers, *Irish-American Units in the Civil War*, 40.
67. O'Grady, *Clear the Confederate Way*, 35–37; Michael Kenny, *The 1798 Rebellion, Photographs and Memorabilia From the National Museum of Ireland* (Dublin: Country House, 1996), 5–8, 34; Terry Eagleton, *Scholars and Rebels in Nineteenth-Century Ireland* (Oxford: Blackwell Publishers Ltd., 1999), 141; Webb, *Born Fighting*, 232; A.T.Q. Stewart, *The Summer Soldiers, The 1798 Rebellion in Antrim and Down* (Belfast, Ireland: Blackstaff Press, 1995), 7–264.
68. Kenny, *1798 Rebellion*, 34, 38–39; O'Grady, *Clear the Confederate Way*, 37.
69. Hayes-McCoy, *Irish Battles*, 99.
70. Rodgers, *Irish-American Units in the Civil War*, 38–39; Lalor, ed., *Encyclopedia of Ireland*, 704–05, 963; Dolan, *Irish Americans*, 99–100; Egan, *Immortal Irishman*, xiv–xv; Paul R. Wylie, *The Irish General, Thomas Francis Meagher* (Norman: University of Oklahoma Press, 2007), 5, 117–19; O'Brien, Irish Americans in the Confederate Army, 53; Dolan, *Irish Americans*, 99.
71. Dolan, *Irish Americans*, 99–100.
72. Thomas Davis Lectures, *The Great Irish Rebellion of 1798* (Boulder, CO: Irish American Book Company, 1998), 12, 80–82; Stewart, *Summer Soldiers*, 237–54.
73. R.F. Foster, ed., *The Oxford History of Ireland* (Oxford: Oxford University Press, 1992), 161–162; O'Grady, *Clear the Confederate Way*, 35–40.
74. O'Grady, *Clear the Confederate Way*, 35–37.
75. Thomas J. Craughwell, *The Greatest Brigade, How the Irish Brigade Cleared the Way to Victory in the American Civil War* (Beverly, MA: Fair Winds, 2011), 18, 38.
76. Dolan, *Irish Americans*, 71–72.
77. Gleeson, *Irish in the South*, 13–16; Dolan, *Irish Americans*, 72; Craughwell, *Greatest Brigade*, 38, 40.
78. Durkin, *John Dooley*, 148.
79. Tucker, *Irish Confederates*, 91–92; O'Grady, *Clear the Confederate Way!*, 279–80.
80. Richard B. Harwell, ed., *The Confederate Reader, How the South Saw the War* (New York: Dorset Press, 1992), 17.
81. Lalor, ed., *Encyclopedia of Ireland*, 729; Tucker, *Irish Confederates*, 94.
82. Lonn, *Foreigners in the Confederacy*, 4.
83. Ibid., 120.
84. C. Vann Woodward, ed., *Mary Chesnut's Civil War* (New Haven, CT: Yale University Press, 1981), 406.
85. Mike Cronin and Daryl Adair, *The Wearing of the Green, A History of St. Patrick's Day* (New York: Routledge Press, 2002), 13–17.

86. Woodward, ed., *Mary Chesnut's Civil War*, 370.
87. Nelson D. Lankford, *An Irishman in Dixie: Thomas Conolly's Diary of the Fall of the Confederacy* (Columbia: University of South Carolina Press, 1988), 69.
88. Woodward, *Mary Chesnut's Civil War*, 589.
89. Ibid., 601.
90. Lankford, *Irishman in Dixie*, 3–5, 42.
91. Guy R. Everson, and Edward W. Simpson Jr., eds., *"Far, far from home," The Wartime Letters of Dick and Tally Simpson, 3rd South Carolina Volunteers* (New York: Oxford University Press, 1994), 14.
92. Diane Miller Sommerville, *Rape & Race in the Nineteenth-Century South* (Chapel Hill: University of North Carolina Press, 2004), 115.
93. Ibid.
94. Rogers, *Irish-American Units in the Civil War*, 13.
95. Lonn, *Foreigners of the Confederacy*, xv.
96. Gleeson, *Irish in the South*, p. 156; Dolan, *Irish Americans*, 99–100.
97. Durkin, *John Dooley*, 114, 117.
98. Barry Cunliffe, *The Ancient Celts* (Oxford: Oxford University Press, 1997), v, 4–9; Foster, *Oxford History of Ireland*, 1–7.
99. Cunliffe, *Ancient Celts*, 4–6
100. Durkin, *John Dooley*, 148.
101. McWhiney, *Cracker Culture*, 35; Webb, *Born Fighting*, 232.
102. John Camden West, *A Texan in Search of a Fight, Being the Diary and Letters of a Private Soldier in Hood's Texas Brigade* (Memphis: General Books, LLC, 2012), 3; Webb, *Born Fighting*, 232; Compiled Military Service Records of Soldiers Who Served in Organizations from the State of Texas, Record Group 109, National Archives, Washington, D.C.
103. Reid Mitchell, *Civil War Soldiers, Their Expectations and Their Experiences* (New York: Viking, 1988), 26–27; McWhiney, *Cracker Culture*, xiii–271.
104. Francis Rufus Bellamy, *The Private Life of George Washington* (New York: Thomas Y. Crowell, 1951), 189.
105. Monroe F. Cockrell, ed., *Gunner with Stonewall, Reminiscences of William Thomas Poague* (Wilmington, NC.: Broadfoot Publishing, 1987), 59.
106. McWhiney, *Cracker Culture*, 7–8, 28–37; Webb, *Born Fighting*, 232.
107. Mauriel Phillips Joslyn, *A Meteor Shining Brightly: Essays on Maj. Gen. Patrick R. Cleburne,* (Milledgeville, GA: Terrill House Publishing, 1997), 1–2, 257–61, 265; O'Grady, *Clear the Confederate Way*, 227–228; Lonn, *Foreigners in the Confederacy*, 60–61.
108. O'Grady, *Clear the Confederate Way*, 228; Gleeson, *Irish in the South*, 142.

109. David Noel Doyle, *Ireland, Irishman and Revolutionary America, 1760–1820* (Dublin: Mercier Press, 1981), xvii–xviii.
110. Ibid., 39.
111. "Maj. Hugh Garvin Gwyn (1839–1925), Find a Grave," www.findagrave.com.
112. Ibid; "James Gwyn (1828–1906), Find a Grave," www.findagrave.com.
113. Lonn, *Foreigners in the Confederacy*, 55; Webb, *Born Fighting*, 232; McWhiney, *Cracker Ways*, 1–50.
114. West, *Texan in Search of a Fight*, 15.
115. Richard Trimble, ed., *The Civil War Letters of William, Thomas, and Maggie Jones 1861–1865* (Macon, GA: Mercer University Press, 2000), ix, 4.
116. Ibid., ix, 40.
117. Lankford, *Irishman in Dixie*, 69; *Huntingdon Globe*, Huntingdon, Pennsylvania, November 18, 1863.
118. Maureen O'Rourke Murphy and James MacKillop, *Irish Literature* (Syracuse, NY: Syracuse University Press, 1987), 3–21, 37, 41; Webb, *Born Fighting*, 232.
119. Simpson, "*Far, far from home*," xi, 208, 284.
120. Ibid., 221.
121. Les Carroll, *The Angel of Marye's Heights, Sergeant Richard Kirkland's Extraordinary Deed at Fredericksburg* (Columbia, SC: Palmetto Bookworks, 1994), 2–10, 29, 33–77.

Chapter 3

122. Lankford, ed., *Irishman in Dixie*, 52.
123. Gregory A. Coco, *On the Bloodstained Field, II, 132 Human Interest Stories of the Campaign and Battle of Gettysburg* (Orrtanna: Colecraft Industries, 2013), 73; Jeffry D. Wert, *A Glorious Army, Robert E. Lee's Triumph 1862–1863* (New York: Simon & Schuster, 2011), 212.
124. Lankford, ed., *Irishman in Dixie*, 79.
125. Ibid., 46, note 50.
126. Ibid., 79.
127. Stephen Sears, *Gettysburg* (New York: Houghton Mifflin Company, 2003), 86, 92, 96.
128. Ibid., 92–93; Wert, *Glorious Army*, 212–13.
129. Sears, *Gettysburg*, 154; Reid, *Civil War Soldiers*, 31.
130. Sears, *Gettysburg*, 138.

131. James Dempsey and Brian James Egen, *Michigan at Antietam: The Wolverine State's Sacrifice on America's Bloodiest Day* (Charleston, SC: The History Press, 2015), 31.
132. Wert, *Glorious Army*, 234.
133. Reid, *Civil War Soldiers*, 30–31; Bellamy, *Private Life of George Washington*, 323–25; James K. Swisher, *The Revolutionary War in the Southern Back Country* (Gretna, LA: Pelican, 2008), 325–26.
134. Durkin, ed., *John Dooley*, 97.
135. Ibid., 67.
136. Ibid; Gleeson, *Irish in the South*, 11.
137. Desmond Guinness and William Ryan, *Irish House and Castles* (New York: Viking, 1973), 7–347; Foster, *Oxford History of Ireland*, 97–147; Gleeson, *Irish in the South*, 11; Golway, *For the Cause of Liberty*, 28–38.
138. Tucker, *Irish Confederates*. 11.
139. O'Grady, *Clear the Confederate Way*, 158.
140. Sears, *Gettysburg*, 17, 58, 95.
141. Durkin, *John Dooley*, 95; O'Brien, *Irish Americans in the Confederate Army*, 88.
142. Sears, *Gettysburg*, 96; Webb, *Born Fighting*, 232.
143. Sears, *Gettysburg*, 96.
144. Lankford, *Irishman in Dixie*, 3, 52.
145. *Buffalo Evening News*, Buffalo, New York, May 28, 1894.
146. James I. Robertson Jr., *The Stonewall Brigade* (Baton Rouge: Louisiana State University Press, 1963), 236; O'Brien, *Irish Americans in the Confederate Army*, 88–89.
147. Ibid., 12–13; CVSR, NA; McWhiney, *Cracker Culture*, 7–8, 28–37; Webb, *Born Fighting*, 232.
148. Haining, *Great Irish Humor*, 14–16; Wallace Nutting, *Ireland Beautiful* (New York: Bonanza Books, 1975), 61–62; Pat Garber, *Heart Like a River: The Story of Sergeant-Major Newsome Edward Jenkins, 14th North Carolina Infantry, 1861–1865* (Lynchburg: Schroeder, 2011), 26.
149. Mary Lasswell, Compiled and Edited, *Rags and Hope, The Memoirs of Val. C. Giles with Hood's Brigade, Fourth Texas Infantry, 1861–1865* (New York: Coward-McCann, 1961), 114.
150. Ibid., 145.
151. Cockrell, *Gunner with Stonewall*, 9; Webb, *Born Fighting*, 232.
152. Cockrell, *Gunner with Stonewall*, 42.
153. Lasswell, *Rags and Hope*, 114; "Robertson, Jerome Bonaparte," The Handbook of Texas Online; Lonn, *Foreigners in the Confederacy*, 13, 23.

154. Charles P. Riddle, "Massacred at Goliad–Joseph P. Riddle," *Alamo Journal*, no. 167 (December 2012): 12.
155. Durkin, ed., *John Dooley*, 96.
156. *Buffalo Evening News*, Buffalo, May 28, 1894.
157. Sears, *Gettysburg*, 90.
158. Ibid., 125–129, 142.
159. Ibid., 128.
160. Ibid., 106–107
161. George Wilson Booth, *Personal Reminiscences of a Maryland Soldier in the War Between the States, 1861–1865* (Gaithersburg, VA: Butternut Press, 1986), 14.
162. Durkin, ed., *John Dooley*, 58.
163. Craughwell, *Greatest Brigade*, 44–45; Tucker, *"God Help The Irish!,"* 19–20.
164. Durkin, *John Dooley*, 96.
165. Ibid., 97.
166. Sears, *Gettysburg*, 91, 110, 115.
167. Ibid., 108–109.
168. Nutting, *Ireland Beautiful*, 95.
169. Doyle, *Ireland, Irishmen and Revolutionary America*, 83.
170. Durkin, *John Dooley*, 97–98.
171. Margaret S. Creighton, *The Colors of Courage, Gettysburg's Forgotten History* (New York: Perseus Books Group, 2005), 35–37, 56.
172. Timothy H. Smith, comp., *Farms at Gettysburg, The Fields of Battle, Selected Images from the Adams County Historical Society* (Gettysburg, PA: Thomas, 2007), 8, 10, 42, 46; Creighton, *Colors of Courage*, 35, 54.
173. Durkin, *John Dooley*, 99.
174. Lonn, *Foreigners in the Confederacy*, 55.
175. Craughwell, *Greatest Brigade*, 8–123; Tucker, *"God Help the Irish!,"* 55–176; Dolan, *Irish Americans*, 86–87; Egan, *Immortal Irishman*, 180, 187.
176. O'Grady, *Clear the Confederate Way!,* 112–26; Tucker, *Irish Confederates*, 56–64.
177. Durkin, *John Dooley*, 116–117.
178. Paul R. Wylie, *The Irish General: Thomas Francis Meagher* (Norman: University of Oklahoma Press, 2007), 181.
179. Carroll, *Angel of Marye's Heights*, 49–51.
180. Gleeson, *Irish in the South*, 33–36, 141, 143; CLSR, NA; James P. Gannon, *Irish Rebels, Confederate Tigers, The 6th Louisiana Volunteers, 1861–1865* (Campbell, CA.: Savas, 1998), ii–iv, x–xiii; Dolan, *Irish Americans*, 86 89.

181. Scott L. Mingus Sr., *The Louisiana Tigers in the Gettysburg Campaign* (Baton Rouge: Louisiana State University Press, 2009), xv, 1–5, 11.
182. Gannon, *Irish Rebels, Confederate Tigers*, ii–202; O'Grady, *Clear the Confederate Way*, 251–52; Tucker, *Irish Confederates*, 29–29; Mingus, *Louisiana Tigers in the Gettysburg Campaign*, 1–8.
183. O'Grady, *Clear the Confederate Way*, 251–253; Tucker, *Irish Confederates*, 28–29, 35.
184. Joseph T. Durkin, ed., *Confederate Chaplain, A War Journal* (Milwaukee, WI: Bruce, 1960), ix, 1–6, 30.
185. Ibid., 80.
186. Ibid., 6, 26.
187. Ibid., 80.
188. Ibid., 34.
189. Mingus, *Louisiana Tigers in the Gettysburg Campaign*, 103–32; Donald L. Smith, *The Twenty-fourth Michigan of the Iron Brigade* (Harrisburg, PA: Stackpole Books, 1962), 126–42; Sears, *Gettysburg*, 172; Charles L. Dufour, *Gentle Tiger, The Gallant Life of Roberdeau Wheat* (Baton Rouge: Louisiana State University Press, 1985), 121; Wert, *Glorious Army*, 236, 239, 243–44.
190. Mingus, *Louisiana Tigers in the Gettysburg Campaign*, 126.
191. Wert, *Glorious Army*, 243–46.
192. Ibid., 247.
193. Ibid., 251–257; Stephen M. Hood, *John Bell Hood, The Rise, Fall and Resurrection of a Confederate General* (El Dorado Hills, CA: Savas Beatie, 2013), 2.
194. Wert, *Glorious Army*, 248.
195. Ibid., 248–49.
196. Ibid., 256–58.
197. Polley, *Hood's Texas Brigade*, 57, 74; O'Grady, *Clear the Confederate Way!*, 190–93; Black Jack Travis, *Men of God, Angels of Death, History of the Rowan Artillery* (private printing, 2008), 12.
198. Travis, *Men of God, Angels of Death*, 13–15.
199. Ibid., 21–75.
200. John W. Stevens, *Reminiscences of the Civil War* (Hillsboro, TX: Hillsboro Mirror Print, 1902), 113.
201. Lasswell, *Rags and Hope*, 131–32.
202. Travis, *Men of God, Angels of Death*, 117–18.
203. Morris M. Penny and J. Gary Laine, *Struggle for the Round Tops, Law's Alabama Brigade at the Battle of Gettysburg* (Shippensburg, PA: Burd Street, 1999), xi–xii, 1–2, 70–94; CASR, NA; Phillip Thomas Tucker, *Irish*

Confederates, The Civil War's Forgotten Soldiers (Abilene, TX: McWhiney Foundation, 2006), 78–80; Rogers, *Irish-American Units in the Civil War*, 20.

204. CASR, NA; Tucker, *Irish Confederates*, 77–86; William C. Oates, *The War Between the Union and the Confederacy and Its Lost Opportunities with a History of the 15th Alabama Regiment and the Forty-Eight Battles in Which It was Engaged* (Dayton: Morningside Boosk, 1985), 214–20, 612–750; Phillip Thomas Tucker, *Storming Little Round Top, The 15th Alabama and Their Fight for the High Ground, July 2, 1863* (New York: Da Capo, 2002), 211–312.

205. Penny and Laine, *Struggle for the Round Tops*, 70–94.

206. Polley, *Hood's Texas Brigade*, 188; Robertson, Jerome Bonaparte, The Handbook of Texas Online.

207. Michael Dan Jones, *Lt. Col. King Bryan of Hood's Texas Brigade, Freedom Fighter for Texas and Southern Independence* (Seattle: CreateSpace, 2013), 1–41, 62–63, 123–36.

208. Travis, *Men of God, Angels of Death*, 117–18.

209. Rufus King Felder, July 9, 1863, Texas Brigade Letters Collection, Harold B. Simpson History Center, Hill College, Hillsboro, Texas.

210. Brian A. Bennett, *A Beau Ideal of a Soldier and a Gentleman* (Lynchburg, VA: Schroeder Publications, 2012), 1–174.

211. CMSR, NA.

212. John C. Oeffinger, ed., *A Soldier's General, The Civil War Letters of Major General Lafayette McLaws* (Chapel Hill: University of North Carolina Press, 2002), 3, 196–197.

213. Ibid., 3.

214. Mingus, *Louisiana Tigers in the Gettysburg Campaign*, 141–87, 239–42; O'Grady, *Clear the Confederate Way!*, 90, 281–83; "Col. Michael Nolan," findagrave.com; O'Brien, *Irish Americans in the Confederate Army*, 93–94; Scott Bowden and Bill Ward, *Last Chance for Victory, Robert E. Lee and the Gettysburg Campaign* (New York: Da Capo, 2001), 350–54.

215. Gannon, *Irish Rebels, Confederate Tigers*, 191–202; O'Brien, *Irish Americans in the Confederate Army*, 93–94; Mingus, *Louisiana Tigers in the Gettysburg Campaign*, 10.

216. Gleeson, *Irish in the South*, 143.

217. O'Brien, *Irish Americans in the Confederate Army*, 94.

218. Ibid., 88–89, 94; 33rd Virginia, Co. E, "Emerald Guard"; O'Grady, *Clear the Confederate Way!*, 288.

219. Alan T. Nolan, *Lee Considered, General Robert E. Lee and Civil War History* (Chapel Hill: University of North Carolina Press, 1991), 98.

Chapter 4

220. Durkin, *John Dooley*, 93.
221. Hunt, *Irish and the American Revolution*, 45–49, 80–81; Doyle, *Ireland, Irishmen and Revolutionary America*, 48; Meade (Philadelphia) Family Genealogy, online.
222. Terry Golway, *For the Cause of Liberty: A Thousand Years of Ireland's Heroes* (New York: Simon and Schuster, 2000), 138.
223. Craughwell, *Greatest Brigade*, 147.
224. Webb, *Born Fighting*, 232; Dolan, *Irish Americans*, 86–89, 96–99; Tucker, *Irish Confederates*, 11–31.
225. Tucker, *Irish Confederates*, 90–94; Dolan, *The Irish Americans*, 99–100; Tucker, *"God Help the Irish!,"* 22–26, 31–39.
226. Dolan, *Irish Americans*, 99–100.
227. Longacre, *Edward G., Pickett, Leader of the Charge, A Biography of General George E. Pickett, C.S.A.* (Mechanicsburg, PA: White Mane, 1995), 116–17; Sears, *Gettysburg*, 47.
228. Durkin, *John Dooley*, 101.
229. CVSR, NA; Lonn, *Foreigners in the Confederacy*, 31–32; Gleeson, *Irish of the South*, 27, 35–36, 38–40.
230. CVSR, NA; Gleeson, *Irish of the South*, 27, 35–36, 38–40; Lonn, *Foreigners in the Confederacy*, 31–43; Tucker, *The Irish Confederates*, 87–94; Webb, *Born Fighting*, 232; O'Grady, *Clear the Confederate Way*, 158–164.
231. Durkin, ed., *John Dooley*, 142–43.
232. CVSR, NA; Gleeson, *Irish in the South*, 39–40, 48; Benjamin H. Trask, *9th Virginia Infantry* (Lynchburg, VA: H.E. Howard, Inc., 1984), 1–10.
233. CVSR, NA; Gleeson, *Irish in the South*, 144; Tucker, *Irish Confederates*, 17.
234. CVSR, NA
235. Durkin, ed., *John Dooley*, 102.
236. *Buffalo Evening News*, May 28, 1894.
237. Ibid; CVSR, NA.
238. CVSR, NA.
239. *Buffalo Evening News*, May 28, 1894.
240. Ibid.
241. Sears, *Gettysburg*, 95.
242. Reid, *Civil War Soldiers*, 30; Phillip Thomas Tucker, *The Confederacy's Fighting Chaplain, Father John B. Bannon* (Tuscaloosa: University of Alabama Press, 1992), 159.
243. Durkin, ed., *John Dooley*, 28.

244. CVSR, NA; Gleeson, *Irish of the South*, 71, 121–29; Nutting, *Ireland Beautiful*, 60–62; Michael Hogan, *The Irish Soldiers of Mexico* (Guadalajara, Mexico: Fondo Editorial Universitario, 1997), 11–245; Webb, *Born Fighting*, 232.
245. Gleeson, *Irish of the South*, 121–129; McWhiney, *Cracker Culture*, 113–31; Noah Smithwick, *The Evolution of a State, or Recollections of Old Texas Days* (Austin: University of Texas Press, 1983), 25, 28, 49; Golway, *For the Cause of Liberty*, 10.
246. Durkin, ed., *John Dooley*, 54–55, 59.
247. James Dinkins, *1861 to 1865, Personal Recollections and Experiences in the Confederate Army, By an "Old Johnnie,"* (Dayton, OH: Morningside Books, 1975), vii, 56
248. Lasswell, *Rags and Hope*, 78–79.
249. Longacre, *Pickett*, 13, 116–117.
250. Archie K. Davis, *Boy Colonel of the Confederacy, The Life and Times of Henry King Burgwyn, Jr.* (Chapel Hill: The University of North Carolina Press, 1985), 40–57, 82, 308–34; *Charlotte Daily Observer*, Charlotte, North Carolina, July 4, 1903.
251. *Charlotte Daily Observer*, July 4, 1903.
252. Davis, *Boy Colonel of the Confederacy*, 328–29; *Fayetteville Observer*, Fayetteville, North Carolina, March 27, 1864.
253. *Charlotte Daily Observer*, July 4, 1903; *Fayetteville Observer*, August 24, 1863.
254. Emory M. Thomas, *Robert E. Lee: A Biography* (New York: W.W. Norton and Company, 1995), 298–99.
255. Durkin, *John Dooley*, 103.
256. Longacre, *Pickett, Leader of the Charge*, 3–14, 116–17.
257. Ibid., 15, 24–27; Lesley J. Cordon, *General George E. Pickett in Life and Legend* (Chapel Hill: University of North Carolina Press, 1998), 27–29; Peter F. Stevens, *The Rogue's March, John Riley and the St. Patrick's Battalion, 1846–48* (Dulles, VA: Brassey's, 1999), 7–276; Hogan, *Irish Soldiers of Mexico*, 183–86.
258. Stevens, *Rogue's March*, 270–76; Hogan, *Irish Soldiers of Mexico*, 187–88.
259. O'Brien, *Irish Americans in the Confederate Army*, 88.
260. Gleeson, *Irish in the South*, 135.
261. Craughwell, *Greatest Brigade*, 44; Durkin, *John Dooley*, 1–2.
262. Longacre, *Pickett*, 27.
263. Ibid., 3–5, 27; Cordon, *General George E. Pickett*, 49, 72.
264. Cordon, *General George E. Pickett*, 26, 28–29,110; Longacre, *Pickett*, 26–27.

265. CVSR, NA; Cordon, *General George E. Pickett*, 87.
266. *Buffalo Evening News*, Buffalo, New York, May 28, 1894; NVSR, NA.
267. CVSR, NA.
268. Rod Gragg, *Covered with Glory: The 26th North Carolina Infantry at the Battle of Gettysburg* (Chapel Hill: University of North Carolina Press, 2010), 155–56.
269. Archie K. Davis, *Boy Colonel of the Confederacy, The Life and Times of Henry King Burgwyn, Jr.* (Chapel Hill: University of North Carolina Press, 1985), 281; McWhiney, *Cracker Culture*, xiii–271; Webb, *Born Fighting*, 232.
270. Gragg, *Covered with Glory*, 149, 155, 158, 175, 192; CVSR, NA; CASR, NA; CNCSR, NA; CTSR, NA; Jean Edward Smith, *John Marshall* (New York: Henry Holt, 1996), 22–23; Gleeson, *Irish in the South*, 143; Donald L. Smith, *The Twenty-fourth Michigan* (Harrisburg, PA: Stackpole Books, 1962), 126; Stephen Dando-Collins, *Tycoon's War, How Cornelius Vanderbilt Invaded a Country to Overthrow America's Most Famous Military Adventurer* (New York: Da Capo, 2008), 7, 117–20, 130.
271. Gragg, *Covered With Glory*, 175; Smith, *John Marshall*, 23, 45–46; Longacre, *Pickett*, 3–5.
272. Gregory A. Coco, *Wasted Valor: The Confederate Dead at Gettysburg* (Gettysburg, PA: Thomas Publications, 1990), 53.
273. Durkin, *John Dooley*, 103.
274. *Buffalo Evening News*, May 28, 1894.
275. Dolan, *Irish Americans*, 99.
276. Glenn Tucker, *Lee and Longstreet at Gettysburg* (Dayton, OH: Morningside Bookshop, 1982), 108.
277. Longacre, *Pickett*, 121.
278. Ibid., 121–122.
279. Ibid; *Buffalo Evening News*, May 28, 1894; Bowden and Ward, *Last Chance for Victory*, 455–56.
280. Durkin, ed., *John Dooley*, 104–05
281. Hal T. Shelton, *General Richard Montgomery and the American Revolution, From Redcoat to Rebel* (New York: New York University Press, 1994), 1–181.
282. David Power Conyngham, *The Irish Brigade and its Campaigns* (New York: Fordham University Press, 1994), 253.
283. Ibid., 60.
284. CVSR, NA.
285. *Buffalo Evening News*, May 28, 1894.
286. Ibid.
287. CVSR, NA, CNCSR, NA; Hunt, *Irish and the American Revolution*, 27–28; Thomas Fleming, *Washington's Secret War* (New York: HarperCollins, 2005),

141–42, 285; McWhiney, *Cracker Culture*, 1–160; Doyle, *Ireland, Irishmen and Revolutionary America*, 51–106; Craughwell, *Greatest Brigade*, 152; Webb, *Born Fighting*, 232.

288. Craughwell, *Greatest Brigade*, 145–46, 152–54.
289. Myles Dungan, *Distant Drums, Irish Soldiers in Foreign Armies* (Belfast: Appletree Press, 1993), 14.
290. Durkin, *John Dooley*, 105.
291. Bruce Catton, ed., *The Battle of Gettysburg by Frank A. Haskell* (Boston: Houghton Mifflin, 1957), 96–97.
292. *Buffalo Evening News*, May 28, 1894.
293. Durkin, *John Dooley*, 105–06.
294. Catton, *Battle of Gettysburg*, 100–01.
295. CVSR, NA.
296. John G. Gallaher, *Napoleon's Irish Legion* (Carbondale: Southern Illinois University Press, 1993), 1–86.
297. Myles Dungan, *Distant Drums, Irish Soldiers in Foreign Armies* (Belfast: Appletree Press, Ltd., 1993), 35; Rodgers, *Irish-American Units in the Civil War*, 43.
298. Durkin, *John Dooley*, 6, note 10, 106; CVSR, NA
299. CVSR, NA.
300. *Buffalo Evening News*, May 28, 1894.
301. Ibid.
302. CVSR, NA.
303. *Buffalo Evening News*, May 28, 1894.
304. Rollins, *Pickett's Charge*, 200.
305. *Buffalo Evening News*, May 28, 1894.
306. CVSR, NA; Lonn, *Foreigners in the Confederacy*, 117; Rogers, *Irish-American Units in the Civil War*, 41; O'Brien, *Irish Americans in the Confederate Army*, 88, 96–99; O'Grady, *Clear the Confederate Way!*, 258.
307. Gragg, *Covered with Glory*, 175–77.
308. *Fayetteville Observer*, August 24, 1863.
309. Ibid.
310. William C. Floyd and Paul Gibson, *The Boys Who Went to War from Cumberland University, 1861–1865* (Gettysburg, PA: Thomas, 2001), 11–13, 28–29, 126.
311. CVSR, NA; *Buffalo Evening News*, May 28, 1894.
312. *Buffalo Evening News*, May 28, 1894.
313. Ibid.
314. Ibid.

315. Ibid.
316. Smith, *Farms at Gettysburg*, 15.
317. Don Ernsberger, *At the Wall, The 69th Pennsylvania "Irish Volunteers" at Gettysburg* (Bloomington, IN: Xlibris, 2006), 11–87, 91; The Dennis O'Kane Project—the 69th Pennsylvania Irish Volunteers," online.
318. James Keir Baughman, *History of the 56th Virginia Infantry Regiment* (Lynchburg: Howard, 2009), 307.
319. Ibid., 213, 269–70.
320. *Buffalo Evening News*, May 28, 1894.
321. Ibid.
322. *Buffalo Evening News*, May 28, 1894; CVSR, NA.
323. Dungan, *Distant Drums*, 18, 21.
324. Ibid., 32
325. Durkin, *John Dooley*, 106.
326. Dungan, *Distant Drums*, 4–5.
327. *Buffalo Evening News*, May 28, 1894.
328. CVSR, NA; Durkin, ed., *John Dooley*, 144; *Irish-American*, New York, New York, August 29, 1863; Tucker, *Irish Confederates*, 91.
329. *Irish-American*, August 29, 1863.
330. Gragg, *Covered with Glory*, 148, 177, 182, 185, 187–96.
331. The Dennis O'Kane Project, The 69th Pennsylvania Irish Volunteers, online; Shiels, *Irish in the American Civil War*, 106–09.
332. Gragg, *Covered with Glory*, 156; *Buffalo Evening News*, May 28, 1894.
333. *Buffalo Evening News*, May 28, 1894; McWhiney, *Cracker Culture*, xiii–271.
334. R.L. Murray, *"Hurrah for the Ould Flag!," Captain Andrew Cowan and the First New York Independent Battery at Gettysburg* (Wolcott: Benedum, 1998), 5–9, 18, 24–102, 117, 119.
335. Dungan, *Distant Drums*, 35.
336. Howard Coffin, *Nine Months to Gettysburg, Stannard's Vermonters and the Repulse of Pickett's Charge* (Woodstock, VT: Countryman, 2011), 20–21, 85, 225–46, 286, 290; Rodgers, *Irish-American Units in the Civil War*, 17.
337. Durkin, *John Dooley*, 106–07.
338. *Buffalo Evening News*, May 28, 1894.
339. Ibid.
340. Ibid; CVSR, NA.
341. Durkin, *John Dooley*, 107.
342. Haskell, *Battle of Gettysburg*, 103.
343. *Buffalo Evening News*, May 28, 1894.
344. Ibid.

345. Ibid.
346. Dungan, *Distant Drums*, 35.
347. Murray, *"Hurrah for the Ould flag,"* 97.
348. *Buffalo Evening News*, May 28, 1894.
349. Lalor, *Encyclopedia of Ireland*, 754; Ernsberger, *At the Wall*, 80–89.
350. Durkin, *John Dooley*, 107.
351. *Buffalo Evening News*, May 28, 1894.
352. Durkin, *John Dooley*, 107; Bowden and Ward, *Last Chance for Victory*, ii.
353. O'Brien, *Clear the Confederate Way!*, 164.
354. Charles W. Turner, ed., *Ted Barclay, Liberty Hall Volunteers, Letters from the Stonewall Brigade* (Natural Bridge Station, VA: Rockbridge, 1992), 91.
355. Durkin, *John Dooley*, 109–10.
356. Ibid., 115; CVSR, NA.
357. *Fayetteville Observer*, August 24, 1863.
358. O'Brien, *Irish Americans in the Confederate Army*, 98–99, 216; O'Grady, *Clear the Confederate Way!*, 263, 277; Edward Younger, *Inside the Confederate Government, The Diary of Robert Garlick Hill Kean* (New York: Oxford University Press, 1957), xv, 79.

Epilogue

359. Gleeson, *Irish in the South*, 156; Webb, *Born Fighting*, 232.
360. Michael Cavanagh, *Memoirs of Gen. Thomas Francis Meagher, Comprising of Leading Events of His Career* (Worcester, MA: Messenger, 1892), 417; Gleeson, *Irish in the South*, 70–73; Golway, *For the Cause of Liberty*, 139; Rodgers, *Irish-American Units in the Civil War*, 43; Mike Cronin and Daryl Adair, *The Wearing of the Green, History of St. Patrick's Day* (New York: Routledge, 2002), 65.
361. *Nation*, Dublin, Ireland, September 7, 1861.
362. Eagleton, *Scholars and Rebels*, 135.
363. Gleeson, *Irish in the South*, 70, 132
364. *Richmond Daily Dispatch*, July 13, 1863.
365. *Irish-American*, New York, New York, August 29, 1863
366. *Richmond Sentinel*, Richmond, Virginia, September 17, 1863.
367. *Irish-American*, September 6, 1863.
368. *Dublin Nation*, September 26, 1863.
369. Durkin, *John Dooley*, 144; O'Grady, *Clear the Confederate Way*, 163; CVSR, NA.

370. Jane Mitchel letter to James Mitchel, June 10, n.d., Gettysburg National Military Park Library, Gettysburg, Pennsylvania; CVSR, NA; Durkin, ed., *John Dooley*, xv.

371. CVSR, NA; Tucker, *Irish Confederates*, 90; Smith, compiler, *Farms of Gettysburg*, 15.

372. Jane Mitchel letter to James Mitchel, June 10, n.d., GNMP; Durkin, *John Dooley*, ix.

373. O'Brien, *Clear the Confederate Way!*, 165.

374. Durkin, *John Dooley*, 142.

375. Cass Canfield, *The Iron Will of Jefferson Davis* (New York: Fairfax Press, 1978), 95.

376. William Rudolf O'Donovan Papers, The Historical Society of Pennsylvania, Philadelphia, Pennsylvania; Craughwell, *Greatest Brigade*, 211; Webb, *Born Fighting*, 232.

377. *Fayetteville Observer*, August 24, 1863.

378. John Fitzgerald Kennedy Address to Irish Parliament, June 28, 1963, John Fitzgerald Kennedy Library, Boston, Massachusetts; Webb, *Born Fighting*, 232. Phillip Thomas Tucker, *How the Irish Won the American Revolution, A New Look at the Forgotten Heroes of America's War of Independence* (New York: Skyhorse Publishing, 2015), 339.

379. Jeffrey Stocker, "Killed at Gettysburg, Letters Reveal Pain of Those Left Behind." *America's Civil War* (September 2017): 30–31.

About the Author

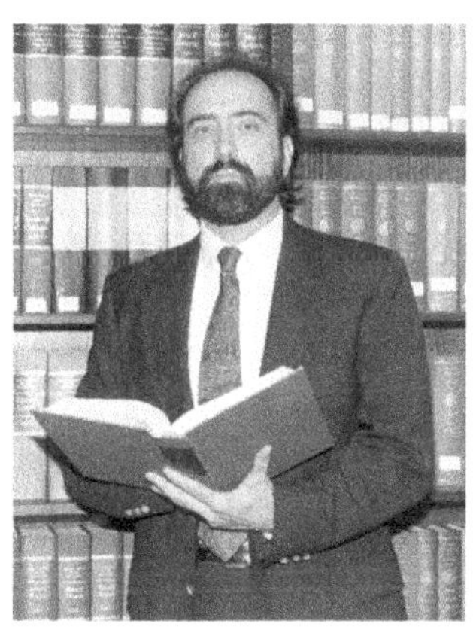

Phillip Thomas Tucker, PhD, is an author and historian of numerous acclaimed books, including *George Washington's Surprise Attack*, *Pickett's Charge*, *Death at the Little Bighorn*, *Miller Cornfield at Antietam* and more. After earning his PhD in 1990, he took a position as a civilian historian with the Department of Defense. The author resides and writes in Upper Marlboro, Maryland. Tucker has written more than thirty books on a wide variety of historical subjects.

www.ingramcontent.com/pod-product-compliance
Lightning Source LLC
LaVergne TN
LVHW052339100826
845147LV00021B/1119

* 9 7 8 1 4 6 7 1 3 8 5 2 9 *